fascinating world.

> —Michael Shapiro, author of *A Sense of Place: Great Travel Writers Talk About Their Craft, Lives, and Inspiration* and *Guatemala: A Journey Through the Land of the Maya*

CRITICAL ACCLAIM FOR ROLF POTTS

"Rolf Potts is at the forefront of a new generation of literary travel writers that came of age with the Internet." —*Bookmarks Magazine*

"He's been drugged and robbed in Istanbul, checked out brothels in Cambodia where prostitutes are identified by numbers, and shopped for donkeys in the Libyan Desert. Rolf Potts usually has an interesting answer to the mundane question, 'So, what did you do today?'"

Examiner

"Anyone ⋯ ⋯ ⋯ ⋯ heyday of
Salon.cor ⋯ flair and
storytellir ⋯ ⋯appened'
travel wri ⋯ l light on
self-aggra ⋯ (Canada)

"Rolf is or ⋯ ⋯ of travel
writers." ⋯ ⋯ick Steves

"Potts en ⋯ ⋯ has been
almost los ⋯ ⋯ im Cahill

"Jack Kerc ⋯ ⋯SA Today

ALSO BY ROLF POTTS

Vagabonding: An Uncommon Guide to the Art of Long-Term
World Travel

SOME OTHER TRAVELERS' TALES BOOKS

Country and Regional Guides

America, Antarctica, Australia, Brazil, Central America, China, Cuba,
France, Greece, India, Ireland, Italy, Japan, Mexico, Nepal, Spain,
Thailand, Tibet, Turkey; Alaska, American Southwest, Hawai'i,
Middle East, Paris, Prague, Provence, South Pacific, Tuscany

Body & Soul

Stories to Live By, The Spiritual Gifts of Travel, The Road Within, A
Mile in Her Boots, Love & Romance, Food, How to Eat Around the
World, The Adventure of Food, The Ultimate Journey, Pilgrimage

Women's Travel

100 Places Every Woman Should Go, The Best Women's Travel
Writing, A Woman's Asia, A Woman's Europe, Her Fork in the Road, A
Woman's Path, A Woman's Passion for Travel, A Woman's World,
Women in the Wild, Gutsy Women, A Woman's World Again

Special Interest

Not So Funny When It Happened, The Gift of Rivers, How to Shit
Around the World, Testosterone Planet, Danger!, The Penny Pincher's
Passport to Luxury Travel, Make Your Travel Dollars Worth a Fortune,
The Gift of Birds, Family Travel, A Dog's World, There's No Toilet
Paper on the Road Less Traveled, The Gift of Travel, 365 Travel, The
Thong Also Rises, Adventures in Wine, The World Is a Kitchen, Sand
in My Bra, Hyenas Laughed at Me, Whose Panties Are These?,
More Sand in My Bra, What Color Is Your Jockstrap?

Travel Literature

A Sense of Place, The Best Travel Writing, Cruise Confidential, A Rotten
Person Travels the Caribbean, Kite Strings of the Southern Cross, The
Sword of Heaven, Storm, Take Me With You, Last Trout in Venice, The
Way of the Wanderer, One Year Off, The Fire Never Dies, The Royal
Road to Romance, The Rivers Ran East, Coast to Coast, Trader Horn

MARCO POLO
DIDN'T GO THERE

STORIES AND REVELATIONS FROM ONE DECADE
AS A POSTMODERN TRAVEL WRITER

MARCO POLO
DIDN'T GO THERE

STORIES AND REVELATIONS FROM ONE DECADE
AS A POSTMODERN TRAVEL WRITER*

WITH SPECIAL COMMENTARY TRACK

ROLF POTTS

TRAVELERS' TALES
an imprint of Solas House, Inc.
Palo Alto

Travelers' Tales and Solas House are trademarks of Solas House, Inc., 853 Alma Street, Palo Alto, California 94301. www.travelerstales.com

Cover Design: Stefan Gutermuth
Page Layout: Cynthia Lamb using the fonts Minion and Mrs Eaves
Cover Photo: Paul Hilts
Author Photo: Catherine Wessel
Illustration Research: Melanie Haage
Production Director: Christy Quinto

Library of Congress Cataloging-in-Publication Data

Potts, Rolf.
  Marco Polo didn't go there : stories and revelations from one decade as a post-modern travel writer : with special commentary track / Rolf Potts.—1st ed.
    p. cm.
  ISBN 1-932361-61-8 (pbk.)
  1. Potts, Rolf—Travel. 2. Travel writers—United States—Biography I. Title.
  G154.5.P68A3 2008
  910.4092—dc22
                              2008019755

910.4092
P OT
  11/08

First Edition
Printed in the United States
10 9 8 7 6 5 4 3 2 1

For my family,
who remind me
how sweet home is
(even if I'm rarely there)

Kublai asks Marco, "When you return to the West, will you repeat to your people the same tales you tell me?"

"I speak and speak," Marco says, "but the listener retains only the words he is expecting. The description of the world to which you lend a benevolent ear is one thing; the description that will go the rounds of the groups of stevedores and gondoliers on the street outside my house the day of my return is another; and yet another, that which I might dictate late in life, if I were taken prisoner by Genoese pirates and put in irons in the same cell with a writer of adventure stories. It is not the voice that commands the story: it is the ear."

—ITALO CALVINO, *INVISIBLE CITIES* (1972)

TABLE OF CONTENTS

Part Three
THE DUBIOUS THRILL OF PRESS TRIPS

Part Four
PEOPLE YOU DON'T FORGET

Part Five
TUTORIAL

Marco Polo Didn't Go There

*"I did not really know where I was going, so, when anyone
asked me, I said to Russia. Thus, my trip started, like an
autobiography, upon a rather nicely qualified basis of
falsehood and self-glorification."*
—Evelyn Waugh, *Labels*

The title of this book is not my own creation: It is a direct
quote from an inmate I met at Bangkok's women's prison in
January of 1999. At the time I had been a full-time travel writer
for less than a month, and I'd been telling people I planned to
travel across Asia in the footsteps of Marco Polo.

Looking back, I'm not sure why I found it necessary to say this.
I guess I was just following the presumed formula of what travel
writers were supposed to do.

Indeed, at the very moment I was setting out from Asia, various travel scribes were researching or publishing books that dili-
gently traced the international footsteps of Captain Cook, Che
Guevara, Moses, Sir Richard Burton, William of Rubruck, John
Steinbeck, Lewis and Clark, Robinson Crusoe, Ibn Battuta,
Robert Louis Stevenson, and Herman Melville. Journeying in the
footsteps of others had, it seemed, become the travel-literature
equivalent of cover music—as common (and marketable) as
Whitney Houston crooning Dolly Parton tunes.

As it turned out, my own "footsteps" ruse lasted less than one
month before I found my way into the visiting room of a women's

penitentiary just outside of Bangkok. As unusual as it might sound, visiting Western prisoners was all the rage among back-packers when I'd arrived in Thailand. In cafés and guesthouse bulletin boards along Khao San Road, photocopied notices urged travelers to take a day off and call on prisoners at the various penitentiaries around Bangkok. Figuring this might be an interesting deviation from the standard tourist-circuit activities, I went to the American embassy and received a letter of introduction to an unlucky drug trafficker named Carla.

Brief acts of presumed kindness carry a whiff of narcissism: As I took a series of buses through the snarl of Bangkok traffic to the edge of the city, I imagined Carla to be a weary, desperate woman who would thank me for the small gift of magazines and the encouragement to keep persevering behind bars. In reality, Carla was a tough, pretty Puerto Rican woman who arrived in the visitor's room fifteen minutes late smelling like shampoo, and regarded me with ambivalent cordiality. After speaking for a while about her own situation (her fateful decision to make a quick buck delivering Thai heroin to New Jersey for an acquaintance; her plans upon her release in nine more months), she began to steer the conversation toward me.

"Why did you come to Thailand?" she asked.

"My primary goal is to follow the route of Marco Polo through the Orient."

"Oh yeah?" Carla said. "Where are you going after Bangkok?"

"North," I said. "Probably to Chiang Mai for a while."

"Chiang Mai?" Carla raised a skeptical eyebrow at me. "Marco Polo didn't go there."

Though I didn't know it at the time, this simple observation was to change the way I traveled, far beyond Asia.

In retrospect, there are a number of reasons why my Marco Polo quest never would have worked. For starters, Carla was right: There is no evidence the famous Venetian explorer ever made it to

Thailand, let alone Chiang Mai. Moreover, I later discovered that William Dalrymple had written a book in the narrative footsteps of Marco Polo a good decade earlier. Dalrymple's *In Xanadu* was not to be confused with Clarence Dalrymple Bruce's classic *In the Footsteps of Marco Polo*—and neither of these books were to be confused with Jin Bohong's *In the Footsteps of Marco Polo* (which was published the same year as *In Xanadu*).

Logistics and marketing aside, however, I came to realize that "Marco Polo didn't go there" was not just a statement of geography: Intentional or not, it was a keen observation about the post-modern reality of far-flung lands. Unlike Marco, my travels were not a simple journey from Home to The Other and back. At any given moment in Southeast Asia, I was likely to run into a Burmese Shan refugee who could quote West Coast hip-hop to illustrate his plight, a Laotian Hmong tribesman who'd recently visited his relatives in Minneapolis, or a Jewish-American Buddhist who'd slept in suburban Maryland thirty-six hours earlier. Whereas Marco had traveled into a mysterious and frightening terra incognita, I was traveling into a globalized Asia that had long since been visited by the oracle of mass media and the shock troops of mass tourism.

I use the word "tourism" intentionally, since it defines how people travel in the twenty-first century. Sure, we all try to convince ourselves that we're "travelers" instead of "tourists," but this distinction is merely a self-conscious parlor game within the tourism milieu. Regardless of how far we try to wander off the tourist trail (and no matter how long we try and stay off it) we are still outsiders and dilettantes, itinerant consumers in distant lands. This is often judged to be a bad thing, but in truth that's just the way things are. Platonic ideals aside, the world remains a fascinating place for anyone with the awareness to appreciate its nuances. Social critics who proclaim that "real travel" is dead are just too lazy to look for complexities within an interconnected planet—and travel writers who seek to diminish their own presence in the tourist matrix are simply not being honest. "Footsteps" might be a nice thematic vessel in which to pour a travel book, but it tends to miss out on the vibrant, often contradictory (and decidedly non-thematic) experience of what it's like to travel in a postmodern world.

This in mind, I scrapped my Marco Polo quest within a week of visiting Bangkok's women's prison. Suddenly liberated from a sober travel-writing mission, I realized that my truest travel urge at that very moment was to crash the set of a Leonardo DiCaprio movie that was being filmed near Phuket. Giving Chiang Mai a miss, I headed south.

The gonzo travel story I penned for *Salon* two weeks later, "Storming *The Beach*," went on to appear in *The Best American Travel Writing 2000*. It also appears as the first chapter of this book, since it set the tone for the stories I would write in the years that followed (including "Backpackers' Ball at the Sultan Hotel," appearing here as chapter 10, which in spite of everything takes place in the Egyptian footsteps of Gustave Flaubert).

Having explained the title of this book, I should clarify the subtitle: "Stories and Revelations from One Decade as a Postmodern Travel Writer."

In a sense, "postmodern" is a confusing appellation, since the word is used in slightly different ways when describing, say, literary theory, or interior design, or TV commercials. I use the word to describe the increasing placelessness that accompanies any information-age journey. Many recurring themes of the travel tales in this book (the weird gap between expectations and reality; the challenge of identifying "authenticity" in post-traditional settings; the realization that unexpected encounters help you better see places for what they are) are the result of this dislocation.

I also find "postmodern" fitting to describe my own writing career, since my earliest travel tales debuted online (in venues like *Salon* and *World Hum*) while I was in the midst of a two-year vagabonding journey across Asia and Europe. Whereas previous generations of travel writers enjoyed comfortable stretches of editorial time and geographical space to achieve a romanticized distance from their stories, I never had that luxury. Mention in an Internet travel story that your Cambodian guesthouse owner served you *twako* pork sausages, and you're bound to get an instant and bewildering array of e-mails—from the British academic who notes that "*twako*" is an incorrect transliteration; to the Arizona vegan who insists that pork is murder; to the Cambodian guesthouse owner himself, who now fears all his guests will demand complimentary sausages. In this environment it's difficult to offer up travel stories as authoritative, self-contained universes. Exotic postcard-panoramas that might once have passed for travel reportage soon become secondary to a more subjective and interactive attempt to draw connections, intuit meanings, and interpret the landscape.

Thankfully, the Internet allows for narrative leeway that isn't always possible in traditional news media or print-based travel publications. Just as international news reporters tend to move in packs from one global crisis to another, travel magazines often build their content around photographs and consumer demographics. And, while hard news and vacation tips have their place, the Internet has afforded travel writers a unique privilege: the simple opportunity to write about their experiences as they see fit, in their own voice, without the constraints of service information or the contrivance of a news hook.

Thus, while my travel-writing career soon advanced into the better-paying world of print journalism, I owe much to my online roots. To this day, I continue to write several stories each year for Internet magazines, as the narrative flexibility more than makes up for the smaller paycheck. Of the twenty stories in this collection, a little more than half originally appeared in online form.

In collecting these stories, I have also added endnotes that reveal the ragged edges behind each tale: how I chose to arrange the facts; what was taken out, and why; what happened just before or after the events described in the story. I realize that this sort of meta-commentary might be seen as a po-mo indulgence, but I find it curiously appropriate for a travel book, especially one that covers a lot of geography. In addition to adding a twist of humor and self-deprecation, these endnotes aim to remind the reader of the gap between story and experience, traveler and writer, truth and presentation. The endnotes reveal things about the journey that—for the sake of good storytelling—one can't reveal in the main text. Just as a photographer might seek to crop out the modern tourists who cluster around an ancient monument, the travel writer ignores those parts of reality that don't serve the threads and themes of his narrative. My endnotes are a reminder that those undesirable-yet-real elements—those fat tourists who screw up the symmetry of the Taj Mahal (so to speak)—still exist.

Hence, my endnotes might be thought of as the book's DVD-style "commentary track" or outtakes—alluding to other things that happened (or, on occasion, things that didn't happen), questioning my portrayal of places and people I invariably knew only for a couple of hours, and reminding the reader that the laws of nature and the laws of storytelling are separate entities.

Some of my endnotes serve different purposes than others. The endnotes to chapters 12 and 13, for example, deal with the wacky ethical and logistical challenges of stories that were funded by "press trips" to Greece and Grenada. The chapter 15 endnotes explain why I left some of the funniest details out of my Beirut tale; the chapter 6 endnotes share some ironic details of what happened to me after I was robbed in Istanbul; the chapter 10 endnotes are primarily a rant in defense of backpacker culture. Other endnotes reveal why I withheld certain details about my expat sojourn in Thailand, how I met one of the characters from Bruce Chatwin's *The Songlines* in Australia, and why I didn't care much for Vietnam. Chapter 20 contains no endnotes at all—but only because the story itself is a self-referential series of endnotes about the travel writing process.

Most all the endnotes contain insights about the writing of the story itself. In this way, *Marco Polo Didn't Go There* might well serve as a quirky travel-writing textbook, since each story is offset by an annotated peek into its own creation.

That said, I must share a few warnings about the endnotes. First and foremost, they are designed to be read *after* the story itself. Just as you don't view the special features on your *Big Lebowski* DVD before you've watched the movie itself, you should avoid dipping into a chapter's endnotes until you've finished its main text. Digest the story first, then read the commentary.

I might add that there's no need to read the endnotes at all if you prefer your travel tales to be self-contained and seamless. One reading strategy might be to read all the stories first, then go back and dip into the endnotes of the chapters that most interested you. These annotations don't form a comprehensive body of work—they only exist to comment on the chapters in question—so they can be read (or ignored) at your discretion.

Keeping this in mind, let us now proceed to some curious corners of planet Earth—places I might never have experienced had I been faithfully following the footsteps of a certain Venetian merchant.

PART ONE

Adventures and
Misadventures

ꨄ 1 ꨄ

Storming *The Beach*

Day Six: January 22, 1999—Storming The Beach *(Prelude)*

It is three o'clock in the morning, and Lomudi Beach is possibly the only stretch of sand on Phi Phi Don island that is completely deserted. The only buildings here are small, sagging bamboo-and-thatch dwellings that probably housed Thai fishermen before the onslaught of sun-starved Europeans and North Americans turned those fishermen into bellboys and t-shirt hawkers. The high tide line here yields a sodden crust of garbage—plastic water bottles, rubber sandals, cigarette butts—but this detritus is only evidence of the boaters, snorkelers and sunburned masses who haunt the other parts of the island. Devoid of dive shops, pineapple vendors and running water, Lomudi is quiet and empty.

I hear the rhythmic thump of a longtail boat somewhere in the darkness, and I realize that my moment is at hand. Gathering up a sealed plastic bag of supplies, I wade out into the shallow waters to meet the rickety wooden craft that will take me across a small stretch of the Andaman Sea to the forbidden shores of Phi Phi Don's sister island—a majestic, cliff-girded island called Phi Phi Leh.

Phi Phi Leh island is not forbidden because of ancient tribal rituals, secret nuclear tests or hidden pirate treasure. Phi Phi Leh is forbidden because it is the current filming location of a Leonardo DiCaprio movie called *The Beach*. My sole mission on this dim night is to swim ashore and infiltrate the set.

I am not a gossip journalist, a Leo-obsessed film nut or a paparazzo. I am a backpacker. The primary motivation for my mission is not an obsession with Hollywood, but simply a vague yearning for adventure. I wish I could put this yearning into more precise terms, but I can't. All I can say is that adventure is hard to come by these days.

Admittedly, I have a daunting task before me. In the wake of ongoing environmental protests, Leo's purported fear of terrorism and the obligatory packs of screaming pubescent females, security on Phi Phi Leh has reached paramilitary proportions. Thus, I have given up on the notion of a frontal assault. Instead, I plan to swim ashore via Loh Samah Bay, change into dry khakis and a casual shirt and—under cover of darkness—hike across the island to the filming location.

I'm not sure what will happen if I'm able to make it this far, but—summary execution excepted—I am prepared to cheerfully deal with whatever fate awaits me.

This attitude has much less to do with optimism than with the simple fact that—after one week of obsessive preparation—I don't really have a plan.

Day One: January 17, 1999—DiCapritation

Thai Air flight 211 from Bangkok to Phuket has been taxiing around for the last twenty minutes, and there seems to be no end in sight. The European package tourists in the seats around me are getting fidgety, but this is only because they have not set foot on actual soil since Stockholm or Frankfurt. I, on the other hand, have been in Thailand for two weeks—and I've already faced the numbing horrors of Bangkok traffic. There, amid the creeping tangle of automobiles, buses, *tuk-tuks*, humidity and fumes, one is left with two psychological options: nirvanic patience or homicidal insanity. Patience won out for me, and I am taking this present delay in stride. In my lap sits a pile of notes and clippings about the movie production—most of it from Thai tabloid newspapers. Considering that culling hard facts from tabloid gossip is a challenge akin to discerning fate from sheep intestines, my mind frequently strays as I dig through the information.

I wonder, for instance, what would happen if Leonardo DiCaprio's fans here were able to overwhelm his bodyguards. In every part of Asia I've visited, I've noticed how young girls act in the presence of their pop heroes, and it's somewhat unsettling. At one level, there is a screamy, swoony, Elvis-on-*Ed Sullivan* innocence to it all—but at a deeper level, I sense an intuitive desperation.

After all, not only is this part of Asia a survivalist bazaar society (where patiently standing in line is not part of the manner code), it also runs on a patriarchal system, where young girls simply have fewer options in life. If Leo's bodyguards ever fail him, I wouldn't be at all surprised by a frenzied display of grim, no-future pathos—a spectacle that, by comparison, would make punk-rock nihilism seem like a gentle tenet from the Sermon on the Mount. I keep getting this picture in my head of the handsome blond movie star being lovingly, worshipfully torn to pieces—of adolescent girls brawling over ragged bits of spleen and femur.

Several weeks before I came to Thailand, I read the Alex Garland novel upon which the movie is based. In the story, a strange man presents the main character (a young English traveler named Richard) with a map that leads to an unspoiled beach utopia hidden in a national park in the Gulf of Thailand. The *Lord of the Flies*-style moral degeneration that results after Richard's arrival on the beach made for a thoroughly engrossing read.

After finishing the book, I toyed with the idea of emulating the plot—of finding some like-minded travelers, hiring a fishing boat into the restricted national park islands, and seeking out an unspoiled paradise. I ultimately discarded this notion, however, when I discovered that tabloid obsession with the film had already rendered my idea unoriginal.

When I arrived in Thailand and the tabloid hype still hadn't let up, a new idea struck me: Why not live *The Beach* in reverse? Instead of seeking out a secret, untouched island, why not explore the most scrutinized island in all of Thailand? Why not try washing ashore on the movie set itself?

The pure novelty of this notion has led me to this very point: seat 47K, Thai Air flight 211, which has now finally begun to accelerate down the runway. As the plane lifts off the ground and banks for its southward turn, a view of Bangkok fills my window.

Below, urban Thailand spans out around the Chao Phraya River in symmetrical brown-gray grids that, from this altitude, look like the outer armor from a 1970s sci-fi movie spaceship. For an instant, the earth looks artificial and foreign, as if it's been taken over by aliens.

The aliens, of course, are us.

Day Two: January 18, 1999—The Hokey-Pokey

Although historically influenced by traders from China, Portugal, Malaysia and India, the beach villages of Phuket island now seem to belong to northern Europe as much as anyplace. Western tourists abound, prices are steep and miniature golf is readily available.

Since the cast and crew of *The Beach* sleep in Phuket, I came here with the intention of scouting out some information before I set off for Phi Phi Leh. Now that I've arrived, however, I'm a bit stumped on just how I'm supposed to scout out information. Mostly I've just been walking around and talking with other travelers, which is not much different from what I did on Khao San Road in Bangkok.

But talking with other wanderers is telling in and of itself, since nobody in the backpacker crowd wants to admit even the slightest interest in DiCaprio or the filming of the movie. Instead, nearly everyone I've met talks about their own travels in wistful terms eerily similar to the characters in Garland's book. It would be difficult to characterize the nuances from each of my beach-front and street-café conversations this afternoon, but I can easily summarize:

Phuket, it is generally agreed, is a tourist shit hole—best served for anthropological studies of fat German men who wear Speedos. For the ghost of Phuket past, try the islands of Malaysia or Cambodia. Laos incidentally, is still charming and unspoiled, like rural Thailand in the '80s. The hill-tribe trekking around Sapa in Vietnam is as full of wonder and surprise as Chiang Mai treks were a decade ago. Goa and Koh Phangan still can't live up to their early '90s legacy; rumor crowns Central America the new cutting edge of rave. Sulawesi is, part and parcel, Bali ten years ago.

Granted, I have condensed what I heard—but for all the talk, you would think that paradise expired some time around 1989.

I am currently staying at the $5-a-night On On Hotel in Phuket City, where a few interior scenes for *The Beach* will be shot in March. Since it is an official movie location, I had secretly hoped it would be brimming with an eccentric array of film groupies, security personnel and rampaging Leo-worshippers. Instead, the open-air lobby is filled with moths, mopeds and old Thai men playing chess.

Earlier this evening, I spent a couple of hours here chatting and sipping Mekhong whiskey with Ann and Todd, a young couple from Maryland. Our conversation started when I heard Ann quoting a book review of *The Beach* from Phuket's English newspaper, which described backpack travelers as "uniformly ill-clad...all bearing Lonely Planet guidebooks and wandering from one shabby guest house to the next in search of banana pancakes, tawdry tie-dies and other trash particularly their own." Since we agreed we prefer the Whitmanesque stereotype of backpack travel—pocketless of a dime, purchasing the pick of the earth and whatnot—this led to a discussion of what actually distinguishes backpack travelers from tourists.

On the surface, it's a simple distinction: Tourists leave home to escape the world, while travelers leave home to experience the world. Tourists, Ann added wittily, are merely doing the hokey-pokey: putting their right foot in and taking their right foot out; calling themselves world travelers while experiencing very little. Todd and I agreed that this was a brilliant analogy, but after a few more drinks we began to wonder where backpack travelers fit into the same paradigm. This proved to be a problem.

Do travelers, unlike tourists, keep their right foot in a little longer and shake it all about? Do travelers actually go so far as to do the hokey-pokey and turn themselves around—thus gaining a more authentic experience?

Is that what it's all about?

The effects of alcohol pretty much eliminated serious reflection at the time, but now that my buzz is gone I can only conclude that the hokey-pokey—whether done well or poorly—is still just the hokey-pokey.

Or, to put it another way: Regardless of one's budget, itinerary and choice of luggage—the act of travel is still, at its essence, a consumer experience.

Do we travel so that we can arrive where we started and know the place for the first time—or do we travel so that we can arrive where we started having earned the right to take T.S. Eliot out of context?

The fact that it's too late to know the difference makes my little mission to Phi Phi Leh less quirky than it sounds.

Day Three: January 19, 1999—Flord of the Lies

Except for the fact that I met the producer of *The Beach* and somehow ended up stealing his Italian-leather screenplay binder, today hasn't been all that eventful. Mostly I've just been rereading Garland's novel. Tomorrow I leave for Phi Phi Don.

This morning's *Bangkok Post* featured a press statement from DiCaprio, who declared his love of Thailand, his affection for the Thai people and his sincere concern for the local ecology. The ecology comment comes on the heels of an environmental controversy that has been brewing since last fall, when 20th Century Fox announced it was going to plant 100 coconut palm trees on the Phi Phi Leh movie set. The reasoning, apparently, was that Phi Phi Leh didn't quite meet the Hollywood standards of what an island in Thailand should look like.

The months following the coconut palm announcement have been fraught with protests, promises, legal action, threatened legal action, publicity stunts and rumor. Thai environmental activists claimed the palms would disrupt the island's ecosystem; 20th Century Fox responded by reducing the number of trees to sixty. When activists derided this as a meaningless gesture, 20th Century Fox (perhaps misunderstanding the difference between ecology and landscape maintenance) paid a $138,000 damage deposit to the Thai Royal Forest Department and planted the trees anyway. Now environmentalists are claiming that producers flaunted their earlier compromise and brazenly planted no less than seventy-three trees at topsoil depths up to a meter deeper than had previously been agreed.

While the precise facts of this controversy would require a Warren Commission reunion, the fact remains that 20th Century Fox's actions are a drop in the environmental bucket compared to the large-scale tourist development that has besieged Southeast Asia's islands over the last decade. Garland alludes to this phenomenon in his novel: "Set up in Bali, Koh Phangan, Koh Tao,

Boracay, and the hordes are bound to follow. There's no way you can keep it out of the Lonely Planet, and once that happens, it's countdown to doomsday."

Countdown to doomsday. Kind of makes a person wonder if Garland was aware of the irony when he sold his novel's film rights to a media entity that makes Lonely Planet look like an obscure pamphlet publisher based out of the back of someone's Vanagon.

Protests aside, the real environmental impact of the filming won't be determined until after the movie appears in theaters and half a million star-struck teenagers in places like Nebraska and New Brunswick simultaneously decide that they, too, are going to buy a ticket to Thailand to seek out the last paradise on earth.

In a perfect world, I never would have had to sneak into the verandah of the Cape Panwha Resort Hotel and skulk around while the cast and crew of *The Beach* ate dinner.

Unfortunately, my more prosaic efforts at intelligence gathering (wandering around town, sending e-mails to friends of friends) had yielded little. Playing spy for a few hours was the only way to accurately gauge what I was up against.

Since I am the type of person who would rather hike eight extra miles than try to charm a park ranger into accepting a bribe, I was not filled with confidence as I took a motorcycle taxi out to Cape Panwha earlier this evening. I'd read on the Internet that the resort had hired extra security guards, and I was not looking forward to schmoozing my way past them.

Miraculously—despite my patchy beard, motorcycle-tossed hair and sweat-salted backpacker attire—none of the hotel personnel gave me a second glance as I strolled past the reception desk and into the verandah area. I immediately spotted the cast sitting at a long table across from the restrooms. Leo was not among them, but I could tell from a glance that everyone there vaguely corresponded to various characters in the novel. Somebody in casting had done his job well.

Overcoming an innate, juvenile sense of dread, I moved to an empty table overlooking the swimming pool and ordered a Manhattan. I had never ordered a Manhattan before in my life—but since it cost more than my hotel room, I figured it probably contained lots of alcohol. I felt extremely out of place, and I needed something to calm my nerves.

I sipped my drink and tried to act aloof. It was easy to tell the film people from the other hotel guests. The movie folks ate and drank and laughed; everyone else peered around silently. I'm sure that half of the people there were waiting around on the off chance that Leo would walk through. I also suspect that—with the possible exception of a chubby little Japanese girl who kept standing up in her chair to gawk over at the cast—those exact same people would pretend not to notice if Leo actually showed up.

By the time Andrew MacDonald arrived and sat down at the table next to me, I'd washed my Manhattan down with a couple of Heinekens. My anxiety was mostly gone, and the only reason I hadn't sauntered over to schmooze with the cast was that it simply seemed like a stupid idea. Instead, I'd chosen the more conservative option of sitting around and doing nothing. I took the appearance of MacDonald—the film's producer—as a good sign.

Aside from DiCaprio, MacDonald was the only person from the movie that I could have recognized on sight. From one table away, he looked even younger and skinnier than he did in the newspaper photos. Sitting there—gangly, boyish and pink-toed in his Birkenstocks—he looked like someone who was sullenly waiting to be picked last for a game of dodgeball. Figuring it was the night's best chance, I feigned courage and walked up to him. "Excuse me," I said, "you're the producer, right?"

"I'm sorry, that's someone else you're thinking of," he replied, looking everywhere but at me.

"No," I told him, "you're Andrew MacDonald."

MacDonald seemed to cringe as he looked up at me. I wasn't sure if he always looks like this or if he expected me to sucker-punch him. Either way, I took it as my cue to keep talking.

I decided to take a neutral, vaguely journalistic approach. "I was wondering if I might interview some of your actors or spend some time on the set of your movie," I said to him. "Is that possible?"

"It's a closed set," he said wearily.

"What about the actors, do you mind if I chat with them a bit?"

"We're not allowing interviews."

"I don't necessarily want to talk to Leo; anyone will do."

MacDonald took out a pen and wrote a phone number down on a napkin. "This is the number for Sarah Clark. She's a publicist. You'll have to go through her if you want to do any interviews. But at most you'll probably just get an interview with me." He didn't look too thrilled by this possibility.

"So are you saying that there's no chance I can get onto the set, even if I swim there?" I said this as a kind of half joke, hoping it might scare up some clues on how to get past the security cordon around Phi Phi Leh.

"No chance on the island. You can apply as an extra, but that won't be until next month in Phuket and Krabi."

"I was once an extra in a movie called *Dr. Giggles*, but that was like seven years ago."

This utterly irrelevant trivia nugget seemed to disarm MacDonald a bit. "*Dr. Giggles?*" he said, smirking.

"Yeah, are you familiar with it?"

"No, I'm not. Sorry." He stared off at the pool, sighed, then absently checked his watch. "It's been a long day," he said, almost apologetically.

I didn't bother him when he stood up to go.

The events that transpired as I tried to leave the verandah make so little sense that they are somewhat difficult to recount.

First, I had a problem paying my bill, since the hotel staff assumed that I was with the movie crew. When I asked the waitress for my check, she just frowned and walked off. When she hadn't returned after ten minutes, I tracked her down to the cash register.

"I need to pay my bill," I told her. I figured it would be bad manners to sponge drinks after having already interrupted the producer's dinner.

The waitress gave me another strange look, then pushed a piece of paper in front of me. "Just write your room number," she said.

"Can I pay now in cash?" I'm not sure why I was being so insistently ethical; one Manhattan and two Heinekens pale in the face of a $40 million film budget.

The waitress shrugged, and I gave her the money. I turned to leave, and as I was passing the reception desk, the waitress came running after me.

"Your friend forgot this," she said, handing me a yellow cloth satchel.

Standing there in the lobby of the Cape Panwha Resort Hotel, the word "friend" caught me off-guard. I couldn't possibly imagine who she was talking about.

I opened the cloth satchel and took out a black Il Bisonte binder. Embossed into the leather cover were the words THE BEACH. And in the lower right hand corner: ANDREW MACDONALD.

Putting the binder back into the satchel, I thanked the waitress and—just moments after my valorous display of Sunday school ethics over the drink tab—walked out the front door.

I spent the motorcycle taxi ride back into Phuket City trying to think of practical justifications for making off with Andrew MacDonald's screenplay binder. Since the binder was empty, I couldn't really think of any beyond using it as a kind of Hail-Mary collateral if things got ugly when I invaded the film set.

Considering that the phone number MacDonald gave me turned out to belong to a confused Thai family in Yala Province, the personally embossed keepsake was the closest thing I had to an asset.

Sitting in my hotel, I imagine myself on the shores of Phi Phi Leh, lashed to one of the illegally planted coconut palms and bleeding from the ears: I am being flogged with rubber hoses by a gang of vigilante set designers, dolly grips and script supervisors. For the sake of reverie, they are all female, vixenlike and dressed in bikinis.

MacDonald swaggers over. He is wielding a scimitar and has somehow managed to grow a pencil-thin mustache in the time since I last saw him.

"Closed set!" he bellows, fiercely raising the blade above his head.

About to lose consciousness, I muster one last ounce of energy. "I have your *personally embossed Il Bisonte Italian leather screenplay binder*, MacDonald," I sneer. "Kill me, and you'll never find out where I've hidden it."

A look of horror washes across the producer's face. "Not my *personally embossed Il Bisonte Italian leather screenplay binder!*" he screams, dropping the scimitar to the sand.

With a sudden look of resolve, he turns to the bikini-clad lynch mob. "Untie the intruder," he commands, "and tell that DiCaprio schmuck that his services are no longer needed." He turns back to me with a flourish. "I think we've found our new leading man."

A bit overdone, as reveries go—but I'll just blame that on the movies.

They seem to make a convenient scapegoat.

Day Five: January 21, 1999—Heart of Dork-ness

I'm starting in on my second day on Phi Phi Don island, but (for reasons that will become obvious) I didn't write anything yesterday—day four—so I'll try to cover both days in this dispatch.

To put it succinctly: Things have gone sour in a way that I had not expected.

From a tactical standpoint, my mission is progressing nicely. The soaring cliffs of Phi Phi Leh stand just two and a half miles across the sea from my roost on Long Beach. A few casual conversations with some Phi Phi Leh dive-tour operators have provided enough physiographical clues for me to devise a landing strategy. I even found a deserted beach (Lomudi) where I can make a quiet departure in the dead of night.

The problem, however, is that I'm having trouble explaining why I want to go there in the first place.

I arrived here yesterday morning to discover that all the affordable lodging on Long Beach had been sold out. Welcoming the ascetic novelty of sleeping on the beach itself, I left my backpack with a friendly restaurant manager and set off to scope things out.

Technically, the island of Phi Phi Don is part of the same National Marine Park system that protects Phi Phi Leh from permanent tourist development. A person could never tell by looking, however, as an unbroken progression of bungalows and beach resorts lines the entire southeastern seaboard. Ton Sai—an old Thai-Muslim village on the isthmus that connects the two halves of the island—is clotted with luxury hotels, dive shops, restaurants, souvenir peddlers and discos. The only evidence of Muslim heritage is that some of the women selling Marlboros and Pringles wear headscarves.

When I met a Danish pair on the longtail taxi-boat from Ton Sai back to Long Beach, I was immediately struck by their similarity to a couple of characters in *The Beach*. In Alex Garland's novel (and, I am certain, in the movie script), Richard travels to the beach utopia in the company of Etienne and Francoise, a young French couple he meets on Khao San Road. Granted, Jan and Maarta aren't French, but they certainly seemed graceful, companionable and adventurous enough to merit a comparison. When I discovered that they, too, were being forced to sleep on the beach that night, I took this as a sign that I should invite them along for my adventure.

I pitched the idea over a *paad thai* dinner on Long Beach. Since they were both familiar with the novel, I skipped straight into my plans to rent a boat and steal over to Phi Phi Leh. When I saw how this idea entertained them, I backtracked a bit and told them about my experience with Andrew MacDonald the day before. By the time I got to my fantasy about the bikini-clad lynch mob, I had the Danes in stitches.

"You Americans have wonderful thoughts," Jan said between gasps for air.

I saw this as my chance. "Why don't you two join me?"

"Yes," Jan said, still laughing, "why don't we join you?"

"Perfect," I said. "This is too perfect. Let's find a boat and leave tonight."

The Danes stopped laughing. "Are you serious?" Maarta asked.

"I am 100 percent completely serious. Let's leave tonight."

"But we thought you were telling, kind of, a joke."

This threw me a little. "Would you rather leave tomorrow?"

Jan and Maarta exchanged a raised-eyebrow look, which I took to mean either "This guy is really daring" or "This guy is a total dork." Judging from the exchange that ensued, I'd put money on the latter.

"If you really want to go to the movie," Jan said, "why don't you just wait until they finish on Phi Phi Leh and go to work as an extra when they film in Phuket or Krabi?"

"That's not the point," I insisted. "The adventure is in going to a place where you aren't supposed to go. The charm is in living the novel backwards—going to an exclusive and secretive beach that also happens to be famous."

"The island is guarded like an army," Maarta said. "You'll never make it."

"Even if you do," Jan said, "what will you do when you get there?"

By this point, I felt like whipping out the novel and showing Jan and Maarta that they were saying the wrong lines. The issue was getting unnecessarily complicated. In the story, Francoise and Etienne were much more agreeable.

"I don't know what I'll do when I get there," I said. "Walk onto the set, I guess. You know, see what happens when I violate their community. Like in the book."

Jan and Maarta conferred for a moment in Danish, then turned back to me.

"Why are you doing this?" Maarta asked, with a tone of concern.

Since I thought I'd already answered that question, all I could do was stammer. Ultimately I changed the subject—to the relief, I think, of everyone present.

In my own mind the reason why I'm doing this should have been obvious.

Or, even more accurately, the reason why I'm doing this should be irrelevant.

Now that I've had time to think about it, I'd say the motivation behind my mission has a lot to do with a kind of traveler's angst I've been feeling ever since I started my Asian journey. I know I'm not the only one who feels it.

In his 1975 essay, "The Loss of the Creature," Walker Percy attributes traveler's angst to the idea that our various destinations have been "appropriated by the symbolic complex which has already formed in the sightseer's mind."

In other words, the angst originates not in watching fat, Speedo-wearing German men defile once-pristine beaches—the angst comes from our own media-driven notions of how those beaches should be in the first place. We cannot hike the Himalayas without drawing comparisons to the IMAX film we saw last summer; we cannot taste wine on the Seine without recalling a funny scene from an old Meg Ryan movie; we cannot get lost in a South

American jungle without thinking of the Gabriel Garcia Marquez novel we read in college. It is the expectation itself that robs a bit of authenticity from the destinations we seek out.

Even the unexpected comes with its own set of expectations: In Garland's novel, Richard interprets what he sees at his beach utopia through the language of the Vietnam War movies he saw as a teenager.

Percy attempts to explain this phenomenon in his essay. "The highest point," he writes, "the term of the sightseer's satisfaction, is not the sovereign discovery of the thing before him; it is rather the measuring up of the thing to the criterion of the pre-formed symbolic complex."

The challenge this poses for the discerning traveler is that— here at the cusp of a new millennium—mass media has not only monopolized the symbolic complex of wonder and beauty, it has recently upped the ante by an extra seventy-three coconut palm trees.

Thus, by storming *The Beach* at Phi Phi Leh, I hope to travel behind the curtain, to break out from the confines of the consumer experience by attempting to break into the *creation* of the consumer experience.

In this way, I guess I could say that my mission is part of a greater struggle for individuality in the information age—an attempt to live outside the realm of who I'm supposed to be.

At least, that's what I would have told the Danes yesterday, had I had my wits about me.

Today I successfully managed to avoid the Danes entirely. After sneaking a shower at a poolside changing room in Ton Sai, I set off to find a boat that would take me to Phi Phi Leh. Since stealth is an important consideration in my mission, choosing the right boat was a painfully difficult process.

Actually, choosing a boat wasn't really a choice at all, since my only realistic option was to hire out one of the longtail boats that transport people and goods among the islands. Considering that these boats cut through the water as gracefully as bulldozers (none of them have mufflers), my only real option was in finding a driver who sympathized with my cause and wouldn't try to cheat me.

Just before dinner, I found a seemingly earnest boat driver who agreed to take me to Phi Phi Leh for 2,500 baht. We leave in a few hours.

It is already well after dark, and I have stashed my backpack under one of the old fishing huts here at Lomudi. In addition to dry clothes, I have sealed my passport and a few traveler's checks into my plastic swimming bag.

Andrew MacDonald's Italian leather screenplay binder, I'm afraid, was too heavy and will have to stay behind.

I pace the shoreline, killing time before the arrival of the long-tail boat. Tiny bits of phosphorescence glow, star-blue, at the edge of the waves, just as they do in the book.

Day Six: January 22, 1999—Storming The Beach at Phi Phi Leh, continued

It occurs to me that I don't know the name of the small, sun-browned Thai man who sits astern from me in the darkness. I hate to write him off as a minor character—"Boat Driver No. 1"—so I have been thinking of him as "Jimmy." He just seems like someone who should be named Jimmy: trustworthy, average, unassuming. Even in the dark, he wears a wide-brimmed cloth cap.

Neither of us has spoken since I waded out and climbed into the longtail back at Lomudi. Both of us know we are breaking the law—that Phi Phi Leh is patrolled by police speedboats for the duration of the movie shoot. I am hoping that our drop-off site at Loh Samah Bay (instead of Maya Bay, where the film set is located) isn't patrolled very closely at 3:30 in the morning.

Unlike most of the longtail operators I met in Ton Sai, Jimmy is a quiet, introspective man. When we were negotiating the trip yesterday afternoon, he nodded silently as I took out a dive-shop map of Phi Phi Leh and told him where I wanted to go. At first I thought he couldn't speak any English, but he cut me short when I tried to use my Thai phrase book on him. "Three in the morning, O.K.," he'd said. "I know Loh Saman Bay." I suspect he is working to support a wife and kids somewhere.

Two thousand five hundred baht—about $70—is no small sum, but I have written it off as an inevitability. Edmund Hillary had to hire Sherpas; I had to hire Jimmy. Perhaps in an effort to accommodate me—or, just as likely, in an effort to conceal me—Jimmy has spread a rattan mat out on the ribbed wooden floor of the boat. Lying on the mat, clutching my plastic bag, all I can see is the bright wash of stars above me. Oddly, the thumping rattle of the outboard motor somehow makes the stars seem closer, like they are a glittering kind of music video that hovers just over the boat.

My thoughts drift as the boat pushes through the water. I think about my first week in Thailand, when I was quick-dosing on an anti-malaria drug called Lariam. Mild psychosis is a side effect of the drug, and—sure enough—on my second day of taking the pills I punched my fist through the door of my hotel room on Khao San Road. It was certainly one of the more violent acts of my adult life, and to this day I have trouble making sense of it. I don't know why I did it; all I remember was how I felt in the moments before security arrived to kick me out of the hotel. It was not a feeling of dread or shock, as one might expect, but rather a bemused, incongruent sense of wonder. Certainly Leonardo DiCaprio must feel the same way each morning when he wakes up and walks into a world that is staring at him.

"What the hell," I remember thinking to myself, "has happened to me?"

After about twenty minutes, Jimmy suddenly cuts the outboard motor. The silence leaves my ears ringing. I sit up on the mat uncertainly.

"Are we there?" I whisper. The boat rocks as Jimmy crawls up to join me on the mat. He pushes his face right up in front of mine, and I see that he is holding his finger to his lips. He rests a hand on my shoulder and peers past the bow into the darkness.

We sit this way for about ten minutes. Strangely, I am not nearly as nervous as I was on the verandah of the Cape Panwha Resort Hotel. Swimming and hiking are tangible activities—far more cut-and-dry than schmoozing and coaxing information.

But swimming and hiking are not the only obstacles that remain: Jimmy curses softly and moves back to the stern of the longtail. Only then do I hear it—the sound of an approaching speedboat. Before long, our wooden boat is awash in the beam of a spotlight. I try to hide myself under the rattan mat, but it's a useless gesture.

Embarrassed more than anything, I lie awkwardly in the bottom of the longtail while Jimmy and someone on the speedboat yell back and forth in Thai. I absently note that the sealing oil on the hull boards has a pleasant, cedary scent.

Surprisingly, Jimmy yells in his apologetic tone for only a couple of minutes before the speedboat cuts its spotlight and leaves.

"O.K.," Jimmy says.

"It's O.K.?" I say, looking out from my hiding place.

"O.K.," Jimmy says.

I crawl out and move to the stern next to Jimmy. He rests his hand on my shoulder. "O.K.?" he says for the third time. I give him the thumbs up; he starts up the outboard and turns our boat 180 degrees. It's a couple of beats before I realize that we are headed back for Phi Phi Don.

"Isn't this where we just came from?" I ask, pointing my finger ahead into the darkness.

"O.K.!" Jimmy says.

It takes me a good five minutes before I can undo the knot on my plastic swim bag. I'm not particularly proud of what I'm about to do, but I feel like I've come too far to give up now.

I crawl back over to Jimmy and I shove the traveler's checks underneath his nose. "Baksheesh," I say, gesturing back at where we last saw the speedboat. Actually, I'm not even sure if "baksheesh" is the correct word for "bribe" in this part of the world. I feel a little doltish as I say it, like I'm trying to speak Spanish by throwing out English phrases in a Speedy Gonzalez voice.

Jimmy puts his hand on my shoulder in what I now take as a wizened parental gesture. He looks down sympathetically at my traveler's checks. "Boat man, O.K.," he says. "Eye-land man, maybe O.K. Movie man: no. Movie man not O.K." He gently pushes my checks away.

"Yes! O.K.!" I say, still waving the traveler's checks, but he just shakes his head.

The very trustworthiness that led me to hire Jimmy is now backfiring on me. Jimmy knows that, even if I manage to bribe my way past the various levels of Thai security on the island, a film crew with a $40 million budget will be less than impressed with my presence. Jimmy is simply trying to save me the money and stress of going through this whole ordeal.

I'm at a loss to convince him how that very ordeal is exactly what I want to experience.

Which Speedy Gonzalez catch phrases could make Jimmy grasp the pitch and moment that drive this enterprise? What can I say that will make Jimmy appreciate the intricate, shadowlike ironies of travel culture? How can I convince him that this "mission" is not merely another variation of the hokey pokey?

My tongue is ineffectual in its pivots; Phi Phi Leh recedes in the darkness behind us.

We go through strange rituals to prove things to ourselves in life.

As we near our trash-encrusted starting point, I insist that Jimmy cut the engine early, so I can jump out of the longtail and swim the last 200 meters back to the abandoned fishing village.

Since simple epiphany doesn't screen well in the test markets, I will tell people that I swam those 200 meters with a defiant sense of triumph. I will tell them that each small step wading ashore was a giant leap for mankind.

I will tell them that I walked through the Valley of the Shadow of Death, and that I feared no evil—for the Valley of the Shadow of Death will soon feature guided tours and a snack bar.

∾

ENDNOTES

1. **Page 4, paragraph 2: *The primary motivation for my mission is not*:** In any travel story, there's bound to be a bit of artifice when it comes to defining the quest. In the case of "Storming *The Beach*," living the adventure was never fully separate from writing about it—and in fact I flew to Phuket knowing that my editor at *Salon* would print the story if my "mission" amounted to anything. Were it not for the narrative possibilities it offered, I would have been less likely to embark on a wacky quest to infiltrate the set of a Hollywood movie.

Few travel "quests" that make it to the written page, I think, exist on a plane of pure desire. Regardless of how artfully the writer presents his thesis, the story itself was invariably a part his initial motivation. This is pretty much a self-fulfilling equation: If you enter into a travel experience taking notes, odds are you intend to write about it—and if your motivation is so pure that you don't take notes, the accuracy of your narrative is going to be suspect.

Nevertheless, some people harbor a sentimental notion of how travel stories ought to work. When "Storming *The Beach*" was selected by Bill Bryson for inclusion in *The Best American Travel Writing 2000*, a book reviewer for *The New Republic* cited my story as an example of how "contemporary travel writing is no longer driven by obsession." Apparently the reviewer didn't think a self-conscious foray into the creation of a motion picture could reveal much about human experience—but I think he'd forgotten to consider how human experience works. In the

1955 book *Tristes Tropiques*, Claude Levi-Strauss noted how anthropologists might miss the true dynamic of a culture if they focus too closely on its perceived purity. "While I complain of being able to glimpse no more than the shadow of the past," he wrote, "I may be insensitive to reality as it is taking shape at this very moment.... A few hundred years hence, in this same place, another traveler, as despairing as myself, will mourn the disappearance of what I might have seen, but failed to see."

In the same way, a gonzo flirtation with popular culture might well reveal something about a pop-culture-obsessed world—and a haunted sense of "obsession" would only serve to obscure the more fickle motivations that drive everyday life.

All of which is a roundabout way of saying that most travel stories are self-referential at a certain level—and this is not a bad thing. When you enter into an experience with the intention of writing about it, you tend to travel the world more creatively and observe it more thoughtfully (even when the experience in question takes place on the fringes of a Hollywood movie production in Thailand).

2. **Page 5, paragraph 2:** *...if Leonardo DiCaprio's fans here were able to overwhelm his bodyguards*: In reading this story, it's useful to understand just how outrageously famous DiCaprio had become one year after the blockbuster success of *Titanic*. Not since Sylvester Stallone's *Rambo* had an American movie star so thoroughly saturated the international imagination. As film director Baz Luhrmann noted, DiCaprio "*became* global culture, in much the same way as the Beatles or Elvis." At the time this comparison was no exaggeration.

Indeed, so far-reaching was DiCaprio's fame in 1999 that the Taliban-led Afghan government arrested no fewer than twenty-two Kabul barbers for Leonardo-inspired moral laxity. Their crime? Peddling a haircut called "The Titanic."

3. **Page 8, paragraph 1:** *...this led to a discussion of what actually distinguishes backpack travelers from tourists*: Two months after this experience, I gained an interesting new theoretical perspective on the traveler/tourist dichotomy. By that time *The Beach* production had moved on to Phuket (where the set was far less secretive and exclusive

than on Phi Phi), and I'd managed to land a job as an extra. On my first night of work, 21st Century Fox's handlers divided all the extras into two groups: "tourists" and "travelers." No actual travel credentials were required; the production assistants simply made their decisions on the basis of fashion.

That is, if you had dreads or wore a sarong or sported tattoos or clutched a set of bongos, you were grouped together with the "travelers." If you kept your hair short or wore nice clothes or had a reasonably neat appearance, you spent your on-camera time as a "tourist." Though my suntan was lacking at the time, I made the cut as a "traveler" on the basis of my hair (which was longish) and clothing (which, while not suitably ethnic, was a bit tattered).

Despite such reductive methodology, I'll admit I felt a small flush of pride as I took my place in the extras' tent with the other "travelers." Just like being picked first for a game of kindergarten kickball, I had proof that I had made the cut: I was a member of the elite.

Sadly, I wasn't a "traveler" for long. Andrew McDonald had recognized me from my adventure at the Cape Panwha Hotel two months earlier, and the film's publicist fired me two hours into my second night on the set.

4. **Page 9, paragraph 2:** *...the Hollywood standards of what an island in Thailand should look like*: The idea that Hollywood producers should travel to Thailand and decide it doesn't look enough like Thailand may sound singularly absurd, but it's not a singular event. Almost forty years earlier, when filming Marlon Brando's *Mutiny on the Bounty* in Tahiti, the film producers didn't like the looks of the dingy volcanic sand in Matavai Bay, so they imported hundreds of tons of more photogenic white sand from New Jersey.

5. **Page 10, paragraph 5:** *...prosaic efforts at intelligence gathering...sending e-mails to friends of friends*: The closest I ever came to useful intelligence about the filming of *The Beach* was a tip from a Canadian girl I met in Phuket, who'd hung out with a British girl on Koh Phi Phi whose deaf cousin had been cast in a minor role in *The Beach*. Using e-mail, I eventually tracked the British girl down on Koh Phi Phi,

but this put me in the decidedly awkward position of trying to figure out how she could possibly help me.

After all, people don't typically feel comfortable offering a complete stranger the services of their deaf cousins in an effort to help him infiltrate the closed set of a major motion picture.

6. **Page 12, paragraph 11:** *...I was once an extra in a movie called* **Dr. Giggles,** *but that was like seven years ago*: In addition to *Dr. Giggles* and *The Beach*, I also worked as "background talent" in the Lindsey Lohan movie *Just My Luck* to earn some extra cash when I was living in New Orleans in early 2005. Those interested in organizing a "Rolf Potts Background-Extra Trilogy" viewing party are advised to provide strong cocktails to smooth the experience, as none of these productions met with much critical approval.

7. **Page 13, paragraph 10:** *...I spent the motorcycle taxi ride back into Phuket City*: This sentence is one of those minor inaccuracies that can sneak into a nonfiction narrative in the interest of keeping things simple.

According to my notes, I didn't hail a motorcycle taxi; I hitched a ride in a pickup driven by a Scottish guy named David, who turned out to be a gaffer for *The Beach*. David wasn't interested in talking about the film, but he did chat me up about the aesthetic difference between real and fake breasts on his various ex-girlfriends before dropping me off at Spark's Pub in Phuket City, where I found some Norwegians I'd met earlier and watched a Thai heavy-metal band crank out Mötley Crüe songs in front of a giant wind-machine.

When I got around to writing the story, it just seemed easier to say I'd taken a motorcycle taxi.

8. **Page 14, paragraph 10:** ... *I didn't write anything yesterday...so I'll try to cover both days in this dispatch*: Recounting a tale such as my storming of *The Beach* requires a fair amount of condensation and elimination of details. In reality, I spent much of that fourth day focused on completely unrelated activities. For instance, I spent several hours that afternoon reading John Pierson's *Spike, Mike, Slackers and Dykes*—a

book about independent filmmaking (purchased in Bangkok days before) that whetted my long-repressed interest in writing a movie comedy set in a high school Spanish class.

Thus, I spent two hours in the middle of my *Beach* adventure making notes on a screenplay I still haven't written.

I only mention this peculiar deviation from my *Beach* mission to bring attention to the fact that any given travel experience is full of details that will never be worthy of a travel narrative, even though they occupy a legitimate place in the travel experience. As Alain de Botton observed in *The Art of Travel*, "the anticipatory and artistic imaginations omit and compress; they cut away the periods of boredom and direct our attention to critical moments, and thus, without either lying or embellishing, they lend to life a vividness and a coherence that [the actual experience] may lack in the distracting wooliness of the present."

9. **Page 20, paragraph 3:** *...I punched my fist through the door of my hotel room on Khao San Road*: After I'd settled the door damage that morning, the chipper Thai-Chinese hotel manager gave me a thumbs-up and told me in halting, phrasebook-grade English that I was very handsome to be able to break the door.

I can't be sure, but I think he meant to say "strong."

❧ 2 ☙

Road Roulette

B y my second day of thumbing rides through Lithuania, I finally feel like I've hit a hitchhiking rhythm, even though my progress (less than 100 miles) hasn't been particularly impressive. Standing at the edge of a town called Marijampole, thumb aloft, I keep my patience—despite the fact that I'm in my third hour of waiting for a ride. The Polish border, my goal for the day, is still a tantalizing twenty miles away.

Regardless of where you are in the world, hitchhiking comes with its own set of basic procedures: choosing a safe roadside hitching spot where traffic is slow enough to stop; refusing to accept rides from drunk or suspicious or crazy people; staying wary, bringing a map, using common sense. Patience, that mossy old virtue, is central to all of this. With the proper amount of patience, hitching can be a safe and interesting way to see Europe and—most importantly—it can allow you to interact with the kind of people you'd never see on well-trod tourist routes.

The inspiration to hitch first struck me two nights ago, while I was researching my Poland guidebook in a McDonald's near the Vilnius bus station. I'd heard great things about Poland from other travelers, but the more I read about places like Gdansk and

Poznan and Czestochowa, the more demoralized I became. From a planning perspective, Poland was just too big and interesting. To tackle the Tatras Mountains in the south might mean missing the Bialowieza Forest in the north; to tour the Renaissance village of Zamosc in the east might mean missing the avant-garde university town of Wroclaw in the west; to experience the cosmopolitan culture of Warsaw or Krakow might mean missing the folk culture of the countryside.

Sometimes, choice presents itself as a glossy act of destruction—of eliminating possibilities in the name of decisiveness. This is why—halfway through a Lithuanian Big Mac—I decided to give Poland up to chance instead of choice: I decided to simply find a highway, stick out my thumb and let fate take me for a ride. Thus, by turning my travels into a kind of road roulette, I could experience each moment of Poland without having to worry about where I stood in relation to point A or B.

Each new ride and random stop-off, I'd hoped, would reveal Poland not as a mere destination—but as a continuously unfolding mystery.

The most immediate challenge upon starting my hitchhiking adventure yesterday came in trying to get out of Vilnius, my starting point. The problem with Vilnius isn't that Lithuanians don't stop for hitchers—the problem is that hitching rides in Lithuania seems to be a wildly popular pastime. On a warm Sunday afternoon in Vilnius, the competition for rides can be daunting. When I arrived at the A1 highway ramp at noon, I was greeted by an outright crowd of Lithuanian hitchhikers strung out down the road. Keeping true to etiquette, I took a place twenty meters beyond the last person, stuck out my thumb and waited.

And waited.

When competing with other hitchers on a balmy Lithuanian day, being male, solo and six foot three is hardly the best marketing formula. After two hours of wagging my thumb at traffic, my arm was sore and my feet were tired. Over a dozen hitchers ahead and behind me had already been picked up, almost all of them females. Male hitchers (myself included) stood forlornly at the front of the queue while female hitchers got whisked off within minutes of arriving.

This ongoing phenomenon was about to drive me into pessimism when a Lithuanian girl stepped off a local bus one block down and walked right up to where I was standing.

"Do you mind if I hitch with you?" she asked. "I have this habit of not hitching by myself."

I looked at the girl and blinked. She had a Betty Boop haircut, a small shoulder bag full of gear, and fantastic green eyes. She'd approached me without a trace of apprehension, and she'd somehow known that I spoke English. Since I'd only seen this kind of luck as a beer commercial plot device, I decided to clarify.

"Why do you want to ride with me?"

"You're American," she said. "Foreign travelers are always a safe bet. Plus you speak English and so do I."

"Yes, but how did you know I spoke English? How could you tell I was American?"

"You look American," she said. "You're wearing white socks."

My new partner introduced herself as Edita ("just like the boss of a newspaper," she said) and went to work. Standing at the edge of the road, she laid one hand across her heart, raised the other into the air and gave her eyelashes an exaggerated flutter—as if she were portraying a coquettish onstage vixen. Within a minute, a white van pulled over and picked us up.

"You're good," I told her as we climbed into the van.

"I got involved in drama at university," she said. "I used to be shy. I still am shy by nature, but acting has helped me become a stronger person. If I ever get into a situation that seems difficult, I can just 'act' my way through it. I was acting when I met you back there, by the way."

"Bravo," I said.

As luck would have it, both Edita and I were headed to the city of Kaunas, where the A1 highway to the Baltic Sea intersects the A5 route into Poland. Had my beer commercial reveries (which had kicked into high gear by this point) been actualized, Edita would have introduced me to a bikinied gaggle of her actress friends in a Kaunas hot tub. Instead, Edita gave me something much more subtle but just as lovely: She took the evening to personally walk me through her city.

Kaunas is a remarkable old settlement tucked into a small gorge at the confluence of the two widest rivers in Lithuania. Some of the buildings and ruins date back to the days before Lithuania—the last pagan holdout in Europe—was Christianized in the fourteenth century. Kaunas has been burned to the ground thirteen separate times in its history, and once served as the national capital when Vilnius fell to the Poles. Kaunas has one street (Laisves Avenue) where it hasn't been legal to smoke a cigarette since the twilight of the Soviet occupation, and it is the only city in the world—to my knowledge, at least—with a museum devoted entirely to folk-art devil figurines.

Following a 700-year-old cobblestone street into the Old Town district, Edita shared with me the secrets of Kaunas: how in 1812 Napoleon launched his ill-fated Russia invasion from a nearby hill; how the embalmed bodies of Lithuanian aviation heroes Tesporas Darius and Stasys Girenas were secretly sealed into the walls of a local medical building during Stalin's reign; how Yasser Arafat once had his private helicopter renovated at the local airplane factory.

Our cobblestone walk terminated at Rotuses Square, where we found a pipe organ concert underway in the baroque-styled confines of St. Francis Church. Admittedly, I know more about Moog tunes than fugue tunes, and I wouldn't recognize a diapason if one hit me over the head. But the complex, sonorous hum of the old pipe organ left me enchanted as I stood with Edita in the back of the crowded sanctuary: I felt like I'd come to Kaunas just to hear that strange music with a green-eyed girl.

Thus far, today hasn't been quite so charmed. Two short rides took me out of Kaunas to the A5 ramp at Garliava this morning; then I had to wait three hours before a man in a blue Mazda took me thirty-five miles to the back streets of Marijampole. All three drivers were friendly, but none of them spoke English or interacted much. Now, at the south edge of town—almost within walking distance of the Polish border—my arm is beginning to tire again.

Pessimism creeps as the traffic whizzes past me. The sun is sinking into its late afternoon groove, and I'm considering my backup plan: to forgo a ride and hike a few hours out of the city limits so I can find a safe place to camp for the night. Since I'm carrying a hammock and a Gore-Tex bivy sack, I figure it will be easy to blend into the forest for an evening's sleep. Then I can walk the rest of the way to the border tomorrow and wait for Poland-bound cars as they pass through the checkpoint.

As I'm pondering this possibility, a white Ford Focus pulls over onto the shoulder and a college-aged girl sticks her head out the passenger window. "Do you speak English?" she asks.

"Sure," I say. "I'm American."

"Good, because my friends and I don't speak much Lithuanian. We're just visiting from Hungary. We're going to Krakow. Where are you going?"

"I just need to get into Poland. Anywhere across the border is fine."

"Well then, please get in. I'm Christina, and this is my boyfriend Ervin and our friend Sepi."

Thanking Christina, I unsling my pack while the Hungarians rearrange things in the car. The Ford Focus is so full of food and gear that it takes them ten minutes before they can shift enough items to clear out a space for me.

"You are very lucky today," Christina says to me as we try to jam my pack into the trunk.

"Why's that?" I ask.

"Because you are the first hitchhiker in Ervin's new car. He used to hitchhike all the time—he even made it to Amsterdam once. Now that he's driving, he finally gets to say thank you for all the people who picked him up. Maybe this will be the best ride of your life!"

Once I wedge myself into the back seat, I have so many sausages and melons and grease-spotted cookie boxes in my lap that I can hardly move. Sepi, a stocky, bearded fellow who shares the back seat with me, assures me that there is one easy way to free up some breathing space. "You look hungry," he says.

Sepi hands out some plastic plates and passes the food around the car as the swampy Lithuanian forestland rolls past. Bit by bit, we eat ourselves some elbowroom.

"Why do you have so much food?" I ask, gnawing at my chunk of watermelon.

"Our Lithuanian friends were married in Marijampole this weekend," Sepi says, cutting a thick slice of ham sausage onto a piece of bread. "Lithuanians are wonderful. When the family of our married friends found out we'd come all the way from Hungary, they treated us like brothers. When it was over, they gave us all this food."

"There was no room to sleep at our friends' house," Christina adds, "so we just slept in the wedding hall. The next morning, all the guests came back and we started eating and drinking and dancing again. So much happiness."

"Too much happiness," Ervin says. "If I didn't have this car to get us home, they would have made us stay there forever."

As we slow to pass through customs, I tell my new Hungarian friends my hitchhiking strategy. "I want to see Poland by thumb," I say. "I was thinking you could just take me to the first Polish city after the border station. The map says it's a town called Suwalki."

"Why do you want to stop there?" Ervin asks.

"Well, I want to discover things as they come in Poland, and that's a good place to start. I just want to keep a laid-back attitude and go where fate and chance take me. That's the best way to discover things, I think. Road roulette."

"Roulette, yes, like gambling," Sepi says. "I think that sounds romantic. But what is 'laid-back'?"

"Relaxed, casual," I say. "Not worrying about goals."

Ervin looks back at me from the driver's seat, a fire of mischief in his eyes. "But how can you be laid back," he says, "if you want to get out of the car at Suwalki and wait for a different ride? That's a goal, yes? We are already going to Krakow. If you are laid back, you will come with us."

Sepi nods seriously. "You must come to Krakow."

"But Krakow is all the way at the other end of the country. If I go there now, I'll miss most of Poland."

"Krakow is not the end of Poland," Ervin says. "Krakow is just the south of Poland. If you want to see more of Poland after Krakow, just hitch north."

"I know roulette," Sepi adds, "and I think you can't change your number now. If Ervin picked you up, then you have to go where Ervin is going."

The Hungarians have me checkmated: To argue otherwise at this point would be to contradict the impulse that led me to hitch in the first place. "Krakow it is, then," I shrug.

A few dozen miles into Poland, the day fades out; we speed south on the darkened road. The Hungarians seem as inspired by my presence as I do by their hospitality, and I soon get a Hungarian-slanted crash course in Eastern European history and politics. Christina, Ervin and Sepi all attend the elite University of Economic Sciences in Budapest, and I am amazed not just by their socio-political knowledge—but by their nonchalant skill at discussing and debating these issues in English.

The most entertaining aspect of this freewheeling culture lesson is that Christina, Ervin and Sepi can't bring themselves to agree on any one interpretation of the world. When Sepi tries to teach me the details of the 1956 Budapest Revolution, Ervin and Christina get into an argument over Imre Nagy's tactical wisdom in standing up to the Soviets. When Christina tries to educate me regarding Hungary's progressive new Gypsy policies, Sepi and Ervin bicker over whether Gypsy social shortcomings are the result of culture or prejudice. When Ervin describes how recent economic growth and reforms have brought Hungary into a new golden age, Christina and Sepi debate whether the last great age in Hungary was the nineteenth century monarchical alliance with Austria or the fifteenth century empire under King Matthias Corvinus. Whenever such debates get too heated, everyone switches over to Hungarian, and I have to wait several minutes before they translate their conclusions into English. I sit spellbound in the back seat under my pile of half-eaten Lithuanian sausages.

Well into the night, about forty-five minutes south of Warsaw, Sepi is talking about the fate of the 3 million ethnic Hungarians living in Transylvanian Romania when Ervin coasts the car to the side of the road. He says something in Hungarian, and Sepi hands him a big plastic cup from the back seat. Very businesslike, Ervin takes the cup, opens his door, and hops outside. I peer out the back window as he takes off running back up the highway like some kind of lunatic superhero.

"What's going on?" I ask.

"We ran out of fuel," Sepi says. "Ervin always forgets to check the gauge on his new car. He says he saw a petrol station a few kilometers back."

While we wait for Ervin to complete his mission, Christina spreads a blanket onto the grass at the side of the road and we snack on some more of the Lithuanian wedding delicacies. Sepi fishes a couple of bottles of red wine from the trunk and mixes the vintage with some Coca-Cola.

"Why are you mixing wine and Coke?" I ask him.

"This is red wine," he says. "It goes best with Coke. Sprite is best for white wine."

"Is this normal—mixing wine and soft drinks?"

Sepi shrugs. "Hungary is famous for wine, and we begin to drink it when we are very young. For kids, it tastes better with Coke. So maybe right now we're just drinking like children."

Sitting at the side of the road, I have my first ever wine-cola cocktail while Sepi and Christina discuss sustainable growth, dismantling state sectors and the best ways to attract foreign investment.

It occurs to me at this moment that I am sitting on a Polish roadside with Hungary's future leaders: that Sepi and Christina (and Ervin) will one day be part of the brain trust that helps bring their country into the new century. And the fact that they are so down to earth and alive—the fact that they would road-trip across four countries to see their Lithuanian friends get married, or teach a hitchhiker about their economy (or, for that matter, sweeten their wine with Coke because it tastes better—an honest populist gesture if I've ever seen one)—makes me suspect that Hungarian democracy is going to do just fine.

Thirty minutes into our picnic, Ervin returns with a full cup of gasoline. He carefully empties the cup into the tank, and we sputter back up the road to the petrol station. As Christina squeegees the windshield and Ervin turns on the gas-pump, I realize that a full day of hitching topped off with wine-cola cocktails has made me sleepy.

By the time Sepi wakes me up, the car is parked on a narrow city street and it is daylight. Though I've been semi-awake all night, I'm still not sure what has just happened.

"We are here," Sepi says as he shakes me awake. "Ervin and Christina have already gone to sleep in their apartment. I'll show you to the dormitory on Horansky, and you can stay in one of the empty rooms there."

Something about this makes no sense at all. "Christina and Ervin have an apartment in Krakow?" I ask.

Sepi laughs. "You have been asleep a long time, I think. This is not Krakow. This is Budapest."

I try to draw a map in my mind—to figure out how Krakow can turn into Budapest without me knowing—but it's too early in the morning for this. "I thought we were going to stop in Krakow," I say.

"We did stop in Krakow, but it was too late to call our friends there, and Ervin felt like driving some more. So we went to Slovakia."

My mental map still isn't materializing. "What happened in Slovakia?" I ask.

"I don't know; I fell asleep before we got there. Slovakia isn't very big, so I guess Ervin felt like driving all the way home. He loves his new car, you know." Sepi pauses for a moment and shoots me a rather apologetic grin. "Who knows? He might even drive you back to Poland, if that's what you want."

I sit for a moment to mull over this unexpected shift in geography. By giving Poland up to chance—by attempting to unravel the mystery of Poland on a thumb and a prayer—it seems as though I have discovered something entirely unexpected: Hungary.

Figuring it's always better to assume you've hit the jackpot than to obsess over what might have been, I yank my pack from the crammed trunk of the Ford. As I follow Sepi to my Budapest crash pad, I feel a small, indescribable welling of joy at the odds that brought me here.

Road roulette, indeed.

∽

ENDNOTES

1. **Page 28, paragraph 3:** *The inspiration to hitch first struck me two nights ago*: To be honest, the urge to hitch didn't suddenly hit me out of nowhere in the middle of a Lithuanian McDonald's. I'd been curious about hitchhiking for years, and Eastern Europe offered me a great opportunity to try it out in earnest.

Before I was a full-time travel writer, when I was teaching English in South Korea, I spent spare moments in my office surfing the Internet for travel information. At the time, Vilnius had an active hitching club with a well organized website, and I'd come to associate the city with thumbing rides long before I traveled there. Thus, while the lure of Poland was certainly a factor in my decision to hitch out of Vilnius, my adventure was equally inspired by random afternoons in East Asia two years earlier.

Since Internet research in a Korean technical college doesn't have the same romantic resonance as hitching by Poland-inspired impulse, I left this detail out of the story.

I'd reckon most carefully constructed travel narratives operate in this way: Because most adventures exist in a complicated web of motivation (including the intention to write about the experience later), it's best to focus on the most compelling motivations when you frame your story.

2. **Page 36, paragraph 8:** *...we sputter back up the road to the petrol station*: While we were at this petrol station, I decided to show my appreciation for the Hungarians by paying for a tank of gasoline. Reasoning that they might refuse this offer if I asked them directly, I went inside and gave the attendant my credit card while Ervin was filling the tank.

By middle-class American standards my gesture might have merited a feeble protest coupled with a nod of appreciation, but Ervin was deeply insulted. Whereas I'd considered paying for the gas a gesture of courtesy (kind of like bringing a bottle of wine when you're invited for dinner), Ervin took it as a grave betrayal of the host-guest relationship.

Later, when I stayed on in Budapest for four more nights, Ervin bought me enough beer to fill the tank a second time. No doubt he did this as a point of honor, but it was also a reminder of the economic dynamic that follows you on the road: When you come from a wealthy country, it's easy to forget how the simplest of gestures might seem patronizing.

3. **Page 37, paragraph 9: ...*as I follow Sepi to my Budapest crash pad***: At a direct experiential level, my four days in Budapest were as interesting as the time I spent hitchhiking. Based out of a spare room in the dormitory, I joined a rotating roster of Hungarian university students on a series of adventures in the city: walking along the Danube while drinking keg wine from plastic bottles; playing stud poker till dawn in the dormitory kitchen; watching Emir Kusturica's *Black Cat, White Cat* at Uránia Cinema while three young Hungarians argued over how best to translate the subtitles into English for me.

In early drafts I tried to include these anecdotes in my narrative, but ultimately I realized the story wasn't about what happened in Budapest: It was about the power of chance, and how it can send you in curious new directions.

❧ 3 ☙

Toura Incognita

W E hike out of the trees and into the shadow of the towering gray cliff, yet even then the entrance to Heup Cave is difficult to make out until we are standing directly in front of it. Then, suddenly, it looks enormous—a rocky yawn of cool air, clean water, and darkness.

The only way into or out of central Laos's Na Valley, our porters tell us, is through this flooded cave, which reputedly stretches more than half a mile under the limestone ridge. Max Arcangeloni, our leathery forty-two-year-old expedition leader, logs a reading on his GPS. In the three days since we crossed the Mekong River from Thailand, Max has been meticulously recording cultural and geographical features along the rocky fringes of the Khammouan Limestone National Biodiversity Conservation Area. The Khammouan does not feature in any history or travel books and has yet to be comprehensively surveyed. This trip is the first attempt to chart it.

Now, having taken our small expedition team fifty miles on foot and by boat up the Hin Boun River, Max is facing a moment of truth. On the one hand, the valley on the other side of the cave could be just another anonymous wrinkle in the landscape of

Southeast Asia. Then again, the Na could very well live up to its reputation as the home of pristine forests, abundant wildlife, the primitive village of Ban Na, and the vine-entangled ruins of a mysterious old city named Aran.

Despite all appearances, however, we are not hauling two hundred pounds of computer equipment, digital cameras, satellite mapping technology, dried food, and climbing gear through Heup Cave in the name of historical or scientific exploration. Rather, Max has been hired by North by Northeast Tours, a Thai travel company, to survey and map the area so that it can be opened up to sustainable tourism. Whatever biological, geological, anthropological, or archaeological curiosities we find will be recorded primarily as potential expedition highlights. I've been trudging along jungle footpaths and boating my way up Mekong tributaries to witness the early development of what is (for the time being, at least) the last frontier of travel. Here, as Max systematically gauges the ecotourism possibilities of the Laotian backcountry, I hope to see how a mere location begins to transform into a destination.

Muntree Paorman, Max's Thai assistant, distributes headlamps to the Lao porters. Giggling at the battery-powered novelty, the teens hoist their loads and wade into the darkness of the cave. I splash into line behind Muntree and Max as the porters' yellow beams of light dance up onto the smooth rock of the cave entrance. After twenty minutes of sloshing our way along the dark stream, we ascend small wooden ladders that lead us up to smooth stone paths worn into the limestone. Cast-off bundles of charred sticks that have been used as torches by recent commuters dot the fringes of our route. Twenty feet up the cave wall, a thin line of mud marks the monsoonal high-water point. Even in complete darkness, pink-leafed shoots of bamboo push up from the stream banks, delicately tilting toward the cave entrance.

After nearly an hour of wading through the darkness, we finally scramble over a jumble of damp boulders and into a blinding slot of daylight. Outside, the mountain-ringed Na Valley reveals itself in a sudden wash of late-afternoon color: green jungle, brown earth, gray rock, blue sky. Teak trees tower up through the canopy, and leaves blanket the forest floor. The air, I note, is more humid than on the Hin Boun side of the cave. A path leads away from the limestone ridge and into a thick stand of hardwoods and tangled underbrush. As we walk, I am filled with nervous anticipation over what awaits us. I also wonder what will happen to the valley once Max collects his data and reports home. After all, this visit stands to change the place forever.

In many ways, tourism is a perfect industry for Laos, a landlocked communist country that has only been open to foreigners since 1989. Unlike its crowded and industrious neighbors (Thailand is home to 54 million people; Vietnam's population is 75 million and growing), Laos has just 5 million citizens and very little commerce or infrastructure. Seventy percent of the land consists of mountains or high plateaus, and 25 percent of Laos is blanketed in primary forest—making it the most pristine country in Indochina. Perhaps seeing value in this, the Laotian government set up seventeen national nature reserves in 1993 (including Khammouan Limestone NBCA), earmarking 10 percent of the Laotian landmass for conservation. And despite the fact that most of these conservation areas are still largely inaccessible, tourism became the top foreign-exchange earner in Laos for the first time in 1999. Theoretically, nature-based ecotourism ventures within the conservation areas could further bolster the Laotian economy at the same time that they preserve the Laotian environment.

The problem with ecotourism anywhere, however, is that it's a difficult activity to define, and an even harder activity to regulate. At a simple level, ecotourism is responsible travel that conserves the natural environment and sustains the wellbeing of the local-people—but even this basic definition can prove full of contra-dictions and loopholes. For example, ecotourism seeks "unspoiled" places that have not been categorized or prepared for tourist consumption, yet ecotourism itself is a form of catego-rization and consumption. Ecotourism promises an escape from the trappings of affluence and information society, yet by attract-ing affluent tourists to isolated points around the globe, eco-tourism spreads the gospel of information society. And while the purpose of ecotourism is to preserve the culture and ecology of far-flung lands, the most efficient way to achieve this is to not travel to those locales in the first place.

In a practical sense, ecotourism isn't the product of design so much as it is the result of market demands. Just as Thomas Cook's pioneering tour-organizing efforts 150 years ago catered to the emerging social and recreational needs of a new industrial age middle-class, ecotourism is a response to information age yearn-ings for uniqueness, isolation and authenticity. Thus, where the traditional aim of tour developers has been to create an exotic, leisurely variation of Paradise, ecotours aim to package a post-modern sort of Wonderland—a place that remains unique to itself, quietly tucked away from the unifying juggernaut of global culture. And such exotic, anonymous isolation is becoming a hot commodity. Depending upon whose statistics you choose to believe, ecotourism has grown to encompass 5 to 35 percent of a tourism industry that generates $2.5 trillion of commerce a year.

Of all the novelties that greet us in Ban Na, the most curious is the village headman's request that we purchase a pig. It seems that this gesture is just a cumbersome method of paying for our room and board, but Max is a bit stumped about what we're expected to do with the pig. I keep imagining him forlornly hik-ing through the forest with a squealing porker strapped to his backpack.

Ban Na itself is little more than two dozen rattan-walled huts perched on stilts in a small clearing. We've arrived during the harvest, and beneath the houses, several old women are threshing rice with big wooden pounders that tilt like seesaws. Most of the villagers are off tending their fields, leaving the dusty lanes of Ban Na to a handful of elderly women, very young children, and a few skinny dogs and chickens. A tiny, straw-roofed schoolhouse sits, half-collapsed, at the edge of the settlement; the headman tells us that classes haven't been held since the teacher stopped coming through the cave from Ban Nakok a few months ago.

Bidding our porters farewell (all of them live in the Hin Boun basin and will return home through Heup Cave while it's still light out), Max, Muntree, and I prepare for a night in Ban Na. It is an unspoken assumption that we will sleep on the porch of the headman's house. The interior of the wood-framed hut is bare save for blankets, clothing, a few mosquito nets, and some faded government-issue public health posters; cooking is done over an open fire in an adjacent outhouse. By all appearances, life is so basic here that I find it hard to believe that Aran—reputedly once a sophisticated settlement—could ever have arisen in this valley. Max, speaking Thai and pidgin Lao, jokes with the small children who've crept up to stare at us.

Indeed—satellite mapping notwithstanding—forging such bonds of goodwill is his most important task here. After all, the locals will know the nuances of the area better than Max's GPS does, and any tour groups that arrive here in the future will depend on their hospitality. In the coming days, he will train various villagers in the art of aesthetically correct trash disposal, slit-latrine construction, and other low-impact methods of hosting visitors. But for now, Max gets out his medical kit and squats at the foot of the headman's house. As people return from the fields in the evening, he attends to their various aches and pains with aspirin and antiseptic.

The sixteen-year-old daughter-in-law of the headman brings him her month-old son. In a soft voice, she explains that the baby has not been taking her breast milk. Lifting the yellow swaddling blanket, she shows how his tiny face has begun to wrinkle from malnutrition. Max suggests that the child be taken through the cave to a clinic downriver, but the headman shrugs off the idea. Perhaps because infant mortality can be as high as 25 percent in settlements like Ban Na, babies are not regarded as full humans until they are old enough to have an active interest in their surroundings. And because the merits of Western neonatal medicine are not understood, it appears that the villagers are prepared to leave the baby's health to local resources. Hoping to help somehow, Max prepares a powdered cocoa solution for the infant.

By nightfall, all hundred or so villagers have returned, and Ban Na is abuzz. Most of the people have never seen *falangs* (non-Asian foreigners) before, and the residents are positively enamored of us. One toothless old lady—who, we find out later, is just fifty-four years old (ancient and matriarchal by Ban Na standards)—solemnly walks up and presents us each with a boiled egg. Max delights them by taking photographs with his digital camera and displaying the images on his laptop.

The people of Ban Na don't conform to the sentimental tourist's idea of what isolated villagers should look like. Instead of colorful ethnic costumes, they sport tattered t-shirts, rubber sandals, Chinese-manufactured woolen trousers, and grimy army jackets. Even the women's wraparound skirts have been fashioned out of mass-produced printed fabrics that probably trickled in from Thailand.

Similarly, there is nothing rich or exotic about the food here. As far as we can tell, wild fruit does not grow in the Na Valley, and the people of Ban Na don't maintain much of a vegetable garden. There are some banana groves nearby, but none of the fruit is ripe right now. Fish, rodents, birds, and even bats are regularly trapped or hunted; on rarer occasions, one of the chickens or dogs is butchered. Thus, tonight's meal of sticky rice, bamboo hearts, and one stringy hen is an enviable feast for these villagers. For Max, Muntree, and me, however, it feels more like an appetizer. We have instant noodles and dried pork among our supplies, but we let our stomachs grumble out of courtesy to our hosts.

Though Max and Muntree know enough Lao to chat with the adults after dinner, I am forced to resort to other forms of inter-action. Since a third of the village is made up of small children, I gather a giggling horde of kids around a bonfire and valiantly attempt to teach them "Old MacDonald Had a Farm." Before long I can recognize the braver kids by their personalities. In my mind, I've given them all nicknames: The doe-eyed eight-year-old waif who preens her way through the proceedings and giggles coyly when I wink at her is Miss Zha-Zha; the handsome ten-year-old who shows me the hand-fashioned trap he uses to catch rodents is Little McGuyver; the naked, scowling six-year-old who skulks around the fire with dirt stuck to his face is Pigpen. By the light of the fire, I feel that Ban Na has grown larger. What by day was a dusty, forlorn village has now become intimate and vividly alive.

Should the ruined city of Aran prove to be more than a rumor, I think as I watch the village settle down for the night, North by Northeast Tours will have a marquee draw to go along with all the area's organic charms, and this expedition will be an automatic success. But once Aran becomes a regular stop on the ecotour cir-cuit, life in Ban Na stands to get a lot more complicated.

Shortly before joining the expedition, I visited North by Northeast's office in Nakhon Phanom, on the Thai side of the Mekong. There, I met with Nick Ascot, the hyperkinetic Canadian who founded the company. "I've been running tours in Thailand for more than two years," he told me. "And that whole time, I've been looking out across the river at those mountains." He nodded toward the distant karst on the Laotian side of the Mekong. "I mean, here we ran a tour company next to one of the world's most impressive biodiversity areas, and nobody seemed to know anything about it."

By questioning local residents and foreign NGO workers, Nick was able to collect enough secondhand information (including rumors about Aran) to justify a formal expedition into the area. Since he didn't have the time or the experience required to explore it himself, he hired Max. That both men make their living in Thailand is telling: The country has been Southeast Asia's most stable and profitable tourist market for the last thirty years. Adventure trekking has been a lucrative niche market in Thailand since the early 1970s, when local guides in the northern mountains began to lead small groups into wilderness areas and ethnic villages. In time, these treks grew so popular that Chiang Mai (typically the staging area) became a tourist hub rivaled only by such canonical draws as Bangkok and Phuket. By the mid-1990s, primitive settlements that had never seen a Western visitor before the Vietnam War were hosting up to thirty-five a night during the dry season.

Tourism transformed northern Thailand. It raised the standard of living for tribal minorities and encouraged the government to build more roads and public facilities. But the hill tribesmen didn't seem so authentic once they started to watch television and eat Pringles. In order to compensate for this eroding "authenticity," trekking companies started to import and invent new attractions: elephant rides, raft trips, opium tents. Bangkok-based tour companies began to wrest business away from local operators, and "hill-tribe rituals" were staged to keep up with the demand. In 1997, wily tour organizers were charging tourists six dollars to take photos of the giraffe-necked Padaung women on the Burmese border; in 1999, a trekking company was prosecuted for adding prostitution to its backcountry repertoire.

Nick was unfazed when I pointed out such shortcomings in the Thai trekking industry. "So many of Thailand's best spots have been ruined because the tourism was unplanned and unregulated," he told me. "My idea in Laos is to get in on the ground floor—for the sake of my business, yes, but also to encourage sustainable tourism in an area so close to home."

"But," I said, "isn't it better—ecologically and culturally speaking—to leave the place to itself?"

Nick thought for a moment, then shook his head. "If we don't explore and sell it, others will," he said. "And if we can agree that change is coming no matter what, then to ignore its approach is wrong. I feel that those of us who care about the place will have a chance to contribute constructively when those changes come."

Our second day in Ban Na begins at 4:30 A.M., when the chickens start screaming and the villagers stir for another day of harvest. Bleary-eyed, I climb down from the headman's porch and join Max. "Muntree and I have a meeting with the headman this morning," he tells me.

"Will you ask him about the Aran ruins?"

"Probably. We have many things to discuss." Max shoots me a wry look. "For example, we should probably discuss why he wants us to buy a pig." I don't understand enough Lao to follow the proceedings, so I wander out into the village. A gaggle of children greets me with jumbled refrains of e-i-e-i-o. Little McGuyver happily leads a pet monkey around on a fraying twine leash. The day has just begun to color the sky above the ring of mountains that encloses the valley, and the morning air is damp, cool, and slightly smoky. I can hardly describe the atmosphere here: I've tasted remoteness before, in the desolate Libyan Desert and on the empty steppes of Mongolia, but this human-inclusive isolation is different—and almost magical. At times it feels as if I'm walking through a dream.

Max climbs down from the headman's house, and from the look on his face, I can tell something's up. "The headman says he's going to take a special trip through the cave when he gets some time," Max tells me. "He wants to buy our pig from Nakok village."

"Did he say what we need it for?"

"A sacrifice," he says, gesturing at the mountains that surround us. "I guess as visitors we need to be 'introduced' to the spirits of the valley. I think it's an animist version of a welcome party. The villagers know where the ruins of Aran are," he adds with characteristic nonchalance. "We'll go there this morning."

Within an hour, we've packed our surveying gear and departed for the ruins. Although the Aran site is said to be close to Ban Na, our journey into the forest becomes somewhat complicated. Every time we get a good hiking rhythm going, the headman scampers off into the trees and returns with some type of root or resin. To my eyes, the dense Na Valley jungle is gorgeously cluttered and indecipherable, but to the people who live here, it is an enormous, leafy convenience store. The headman seems particularly pleased when he finds a thick vine that he calls *kheua yan-nang*, whose bark, he says, can cure insomnia when boiled into a tea.

The more he dallies, the more I suspect that Aran will prove to be little more than a few decade-old abandoned bamboo huts. Though supposedly an ornate stone city swallowed up by the jungle of the Na, Aran sounds like a fairy tale. After all, urban settlements have never been common this far inland from the Mekong.

My skepticism, however, does not last much longer. Less than two miles outside Ban Na, we veer just a hundred yards off the path to discover a square gray pillar tilting out from a small stand of trees and vines. The pillar is part of a mossy, mostly decayed brick-and-mortar temple building. Atop the small temple mound, toppled circular pillars and stray red bricks share space with rotting leaves and vigorous shrubs; tree roots as thick as my leg zigzag through the brickwork foundation.

On the far side of the mound, a second square pillar has fallen to the ground, its once-ornate lotus-flower fluting pressed deep into the mud.

While Max photographs the ruins with a digital camera and marks our location on the GPS, Muntree and I search for more Aran remnants. We find another group of the toppled round pillars and a small pile of bricks but nothing that compares with the temple mound. In all likelihood, it was the city's only brick-and-mortar building, and whatever other structures once stood here are long gone. The headman picks up a brick and says that the mud used to make it was probably carried in through Heup Cave. A smaller cave nearby, he adds, served as an oven to bake the bricks. Aside from this, however, he doesn't seem to know anything about the site. Indeed, we have yet to meet anyone (or find any literature) that can tell us about its origins. Consequently, Aran tantalizes visitors into doing their own circumstantial-historical detective work. Since the site is not terribly old (less than two hundred years, it seems, given its architectural similarity to nineteenth-century temples in the Mekong Valley), I'd wager that Aran was built as a refuge for besieged Mekong Valley Lao during the Thai-Vietnamese power struggle in the 1830s. At that time, the local Lao seemed likely to sympathize with the Vietnamese in the event of war, so the Thais began a policy of forced relocation in the Mekong. For fifteen years, with entire villages seized and moved to Thai territory, Lao families sought refuge in the rugged limestone mountains of what is now central Laos.

The *Pheun Vieng Chronicle*, a poetic historical account of the period, vividly speaks of these dramatic events: "The Lao... escaped through the mountain crevices, / Crawling up the cliffs of the highest peaks, / Hiding in those mountains, / There only to be followed, captured, and bound."

I can imagine how the temple (and the city that once surrounded it) might have been built as a sanctuary. Heup Cave would have provided a natural defense and camouflage against the Thai raiders, and the brickwork technology could have been imported from a more sophisticated Lao settlement in the Mekong Valley. Looking at what's left of the site, I wonder if Aran was evacuated peacefully when the relocation raids ceased or if it met a violent end at the hands of Thai invaders. I can't be sure of this theory, of course, but I find giddy fascination in the idea that Aran could be the most dramatic physical evidence of that violent era in Lao history: a silent, brick-and-mortar *Pheun Vieng Chronicle* that sits draped in moss, waiting to be read.

As far as Max is concerned, the history will sort itself out. Aran neatly completes the equation that will make the Na Valley a key attraction for North by Northeast Tours. He remains stoic on our hike back to Ban Na, but his enthusiasm occasionally shines through. "If you talk to Nick before I do," he says to me, "tell him that this valley is a gold mine."

It's not until our final night in Ban Na that we are reminded about the sacrificial pig and the jealous spirits of the Na Valley. We have been joined by Knut Bry and Gilles Tondini, who've come to photograph the expedition. Now that four *falangs* are staying in the village, our evenings have taken on a kind of carnival atmosphere. Tonight, I continue my efforts to teach the kids "Old MacDonald," while Knut instructs a group of teenagers in the art of the high five. In the headman's hut, Max types on his laptop in front of a rapt audience of two-dozen villagers. We have proved to be as much of an attraction for the people of Ban Na as this valley is for us.

We are halfway through our dinner of boiled chicken and sticky rice when the moaning starts. At first I think it's a sick dog, but then I notice that people are congregating at the door of a neighboring hut. Max asks a few questions in Lao, then trots off to get his medical kit. "Sounds like someone has food poisoning," he tells me. I follow him up onto the porch, but the villagers stop us at the door. Inside, I see an alert old man casually pressing loose tobacco into a square of notebook paper. Across from him, a wild-eyed woman rocks back and forth in front of a flickering oil lamp, groaning loudly in rhythm with her movements. Still nonchalant, the old man rolls up his cigarette and begins to talk soothingly to the woman. Timing his syllables to the rhythm of her motions, he looks her in the eye as he lights his cigarette in the flame of the oil lamp.

Max interprets the situation for me in bits and pieces. Apparently, the moaning woman has been possessed by *phii*—the spirits of the valley. The man with the cigarette is the shaman, and he's trying to determine what the spirits want. Gradually (and somewhat chillingly), it is revealed that the spirits are upset by the presence of the four *falangs*. Because the Ban Na headman didn't have time to go through the cave and buy a sacrificial pig from Nakok, we were never properly introduced to the *phii*. Moreover, the spirits didn't even know of us until one of the village boys shot stones at some jungle birds when we were hiking through the valley that afternoon. The birds apparently spilled our secret—and now the spirits want to know who we are and why we are here.

The moaning lasts long into the night, and I have trouble falling asleep. At one point, I climb down from my corner of the headman's porch and—perhaps because of the spirits, or maybe out of random workaday sickness—vomit onto the Ban Na dirt.

When the sun finally comes up, our group begins to prepare for the planned hike out of Na Valley. One of our last items of business is to pass out a few gifts—t-shirts, notebook paper, butane lighters—to the villagers. Max prepares a supply of powdered milk for the headman's baby grandson. Once Max has finished giving preparation instructions to the young mother, I ask him how he thinks the village will change once tourists start to come. "I'm a pessimist," he replies, "especially in this part of the world. Tourism is a shortcut to development; things happen too fast."

Since I've always taken Max for a grizzled idealist, I challenge him a bit. "By the time that sick baby becomes a teenager," I offer, "tourism could be giving him access to the sort of health and education that these people have never dreamed of."

"Yes," Max says. "But he'll be getting his dreams from television and the outside world. He'll lose interest in this valley and move to Thakhek or Vientiane because there's more money there. I've seen it happen before, and I can't see how it will be any different here."

An hour later, we finish packing our group gear, hire half a dozen villagers as porters, and hike out of the Na Valley. In another week, we'll receive word that the headman's infant grandson has died.

Though frequently used (and awe-inspiring) Heup Cave is not the only way out of Na Valley. Southeast of Ban Na, a second trail zigzags up one of the lower ridges and leads us onto a plateau fringed with razor-like limestone peaks. Beyond the valley, we encounter quirky villages, the dust-covered French colonial hill station of Phontiou, and an eccentric array of natural wonders.

Seven days after having left Ban Na, we emerge from the wilderness near Konglo Cave, which, because it gets about five visitors a month during the dry season, is currently the most heavily touristed destination in the entire Oahu-sized expanse of the Khammouan.

Just a few valleys east of Konglo Cave—in a region far more isolated than any place I've visited in recent days—lies the Nakai-Theum River NBCA, the largest of its kind in Laos. Stretching along the mountainous border with Vietnam, the Nakai-Theum River reserve is over twice as large as the Khammouan Limestone NBCA, and features clouded leopards, wild elephants, Indochinese tigers and scattered hilltribe settlements representing twenty-eight different ethnic groups. If, as has been suggested, these two central Laotian reserves were linked with the Hin Namno NBCA (an important primate conservation area) to the south, Laos would find itself home to one of the most important biological and cultural conservation regions in the world. In this way, central Laos is like an equation waiting to be added up—and for now, it's too soon to say how tourism will factor in.

The only thing I can say for certain is that the arithmetic has begun.

∽

ENDNOTES

1. **Page 40, paragraph 2:** *This trip is the first attempt to chart it*: This trip was also my first story assignment for a glossy travel magazine. After "Storming *The Beach*" was published online in *Salon*, an editor from *Condé Nast Traveler* contacted me by e-mail and told me she wanted me to write a similarly wacky-yet-insightful "travel stunt" story for her magazine. Over the course of the next year, I sent her dozens of "travel stunt" ideas, from training as a space-tourist, to living on airport food for a week, to wandering the Judean Desert for forty days and nights. None of these ideas ever turned into a story assignment.

While I was sending off stunt ideas, however, I continued to travel across Asia and write about my experiences for *Salon*. In Laos I met Nick Ascot at a Buddhist shrine near Luang Prabang, and he later contacted me for advice on how to write a press release about Max's Khammouan expedition. On a lark, I mentioned the expedition to my *Condé Nast* editor, and she was fascinated by the notion of an exploratory trek that sought to chart an untraveled region for ecotourism. Two months later the magazine flew me from India to Laos to report the story.

After Laos I went on to write a few other adventure-slanted stories for *Condé Nast Traveler*, though to this day I still haven't done a "travel stunt" for them.

2. **Page 40, paragraph 3:** *…having taken our small expedition team fifty miles on foot and by boat*: Though my editor and I ultimately determined this story worked best by focusing on the five days I spent in the Valley of Na, the expedition actually played out over the course of fifteen days, and most of the journey wasn't documented in my article.

For example, we spent the first two days of the expedition under the watchful eye of a government official from Thakhek, the regional capital. Short and pudgy, with thick glasses and a hip-pack, he looked like a bumbling assistant to some evil superhero nemesis. Like most officials in Laos, he was a member of the communist party, and when Max told him I was a writer, he exclaimed, "Lenin was a writer too!" Sadly, the chipper little commie lasted less than forty-eight hours with us before early mornings, long hikes, and Spartan meals sent him trudging back to Thakhek in resignation.

The night before he left, he got drunk on rice wine and told us how the city of Thakhek had been founded by Chao Sikhot, a normal man who'd gained Herculean strength and conquered much of Laos after eating a bowl of magic rice. Like Achilles, neither spears nor swords could penetrate Sikhot's body. Unlike Achilles, his only point of weakness was his anus. On learning this, the King of Vientiane managed to kill Sikhot by placing an assassin in his pit latrine and shooting an arrow up his ass.

At first I thought this tale was just the rice wine talking, but it turned out to be true. Sikhot is a major figure in central Laotian folklore, and there's even a shrine to him near Thakhek.

3. **Page 43, paragraph 2:** *...Thomas Cook's pioneering tour-organizing efforts 150 years ago*: Since this particular story examined the arrival of tourism to a seldom-traveled part of Laos, it made sense to study the history of tourism during the research process. Even in stories that aren't explicitly about the tourist trade, it's useful for travel writers to become familiar with the history, economics, and sociology of tourism, since (whether we like it or not) so many journeys take place within a tourist setting. A number of academic and industry publications track trends in tourism—though one can find a wealth of useful information by simply Googling "history of tourism" or "tourism studies" in the context of a given destination. The trick is to include research details with a light touch, since too much clinical information can stifle the flow of the story (and I often require several rewrites before I can find the proper balance between information and narrative).

4. **Page 52, paragraph 3:** *...I climb down from the headman's porch and...vomit onto the Ban Na dirt*: The woman's melodramatic

possession by *phii* spirits was quite disturbing at the time, and it's still a little unsettling to remember. A part of me wants to believe that *phii* really were watching over that valley, but in truth I was probably witnessing something far more banal.

Indeed, the *phii* woman had acted strangely from the moment we'd arrived in the village, and some of the villagers had mentioned she was "weak." In local terms this meant it was easy for the spirits to possess her; a medical diagnosis might have revealed a predisposition for mental and emotional instability. As for the sacrifice, it's true that the headman never got around to purchasing a pig, but the fallout was probably more political than spiritual. After all, 500 baht was a lot of money in that part of Laos, and many villagers were no doubt chagrined that the headman hadn't thrown us a welcoming party (which, in a sleepy little village like that, might well have been the most memorable event of the year).

When the *phii* lady lost her marbles, I'd reckon that was just her way of publicly shaming the headman for pocketing the pig money.

5. **Page 53, paragraph 3:** *...we'll receive word that the headman's infant grandson has died*: Though it only merits half a sentence in the story, I was deeply saddened when I heard this news. Since that day, I've often thought about what we might have done to help save the infant's life. I suppose we could have been more forceful about taking the baby out of the valley and downriver to a hospital in Thakhek—but when we suggested this the villagers acted like is was a stupid and self-indulgent gesture.

I didn't understand this attitude until I read an anthropological study on central Laos while I was writing the story. "In some places," it read, "it is the practice not to register babies below the age of thirteen to eighteen months. Until then, i.e. until the baby begins to walk and show signs of individual personality (for example, by smiling and taking an active interest in its surroundings), the baby is regarded more as being an appendix to its mother than an individual human being."

No doubt this attitude is a pragmatic measure in a place where health resources are few and infant mortality is one in four. It's also the most compelling argument for how contact with tourists (and the money/information they bring) stands to improve the quality of life in places like the Valley of Na.

6. **Page 53, paragraph 4:** *Beyond the valley, we encounter quirky villages...and an eccentric array of natural wonders*: Though it only tangentially related to the story, my seven days' journey beyond Ban Na was an adventure in itself. The farther I hiked into central Laos, in fact, the more I realized how many fascinating little places exist off a country's well-trod tourist route.

The faded French colonial tin-mining hill-station of Boneng, for example, felt like something from the early industrial age: ramshackle wooden buildings along the road; stoop-backed old women panning for tailings in the muddy waters below the mine; red dust covering everything, from motorcycles to cats. Beyond Boneng, the village of Phontiou (which gets just the slightest mention in the story) was home to an anachronistic Cold War-era mining venture; stone-faced North Korean overseers followed our every move there.

Later, when I was staying in a village called Houana, a little girl came up to the headman's house bearing three dead bats, and I watched in fascination as they were boiled, peeled, and eaten for breakfast. The following day we hiked into the mountain village of Kouankacha, where I found a pile of unexploded Vietnam War-era cluster bombs sitting in the schoolyard (Max later saw to it that an international munitions team went up and removed them). As we hiked from village to village, we rarely used cash; most of our food and assistance was paid for with pocketknives, ballpoint pens, digital wristwatches, and medical supplies.

Even in Konglo Village, where villagers owned motorcycles and accepted paper money, I was reminded of my isolation when an elderly man walked up and lifted his shorts to reveal thighs thickly laced with ornate tattoos of elephants, birds and dragons. At first I couldn't remember how I knew about this dying Laotian custom, and it wasn't until days later that I recalled having read about it in Marco Polo's *Travels*.

﹌ 4 ﹏

Be Your Own Donkey

B y the afternoon of my second day in the Libyan Desert, I finally found the sense of isolation I'd been looking for. The faint white ridgeline that marked the far edge of Dakhla Oasis thirty-five miles to the north had just dropped beneath the horizon, and I found myself adrift in a sterile sea of yellow dunes. Inspired by the gorgeous absence of everything but curves and light, I unslung my pack, tossed it into the sand, and sat down for a much-needed breather.

Though it seemed innocuous at the time, this was probably the act that turned the next ten hours of my life into a wearying mix of self-loathing and dull paranoia.

Up until that moment, my hike into the sandy fringe of the world's largest desert had been full of simple discovery and fascination. In the utter emptiness of the landscape, I found myself vividly aware of slight details: telltale irregularities in the texture of the sand; the metallic ping of the odd rocks beneath my boots; a lone ant marching up a dune, its abdomen tilted skyward. I noted a complete lack of odor in the dry air; I watched the rippled shadows of the landscape dissolve at mid-day, then deepen again with the afternoon.

This all changed just before sunset, when I opened my pack to find my gear slathered in a sodden brine of damp grit and filmy garbage. Beneath this water-slicked gear, I found my last bottle of Baraka mineral water—its thin plastic shell burst open in the middle, its contents mostly empty. Unthinking, I sloshed the excess water out from the bottom of my pack and started spreading things out to dry in the sand.

It wasn't until I'd begun to tally my gear that I realized the problem: two days into the desert, I only had one bottle of drinking water remaining, and that bottle was half-empty.

There are some moments in life when unexpected situations call for momentous, life-changing acts of resourcefulness and endurance. This was not one of them. Granted, I was hiking into one of the emptiest areas in the world: to my south and west, nothing but sand and rocks lay between me and the distant, barren borders of Sudan and Libya. To my north, however, a village called Mut—the southernmost outpost of Egypt's Dakhla Oasis—was no more than a twelve-hour trudge away. Outright stupidity on my part excluded, I'd not likely be forced to jettison my gear, drink my own urine, or flag down passing airplanes in the effort to survive.

Rather, my situation was far more representative of prosaic day-to-day life: it didn't require outright heroism so much as it required thankless, forgettable drudge work. A twelve-hour forced march to Mut on a half-liter of water was certainly do-able; it just wasn't desirable.

Sitting in the sand, the day going dark, I pondered other options. The only unknown factor at the time was what lay to my east. The map in my guidebook (which, I'll confess, was not designed to aid desert trekking) showed a dotted line dropping south out of Mut—evidence of the old caravan route that once arced down to the distant sands of Sudan. By my own estimation, I could cut due east in the cool of the night and arrive at the caravan road in less than five hours. If this road were still in use, I could wait there the next morning and hitch a ride on a truck (or, I secretly hoped, on a camel), thus neatly avoiding the tedious slog to Mut. If this road were disused on the other hand, I would double both my hiking distance and my odds of being forced to swill my own urine.

Gathering up my gear, I took an eastward bearing off my compass and rolled the dice.

Except for certain situations involving science, warfare or divine prophecy, there is never really any practical reason to go wandering off into the desert—and this is likely the very reason why so many people are inclined to do it.

Nearly 2,500 years ago, the Greek historian Herodotus wrote that, among the Nasamon tribe of western Egypt, there lived some "wild young fellows, who planned amongst themselves all sorts of extravagant adventures, one of which was to explore the Libyan Desert and try to penetrate further than they ever had before." These youths, Herodotus noted, eventually came upon an isolated oasis, where they were attacked and imprisoned by a marauding band of dwarves.

Twenty-five centuries later, the idea of exploring lifeless stretches of sand for no good reason still carries a visceral appeal—dull dangers of dehydration and attack-dwarves notwithstanding.

In the deserts of the Arabic world, much of this mythic appeal has been perpetuated by the tales of classic explorers such as T.E. Lawrence, Wilfred Thesiger and Sir Richard Burton. When I traveled to the western sands of Egypt, however, I had yet to study the exploits of these steely, turban-wearing Brits. Rather, my desert canon consisted primarily of eclectic American fare: Edward Abbey's Utah solitaire; the cinematic fantasies of Lucas and Spielberg; wisecracking vultures in Far Side cartoons; NASA photos of Mars. Perhaps as a result of this, my inclination toward epic exploration in the Libyan Desert was offset by equal inclinations toward fantasy and irreverence.

Thus, my first impulse upon arriving in the desert town of Farafra had been to buy a donkey and ride it into the sandy unknown.

On paper, riding a donkey into the desert is a perfectly legitimate low-tech adventure. Not only are donkeys less expensive than camels and more authentic than Jeeps, I figured I could sell off my beast at the end of the trip and break even for the experience.

As any layman who's tried it will know, however, shopping for donkeys in Egypt is a resoundingly humiliating experience. Not only does the American higher education system leave its graduates with very few practical skills in assessing the market value of donkeys, it would seem that the inhabitants of Egypt's oases aren't used to selling their animals to foreigners. During my first morning of wandering through the dusty outskirts of Farafra, I spent two hours startling and bewildering farmers before I finally found someone who was interested in my proposition.

After a bit of sign language, a smiling old farmer hauled a load of green reeds from the back of his donkey and motioned for me to get on. Once I'd swung my legs onto the beast, the farmer smacked it on the rear, and I went bouncing idiotically down the dirt road.

The donkey stopped after about fifteen meters, so I climbed off and flashed the farmer a thumbs-up. I wasn't really sure what to do next (slam the doors? kick the tires?), so I decided cut straight to the bargain. "O.K.," I said to the farmer. "Bikam? How much do you want for it?" I wasn't ready to buy it, necessarily, but I wanted to get a feel for price.

"Pen," he said.

Not sure what he meant, I took out a pen and some paper so he could write down the price. Smiling, he handed the paper back and pocketed the pen. As the farmer merrily returned to his work, it dawned on me that I had just purchased one twenty-second donkey ride.

Since this flavor of commerce wasn't likely to get me very far, I tried to indicate that I wanted to actually purchase the entire animal with cash. Every time I waved some money around in an effort to pantomime my desire, however, the farmer just shook his head and gestured to the donkey. "Pen," he repeated cheerfully.

Motioning my intention to come back, I jogged over to my hotel to find a translator. Mohammed, a temperamental middle-aged fellow who worked the front desk, was my only option at the time. After exchanging a few pleasantries, I got down to business.

"I need you to help me buy a donkey," I told him.

Mohammed scowled. "Why you want to buy a donkey?"

"I want to ride it into the desert."

"A Jeep or camel is better. I'll arrange you a trip."

"I'm not really interested in that; I want to try and do it on my own."

Mohammed raised an eyebrow in irritation. "You know how to keep a donkey?"

"What do you mean?"

"Food! Water! So it does not die!"

I realized that I'd never considered this. "No," I said. "Is it difficult?"

The grumpy clerk grinned at me sarcastically. "You want a desert trip by yourself?" he said walking his fingers across the countertop. "You be your own donkey."

Though I never did any more donkey shopping in the Egyptian oases, it took me two days before I had rationalized the disappointment and moved on to other options.

By that time, I'd continued on to Dakhla—the southwestern-most of Egypt's big oases—and I was sharing a dorm room at the Al Qasr Hotel with a German political-science student named

Tomas. Tomas enjoyed the tale of my Farafra donkey encounter, but he couldn't seem to understand my initial motive.

"Why did you want a donkey?" he asked me.

"So I could travel out into the desert," I said.

"Why did you want to travel out into the desert?"

"So I could be away from things. I wanted to go to a place where nothing has ever lived. I wanted to be isolated."

"Isolated? What about the donkey?"

"Well, the donkey would just be a funny detail. You know, part of the challenge."

"So the isolation part wasn't really that important."

"No, I wanted to be isolated. And the donkey would have been part of that isolation, considering I really don't know much about donkeys."

"So did you want to be isolated or did you want to feel isolated?"

"I wanted to be isolated."

"Yes, but really. How is being isolated all that different from feeling isolated?"

After fifteen minutes of simple logic, Tomas had talked me into dreaming up a new journey—a walking trek into the Great Sand Sea.

Unlike the rest of the Libyan Desert, where blowing sands mix with dry buttes and rocky moonscape, the Great Sand Sea is nothing but dunes. Covering an enormous sprawl of territory along the Egypt-Libya border, this area went unexplored and uncharted for centuries on account of its complete isolation and lack of water. In 1874, the first man to cross these dunes—a German geographer named Gerhard Rohlfs—nearly died in his attempt to lead seventeen camels over 420 continuous miles of waterless desert. "It was as if we were on a wholly lifeless planet," wrote Rohlfs of the experience. "If one stayed behind a moment and let the caravan out of one's sight, a loneliness could be felt in the boundless expanse such as brought fear, even in the stoutest heart.... Here, in the sand ocean, there is nothing to remind one of the great common life of the earth but the stiffened ripples of the last sandstorm; all else is dead."

Conveniently for my purposes, a thin tongue of the Great Sand Sea stretches out into the western fringe of Dakhla Oasis. Here, I'd hoped, I could enjoy this feeling of boundless isolation without the danger of actually being isolated. Here, in relative safety, I could be my own donkey.

Using my guidebook map, I plotted a course that would start in Al Qasr village on the northern fringe of Dakhla, curve west and south through the dunes, then boomerang back into the southern oasis village of Mut three days later.

Packing enough food and water to last the duration of the journey, I struck out for the dunes the following morning.

Tomas joined me for the first leg of the hike, since he was interested in exploring the Al-Muzawaka tombs two hours west of Al Qasr. There, we found a small network of caves that had been hollowed-out by some long-ago inhabitants of the oasis. Unlike the famous tombs of Egypt's Nile valley, there were no admission booths, souvenir stands, or rifle-toting guards at the site. The only soul we saw there was an old man who walked out from a lone stone house to take us by the arm and shine a flashlight into the caves. When we tipped him fifty piasters each, he smiled and took us to an open-faced cave that contained five dusty, brittle adult mummies.

Beyond Al-Muzawaka, Tomas followed me into the first cluster of yellow dunes before turning back for Al Qasr. For the rest of the afternoon, I maintained a sloppy southwestern bearing, zagging my way up and over the grand piles of sand. Still within sight of the oasis, the desert sand was abuzz with activity: shiny blue beetles, fat black flies, faded pink garbage bags. Every so often, the sand would yield broken pieces of pottery, or heavy brown stones.

As recently as fifty years ago, explorers in this part of the

Egyptian desert were likely to find all sorts of artifacts preserved in the sand, from flint-knives to broken ostrich eggshells to rock paintings. Mixed in with the pre-historic relics was evidence of more recent visitors: camel bones, bits of clothing, human skeletons. In 1999, a group of American tourists crossing the desert near Bahariyya found the remains of three German soldiers—all members of a flight crew that had disappeared on an exploratory mission during World War II.

Though I'd secretly hoped to find something ancient or macabre in the desert, I never was that lucky. At one point, I found a copper bullet-slug in the sand and put it in my pocket, thinking perhaps I'd drill a hole in it and hang it on a necklace. Five minutes later, I found two more bullet-slugs, then another. By the time I'd collected seven bullet-slugs, they didn't seem so special any more, so I threw them all away.

The sun went down just after six, and—since I had no stove and there was obviously no firewood—I set in for the night in the lee of a huge dune. After spooning up a can of tuna for dinner, I pulled out my sleeping bag and stared at stars until I fell asleep. I woke up at first light and resumed my journey.

For the most part, the curved sameness of the Great Sand Sea precludes narrative. My second day in the dunes proceeded much like the first—the only difference being that the insects became fewer and the view of Dakhla's ridgeline became fainter as the day went on. I filled the emptiness of the landscape with my wandering mind, stopping occasionally to take compass bearings or photograph my footprints.

In a weird way, though, I don't really recall making any progress until I opened up my water-soaked backpack at dusk and found myself with a tough decision on my hands.

Though I didn't know it at the time, the area beyond my little tongue of the Great Sand Sea was once thought to be a possible location for an elusive oasis town called Zerzura. Reputedly a place of palms, fresh-water springs, and white birds, Zerzura's location never could be pinned down once explorers started systematically mapping the desert a hundred years ago. Early Arab historians placed it south of Siwa Oasis near the Libyan border; early British adventurers placed it west of Dahkla. Murray's 1898 *Guide to Egypt* placed it in four different locations in the hinterland of the Egyptian southwest. Over the years, various wanderers, bandits, and pilots claimed to have seen Zerzura while headed elsewhere, but none could ever find his way back.

In his classic 1935 book *Libyan Sands*, British explorer Ralph Bagnold (who was a member of the British Long Range Desert Group loosely portrayed in Michael Ondaatje's *The English Patient*) conceded that Zerzura would probably always be a lost oasis, having long ago been mapped under a different name and absorbed into the Egyptian geography. Still, he held on to the idea that it was out there in one form or another.

"I like to think of Zerzura as an idea for which we have no apt word in English," he wrote in the conclusion to his book, "meaning something waiting to be discovered in some out-of-the-way place, difficult of access, if one is enterprising enough to go out and look; an indefinite thing, taking different shapes in the minds of different individuals according to their interests and wishes."

This in mind, I suppose I discovered my Zerzura when I lost my last water bottle in the depths of my pack. What had before been an adventure of fancy had now turned into a matter of real consequence. My Lucas-Spielberg reveries gave way to reality, and I discovered the desert all over again.

Of course, this is an assessment of hindsight. Under the pressure of the decision itself, I wasn't so philosophical as I trudged my way east. Having been raised to make the more conservative choice in this type of situation (i.e., enduring the direct slog to Mut), I found myself unconsciously veering to the north. Every so often I would catch myself and resume my eastbound progress.

Hiking through the desert under the light of the moon was quite similar to hiking the dunes in daylight. The only difference was that the air was cool, the sand was gray, and the mood was spooky. After a while, my footfalls didn't sound like they were coming from my own feet anymore; I kept turning around to see if I was being followed. Even sudden patches of soft sand would give me an occasional start in the dim silence.

Eventually, my paranoid habit of veering north caught up with me, when—just short of midnight, I found a jeep track in the sand. Since I'd been hiking what I thought was east for nearly six hours, I assumed that I'd reached the caravan road. In retrospect, this was a silly assumption: Given that Mut is the last sizeable human outpost in that corner of Egypt, it would make sense that a southbound road toward Sudan would be large and well maintained. At the time, however, I wasn't so confident. Not sure what to do, I snuggled into the slope of a nearby dune and waited for someone to show up.

After a ten-minute doze, I heard what sounded like footsteps coming my way. Suddenly nervous, I dug my headlamp out of my pack. The sound got louder, then stopped. It started again, stopped again, then started once more, even louder than before. It sounded like someone was stumbling through the sand in a ragged pair of scuba-flippers. Too spooked to say anything, I turned on the headlamp and stood there with my fists clenched—looking, no doubt, like some kind of spelunker-ninja madman. Finally, I spotted the culprit: a heavy paper-and-plastic cement bag, drifting its way down the jeep track on a hiccupping migration to Sudan. I turned off my headlamp and sat back down.

As I listened to the cement bag flop off into the night, I caught the hint of another sound: a truck downshifting somewhere in the distance. Shouldering my pack, I crossed the jeep track and continued east. Within thirty minutes, I could see a set of headlights; an hour later I was standing on the blacktop caravan road to Mut.

My eastbound gamble had paid off: I'd found my lost oasis in the form of an asphalt road. In an indulgent show of celebration, I took a long pull from my water bottle.

Finding a flat spot far enough from the road so the nighttime trucks wouldn't disturb me, I spread out my sleeping bag and dozed for a few hours. Just past dawn, I packed up my gear and hitched a ride into the only place there was to go in that humble fringe of the Libyan Desert.

∾

ENDNOTES

1. **Page 59, paragraph 3: *...acts of resourcefulness and endurance. This was not one of them***: To be sure, my forced slog in the Libyan Desert was all dull fear and drudgery; I never once thought of it as an adventure when I was living it. Fortunately, as Jean-Paul Sartre wrote in *Nausea*, "for the most banal event to become an adventure, you must (and this is enough) begin to recount it."

Note that the first section of this story creates a key narrative question: What will happen as Rolf tries to hike back to Mut on half a bottle of water? In creative writing workshops, this is known as the story's "engine"—the unanswered question that invariably keeps the reader reading. Essentially a variation of "what's going to happen next?", the engine creates the narrative tension that allows the storyteller to digress and give background information.

Not all of the stories in this book have such an explicit "engine," but many of them do. In chapter 1, the engine revolves around whether or not I'll be able to infiltrate the set of *The Beach*; in chapter 11 the engine focuses on what has become of Mr. Benny. In analytical retrospect these narrative hooks might feel a bit obvious, but readers scarcely notice them in well-structured tales (perhaps because stories have been organized this way for as long as humans have told them).

2. **Page 61, paragraph 2:** *...my first impulse...had been to buy a donkey and ride it into the sandy unknown*: Part of the reason I wanted to ride a donkey into the desert is that I thought it might make a funny story, since at the time I was writing a biweekly travel column for *Salon*.

The other story idea I'd toyed with in Farafra involved the "mystic poets" who supposedly lived there. I'd heard about these desert bards from a Dutch girl I'd met in Cairo the previous week. She'd told me how these men would drive deep into the desert at night, build bonfires, and compose beautiful verses. When I arrived in Farafra and tracked down the "poets" she'd mentioned, these men had absolutely no interest in talking about poetry with me. As it turned out they were a bunch of horny young Egyptian guys who worked at the local tourist hotel and used a handful of stock verses to seduce Western backpacker girls in the desert. It was actually a clever ruse, and the guys seemed to be doing quite well with it (and in retrospect I realize there may have been a story in that).

My hike into the Great Sand Sea was a whimsical diversion after the poets and donkeys didn't pan out—and had it not turned into a misadventure I might never have written about it.

3. **Page 64, paragraph 6:** *...Tomas followed me into the first cluster of yellow dunes*: While we were in these dunes, I had Tomas take a photo of me hiking in the desert. This picture later appeared on the cover of my first book, *Vagabonding*.

4. **Page 65, paragraph 6:** *...an elusive oasis town called Zerzura*: In *Desert Sands*, Bagnold wrote how, "for the less scientifically minded [Zerzura] may be still more vague; an excuse for the childish craving so many grown-ups harbor secretly to break away from civilization, to face the elements at close quarters as did their savage ancestors, returning temporarily to their life of primitive simplicity and physical vigor; being short of water, to be obliged to go unwashed; having no kit, to live in rags, and sleep in the open without a bed."

That pretty much sums up my impetus for wandering into the Libyan Desert.

5. **Page 67, paragraph 1: *…I kept turning around to see if I was being followed*:** If you've never hiked alone in a desert before, it can be hard to understand just how spooky it can be at night. At times, it literally *feels* as if there are people all around you, even though the landscape appears completely empty.

This feeling actually factors in a lot of travel accounts over time. Arab geographer al-Mas'udi wrote of the *ghuls* that appeared to desert travelers by night; Roman historian Pliny the Elder wrote of phantoms that appear and vanish before wanderers in the Sahara; Venetian explorer Nicolo de Conti reported being awakened at midnight by the noisy "demons" of the Chaldaean desert. Even Marco Polo reported how, in the Gobi, stray travelers would "hear spirits talking, and will suppose them to be his comrades…and thus shall a traveler oftentimes be led astray."

❧ 5 ❧

Something Approaching Enlightenment

OR weeks after returning from my ill-fated journey to the Indian Himalayan village of Kaza, I had difficulty explaining to people why I'd wanted to go there in the first place. Sometimes I'd claim it had something to do with the Dalai Lama—though someone would always point out, correctly, that the Dalai Lama lived in the Tibetan exile capital at Dharamsala, not in some obscure mountain outpost several days in the other direction.

I had no easy answer to this seeming discrepancy. Granted, the Dalai Lama was reputed to travel to Kaza once each summer—but I'd gone there in the winter. And, while rumor had it that the Dalai Lama planned to spend his twilight years in a monastery just up the valley from Kaza—the famous Tibetan holy man was nowhere near retirement at the time. In the end, I suppose my decision to gain an understanding of the Dalai Lama by going where he *didn't* live was grounded in a vague fear of disappointment—a fear that (as with other religious destinations I'd visited in India, such as Varanasi and Rishikesh) Dharamsala had become so popular with other Western travelers that any spiritual epiphanies I found there would feel forced and generic.

By contrast, the Indo-Tibetan burg of Kaza was the remotest Himalayan town I could reach by road in late winter. There, in the cobbled alleyways of an ancient and windswept Buddhist village, I imagined I might find a more authentic vision of what the Dalai Lama represented. Far from the well-worn lanes of Dharamsala, I hoped I might better be able to discover something approaching enlightenment.

Thus, from the northern Indian hub city of Shimla, I'd walked to the far end of the bus terminal—past the backpack-toting crowds of Westerners headed to Dharamsala—and boarded the first in a series of buses that would take me to my far-flung Himalayan Shangri-La.

While still within the fog of my initial inspiration, it was fairly easy to rationalize a three-day bus ride through the remote Himalayas. Once I was actually en route to Kaza, however, I immediately realized that my whimsical pilgrimage could very well get me killed. The copy of the *Hindustan Times* that I'd bought in Shimla, for instance, devoted an entire front-page story to grisly mountain bus crashes. "At least forty people were killed when a bus plunged into a tributary of the Ravi River yesterday evening," the article read. "Earlier in the day, eight people died and thirteen were injured when a truck carrying them fell into a gorge thirty-five kilometers from Manali."

The Indian highway signs were not much more encouraging, as (in lieu of, say, shoulders or guardrails), dangerous curves on the mountain featured boulders with white-painted slogans that read, "O God help us!" or "Be safe: Use your horn." I kept staring out at the river valley a thousand feet below and imagining our driver cheerily honking the horn as we all plummeted to certain death.

The most alarming part of the Himalayan bus ride, however, was the road itself, which seemed to be buried under massive mudslides at fifty-mile intervals. Indeed, every couple of hours or so, our bus driver would screech us to a halt, and I'd peer out the window to see what had formerly been the road lying in a crumpled crust sixty feet down the mountain. Invariably, several dozen Indian highway workers would be making a frenzied effort to carve a makeshift dirt track into the flank of the mud wall in front of us. My fellow passengers would disembark and smoke cigarettes at the edge of the cliff, watching without interest until the laborers gave a shout, and our bus driver rumbled across the improvised mud-road. Along with the other passengers, I'd then follow on foot at a safe distance, climbing back into the bus once the normal highway resumed. My main solace amidst all this was the optimistic promise of Kaza, and the serene Buddhist environs that awaited me there.

After two days of nonstop travel, I'd made it deep into the Tibetan border region before the transmission dropped out of the bottom of my bus near a town called Pooh. Folks in Pooh informed me that there were no more onward buses that day, but that I might be able to find transportation out of Kob, ten kilometers farther up the road. Feeling optimistic in the early afternoon sunshine, I set off for Kob on foot.

In retrospect, the early hours of my hike to Kob were the happiest of my entire Himalayan sojourn. Outside of Pooh, the altitude snaked up to above 10,000 feet; hand-planted cherry trees along the roadside had just begun to sprout pink blossoms. Before long, I was trudging into a massive canyon of gray-tan rock, the highway reduced to a narrow slot dynamited out of the cliff-side. The Spiti River was barely visible below, but I knew it was the same river that roared down from Kaza—a place where I envisioned cool air, welcoming locals, and the soft tinkling of monastery bells.

Unfortunately, the transit town of Kob never materialized, even after four hours of hiking. I trudged an additional hour in the dark before I spied an abandoned blockhouse at the side of the road. Figuring it as good a place as any to bivouac, I pulled on several layers of warm clothing, curled up on the dirt floor, and—exhausted—fell asleep. When I woke up, my watch told me it was just past seven o'clock. Encouraged to have gotten a full night's sleep, I walked outside to catch the sunrise.

I must have stared at the darkened eastern horizon for half an hour before I re-checked my watch and noticed the small "PM" over the time-code.

Nervous about the gathering mountain cold, I began a search for firewood—but all I could find was the old wooden blockhouse door, which had long since fallen off its hinges. When repeated attempts to smash the door with rocks resulted in nary a dent, I tried tossing it into the air and breaking it over the large roadside boulders.

I had been tossing the door onto the boulders without success for about fifteen minutes before I realized that a half-dozen bewildered-looking Indian army soldiers were watching me. Not knowing what else to do, I put my hands above my head. One of the soldiers grabbed my backpack, and the others marched me half a mile up the road to their transport truck, where I met a no-nonsense lieutenant who (apart from the beard, turban and Punjabi accent) looked somewhat like movie star Vin Diesel.

"My soldiers tell me you were taking photographs," he said. "Is this true?"

"No," I told him. "I was trying to smash up a door."

Lt. Diesel shot me a suspicious look. "This is a dangerous border, and it's not for tourists. Why did you bring a door?"

After a witheringly absurd ten-minute interrogation about my motives for trying to destroy a door in total darkness along the Indian-Chinese border, Lt. Diesel consented to drive me back to his army base near Pooh. There, I was allowed to sleep on a bench in a small administrative office. "If anybody asks," the lieutenant told me gravely, "tell them you were taking photographs."

The following day, I hitched a ride on a troop transport to the village of Yangthang, where I was finally able to catch a bus that took me over a final stretch of highway switchbacks and road washouts to my high-mountain destination. As I stumbled out of my bus at the Kaza depot, I marveled at the stark simplicity of the town, which consisted of whitewashed houses and small store-fronts spread out along a talus-strewn basin. Two monasteries perched on the hillsides above the town, and I noticed with delight that the stones along the walkway had been carved with Buddhist prayers. The place looked like a picture postcard of Tibetan authenticity.

Wandering into the center of town, however, I was disap-pointed to find that—save for wandering packs of stray dogs—Kaza was largely deserted. All the guesthouses were shuttered for the winter, and the few ethnic Tibetan residents I passed on the street couldn't understand my English queries. The only person in town who took an interest in me was a chubby, balding man at the government-housing complex, who introduced himself as Mr. Singh.

"Come and drink with us!" he hollered happily. "Today we cel-ebrate the Holi festival. It is very important to Hindus." I politely declined Mr. Singh's offer, explaining that I had come to Kaza to experience Buddhist culture.

Since the local monasteries were as empty and gated as the hotels, however, I was quickly running out of options. Stopping to check my guidebook, I noticed that Ki Gompa, a historically iso-lated 1,000-year-old monastery, was just fourteen kilometers from Kaza via a mountain trail. Realizing that all my travails up to that point might really just be hints of fate leading me to the halls of Ki Gompa, I shouldered my pack and headed to the foot-path at the edge of town.

As I walked, I felt a slight twinge of pity for all the travelers who went to Dharamsala seeking the Dalai Lama, only to wind up in guesthouses and Internet cafés full of travelers from Berkeley and Birmingham and Tel Aviv. By contrast, I reckoned my final push to Ki Gompa would transcend such tourist banality and lead me into the true heart of Tibetan spirituality.

Less than two hundred meters up the mountain—with these happy delusions still floating in my head—a giant mastiff charged out from behind a rock, bared his teeth and tore off my right pants-leg at the knee. Spooked, I ran all the way back down into Kaza, blood oozing into my socks. Since I didn't know of any other options, I jogged over to the government-housing complex.

"You have come back to celebrate Holi!" Mr. Singh exclaimed upon seeing me.

"Actually, a dog bit me and I need some first aid." I pointed down at my bleeding wound.

With the formal air of a person who is doing his best to feign sobriety, Mr. Singh stumbled out, shook my hand in sympathy, and led me to a small cinderblock hospital just up the road. One tetanus shot and one roll of gauze later, I was back in the housing complex, being introduced to Mr. Singh's colleagues—Mr. Gupta, who was as bald and chubby as Mr. Singh, and Mr. Kumar, a thin middle-aged man with hunched shoulders and owlish eyeglasses. Mr. Singh merrily explained that they were all road engineers from the Delhi area, and that they hated living in Kaza. "This is an ugly place," he said, "and it is filled with country people who have no culture or sophistication."

Mr. Gupta proposed they give me a Holi blessing, so I followed them into Mr. Kumar's room, which (with its stovepipe oven, peeling wallpaper, and magazine photos of Bollywood starlets) looked like a cross between a college dorm and a miner's cabin. Three bottles of Director's Special whiskey sat empty on the top of a dresser. Mr. Gupta produced a jar of chalky red pigment and smeared a *tikka* mark onto my forehead; Mr. Singh twisted open a fresh bottle of Director's Special and poured me a glass.

"So why do Hindus celebrate Holi?" I asked.

"It comes from a story in our ancient book, the *Mahabharata*," Mr. Singh slurred. "Exactly one million years ago there was a goddess who tried to torture her brother to death. So now we celebrate."

"It is a very enjoyable holiday," Mr. Gupta added.

"What do you do when you celebrate Holi?"

"Sometimes we throw buckets of colored water at our friends or at strangers. But today, since you are our guest, we will watch movies of the color blue." Mr. Singh shot me a conspiratorial look. "Of course you know which movies I mean."

"I don't think so," I said. "Are they movies about the *Mahabharata*?"

"No, these movies are much more interesting." Mr. Singh gestured to Mr. Kumar, who popped a videotape into the VCR. Throbbing synthesizer music crackled out of the TV speaker, and a fuzzy image shuddered onto the screen. The movie had such poor picture quality that I could barely tell what was going on— though it appeared to be the writhing of two or more naked bodies. Presently, the synthesizer music was offset by slurping, slapping, and moaning noises. "Oh yeah," a voice from the TV said. "Ride me harder!"

I shot Mr. Singh a quizzical look, and he giggled boyishly. "Mr. Kumar wants to know why that man has such a long penis," he said.

"Long and fat," Mr. Gupta said.

I looked back at the TV, but still couldn't make out a clear image. Apparently, these men had rewound and fast-forwarded the movie so many times that it had deteriorated into jumbled images of static and fuzz. Only the soundtrack remained.

Assuming it was a fairly standard porno movie, I considered my answer. "I guess it's part of the job qualification," I said. "Men in blue movies need to have big penises, just like men who build roads need to have engineering degrees."

Mr. Singh translated this for Mr. Kumar; the men nodded seriously.

"What about this," Mr. Singh said, gesturing at the screen. "Is this normal for married men in America?"

I squinted at the TV, but couldn't make out what was going on. "Is *what* normal?"

"To have two women licking one man's penis," Mr. Gupta said.

"Only one of them is his wife," Mr. Singh clarified, "and the other woman brought them a pizza on her motorcycle."

"Oh my God!" the TV crackled. "Don't stop."

"Listen," I said, "these kind of movies are just fantasies. You can't assume they represent anything about normal American life. I mean, what if everyone thought life in India was exactly like a Bollywood musical?"

"Bollywood movies are very accurate!" Mr. Singh exclaimed. "They show many good things about India."

"But certainly they don't represent normal Indian life," I said. "I mean, do you and Mr. Gupta and Mr. Kumar break into song and dance every day at work?"

"I like to sing and dance!" Mr. Gupta offered.

"That's right," the TV interjected. "Give it to me, you big stud!"

Before the conversation could deteriorate any further, there was a knock on the door, and a teenage boy walked in to serve us bowls of dal. "This is Vikram," Mr. Gupta said. "He is a student of English."

"He will look at this movie, and then he will want to run off for hand practice," Mr. Singh giggled, making a wanking motion.

Vikram gave me a sympathetic look as he handed me the dal. "These guys are hammered," he whispered. "Just let me know if they start to bother you."

Ten minutes later, I caught up with Vikram in the housing-compound kitchen. "Look," I told him. "I traveled for three days on some of the worst roads I've seen in my life just to get to Kaza. I have nothing against Holi or Hindus, but I was hoping to meet some Tibetans here. Do you know of any way I can stay at one of the Buddhist monasteries?"

"You've come here at the end of winter," he said. "Only a handful of trucks and buses have made it through since November. The monasteries are running low on food this time of year, and the guesthouses won't want to turn on their generators for just one person. You should just stay the night in Mr. Kumar's room. It's pretty comfortable."

"But isn't there any way to meet some Buddhists while I'm in Kaza?"

Vikram shrugged. "Maybe, but people stay indoors this time of year. And they don't know much English. You'd probably get bored if you don't speak any Tibetan. You should come back in June or July. That's the best time for tourists."

For some reason, the word "tourists" triggered an instant and vivid fantasy. I imagined myself off in the streets of Dharamsala—eating muesli, flirting with Norwegian backpacker girls, sending e-mails to friends back in the States, and swapping Dalai Lama-sighting stories with star-struck Canadians. Suddenly, this scenario didn't seem so bad at all.

Resigned to my fate, however, I returned to Mr. Kumar's room. There, as we fast-forwarded through several more scenes from the movie (which appeared to be about a team of unusually libidinous pizza delivery women), I served as an informal ambassador of American marginalia.

"Yes," I told them, "I'm pretty sure Viagra works. No, I haven't tried it. Yes, I'm aware that Bill Clinton and Monica Lewinsky had sexual relations. No, I don't think they still keep in touch. Actually, I don't think they were ever in love to begin with. Yes, there are many famous black Americans named Michael. Yes, I know all about Michael Jackson's career. No, I don't think that would make Michael Jordan want to get plastic surgery."

Eventually, Mr. Singh and Mr. Gupta staggered off to bed. I slept on Mr. Kumar's floor, next to the woodstove. A little after midnight, I awakened to see the stoop-shouldered Indian sitting at the edge of his bed, intently watching the snowy image of a

naked man and woman engaged in a sexual act that was technically outlawed in numerous states and countries.

Seeing that I was awake, Mr. Kumar grinned over at me and,
with a knowing wobble of his head, said: "Back-door entry!"

This was the only English I ever heard him speak.

Sometime before sunrise, Vikram came into the room and
shook me awake. "I know of a fuel truck that is leaving in ten minutes. It can take you as far as Pooh, and you can catch a normal
bus from there." He paused for a moment. "Or, if you want to stay
in Kaza longer, the regular bus leaves next week."

Two minutes later, I was fully packed and sprinting for the fuel
truck.

The ensuing three days were not that eventful. Though the
muddy Himalayan highway was just as precarious as it had been
on my inbound journey, I didn't let it get to me; I merely looked
forward to getting back to the well-worn grooves of the tourist
trail. As a new series of buses rattled me back down toward
Shimla, I stared out at the steep mountain canyons with Zen-like
patience.

I had indeed, it seemed, achieved something approaching
enlightenment.

ENDNOTES

1. **Page 71, paragraph 1:** *...ill-fated journey to the Indian
Himalayan village of Kaza:* Of all my global wanderings in the past
decade, this Himalayan misadventure has proven to be my second-
favorite source of barroom anecdotes (for the #1 best source, check out
the endnotes to chapter 14).

For years I only told this story when someone asked me to share my
weirder travel experiences—though I eventually set it down on paper for
a Lonely Planet humor anthology in 2005. The ongoing refrain about

wanting to experience Tibetan Buddhist culture in Kaza (which on the printed page might at times feel overstated) is a remnant of the story's original spoken-word rhythm.

2. **Page 74, paragraph 8: *…I was allowed to sleep on a bench in a small administrative office*:** This office had a wood-burning stove, and the officer on duty had a young orderly drop by at several points during the night to stoke the fire. When the boy first came in to check the stove, he wordlessly presented me with a roll of toilet paper.

I found this curious, since Indians don't typically use toilet paper. In most Indian toilets (which often consist of little more than a hole in the floor), buckets of water are provided for the purpose of "wiping." The thought of cleaning your butt with some water and your fingers might seem unsanitary to Westerners, but Indians will insist it's a superior method. After all, they note, would you wash yourself with paper if you had dung on your face? Of course not—you would use water, then thoroughly wash your hands when you've finished. The same principle applies to the cleanliness of your butt.

It's a sensible argument, though I confess I still haven't broken the paper habit.

Anyhow, I suspect the duty officer had told the boy that Westerners have this bizarre method of cleaning their asses, and that he should remember to be culturally sensitive in their presence. In this sense, breaking out a roll of toilet paper at an Indian military post was quite the grand gesture—the socio-hygienic equivalent of presenting me with a bottle of champagne.

3. **Page 77, paragraph 1: *…there was a goddess who tried to torture her brother to death*:** I never bothered to confirm this story until right now, but it's actually somewhat true.

According to Hindu tradition, a demon king named Hiranyakashipu was granted near invincibility by Brahma, but he became arrogant with his new power and demanded that people start praying to him instead of the gods. Hiranyakashipu's son Prahlad stayed faithful to the god Vishnu, however, and Vishnu protected him from his father's wrath. When other attempts to kill his son failed, the demon king ordered Prahlad to sit on a pyre with his sister Holika, who was protected from the fire by a magic shawl. Hearing Prahlad's prayer for safety, Vishnu moved the shawl to cover him, and Holika was consumed by the fire.

Holi is a celebration of Holika's immolation. Despite its morbid-sounding origins, the holiday is a cheerful spring festival where celebrants throw colored chalk and water at one another.

(Presumably, getting drunk and watching "blue movies" are optional holiday activities.)

4. **Page 79, paragraph 5: *…I served as an informal ambassador of American marginalia*:** In reality, my conversation with the Hindu road engineers veered into all kinds of strange directions too numerous to fit into a concise story. Based on my notes of the experience, here are a few curious details that didn't make the cut:

> While Mr. Singh was remorselessly downbeat about living in Kaza, Mr. Gupta occasionally threw out peppy, chamber-of-commerce-style facts about the town's scenic views and monasteries. The drunker he got, the more he repeated these facts. He must have told me twenty times that Kaza boasted the world's highest retail gas pumps.

> Mr. Singh and Mr. Gupta told me Mr. Kumar loved Nepali prostitutes because Nepali women were "very strong" in bed. I never could tell if they were stating this as a fact, or just playing a backhanded joke on Mr. Kumar because he didn't speak English.

> At one point, Mr. Singh let it slip that he made as much as 3,000 rupees a month for "special contract work." On hearing this, a mortified Mr. Gupta yelled at him in Hindi for a good ten minutes.

> When I shared my story about getting detained by the Indian army in the town of Pooh, Mr. Singh declared that he would write a letter to the regional government, protesting the military's mistreatment of tourists. I tried to explain how the army patrol had probably saved me from freezing to death that night, but Mr. Singh managed to write several grandiose paragraphs before his attention drifted back to the pornos. I'm guessing he never mailed the letter.

ಲ 6 ೬

Turkish Knockout

I.

When the date-rape drug finally wore off to the point where I could think and function, I found myself face down in a darkened park not far from Istanbul's Blue Mosque. For an instant, it was as if I'd been born all over again, erased and re-rendered. I remembered nothing: who I was, why I was there, what I'd ever been doing before that moment.

Instinct told me to stand up. Shaking like a junkie, I drew myself up to my haunches and pushed with my legs. I rose to my full height for just an instant before something malfunctioned and my whole body veered rigidly to one side. I fell over like a windup toy on a rumpled bed sheet; my shoulder hit the pavement first, then my face.

Blood welled on my cheekbone as a hazy understanding began to form. I patted down my pockets: my petty cash was gone, as was my wallet, my leather belt and my Swiss Army knife. I felt along my belly for my hidden money belt, but it was gone too—passport, traveler's checks and all. Oddly, my red spiral notebook and my recently purchased Penguin anthology of Middle Eastern mythology were still jammed into my back pocket.

Pulling myself into an upright position, I took a few deep, deliberate breaths. Sitting there, drugged and dazed in the dim park, I strained to reconstruct what had just happened.

Up until the moment I lost consciousness, my day in Istanbul had already been exceptional—enlivened by unexpected cama-raderie, by uncommon novelties. In one afternoon, I'd met more strange people than the rest of my brief days in Turkey com-bined. Trying to determine at what point I went wrong would be no easy task.

Technically, I wasn't supposed to be adrift in the city that day, since I'd been scheduled to join a pre-planned Cairo-bound over-land trip the day before. However, when the truck and trip leader never arrived for the pre-departure meeting, I found myself with an extra day to kill in Istanbul.

Since I'd already spent three days touring Istanbul's marvelous historical attractions—from the lavish Ottoman halls of Topkapi Palace to the crowded dagger-and-hookah-pipe stands of the Grand Bazaar—I decided to devote my extra day in Istanbul to ran-dom wandering. Strolling the parks and alleys of the Sultanahmet tourist district with no particular goal, I spent my morning taking in the details I'd been too busy to notice when I first arrived.

Istanbul has long enjoyed a reputation of mystery and intrigue—of East and West co-mingling in grand palaces and smoky alleyways: a place where dreamers, schemers and pilgrims go to lose themselves. As I walked that day through the ancient neighborhood where the Bosphorous and the Golden Horn meet the Sea of Marmara, everything I saw seemed to contain a hidden currency. When a tout in Sultanahmet Square bullied me into his carpet shop, I was interested less in the Persian-styled rugs than the 1,500 year-old Byzantine column that slanted crazily through the recently poured concrete floor of the showroom. When I asked an old Turkish man how I might find an *eczane,* he gave me directions to the pharmacy in shrill, German-inflected

English that made him sound like Colonel Klink from "Hogan's Heroes." When I walked past the earthquake refugees camped out in the grass along the Hippodrome, I noticed that several of them clutched cell-phones. A little gypsy girl selling candy near the tram station wore an oversized Metallica concert shirt cinched at the waist like a dress. Cats crouched in doorways and alleyways; seagulls soared over the minarets of the Blue Mosque. A neatly dressed Turkish boy sitting on the tram grinned shyly at me and whispered "fuck you," as if in greeting.

Sometime around noon, an African teenager approached me near the Galata Bridge. His skin was as black as coffee, and he flopped after me in a loose-fitting pair of rubber sandals. "Hey man," he called to me. "Where are you going today?"

Since this same guy had already approached me two other times in the past three days, I decided to yank his chain a little. "I'm going to Senegal today," I said. "Don't you want to come with me?"

A look of confusion came over the boy's face. He'd told me he was from Senegal two days before, but no doubt he'd told dozens of other people since then. It was a few beats before he smiled in recognition. "Oh hey, I remember you. You're Mr. America. You're always alone, and you never want to meet any girls. Maybe you could meet a girl today, huh? You have a place to stay?"

"Yes, I still have a place to stay," I said. "And no, I don't need to meet any girls. I'm just looking for some place to eat lunch."

"Why don't you go to McDonald's? American food for Mr. America, yes?"

"But Mr. America is in Turkey now," I said. "So maybe he'll eat Turkish food."

"Turkish food is for Turkish people. McDonald's is better for you. Maybe you can buy me a hamburger, O.K.? I want to try a McDonald's."

"You've never eaten at McDonald's before?"

"McDonald's is for Americans. I am so poor!"

Against my better judgment, I decided to indulge him. "What kind of hamburger do you want?"

"A big delicious one. And a Coca-Cola. I will wait right here until you come back."

"If I buy you a hamburger, you have to come to McDonald's and eat it with me."

The Senegalese boy seemed to hesitate for a moment before falling into step with me. On our way to the restaurant, he told me his name was Ahmad. "Do you think I am very handsome?" he asked.

"I'm just buying you a burger, Ahmad. I don't want to be your boyfriend."

Ahmad let out an embarrassed laugh. "No, no," he said. "I want to know, am I very handsome? Could I go to Sweden do you think?"

"What does Sweden have to do with whether or not you're handsome?"

"I think rich Sweden women like boys from Africa. I want to go to Sweden with a rich woman."

"Sweden is cold, Ahmad."

"But I think rich women are very warm!"

At McDonald's, I ordered two Big Mac meals. Ahmad temporarily forgot his hustler persona as he devoured the food in silence and stared around at the spotless, mass-produced interior. "That was my best food ever," he said, somewhat dispassionately, when he'd finished. "Now I will help you find a pretty girl."

"I was thinking of something else, Ahmad. How would you like to go out for a smoke?"

Ahmad's face lit up and he leaned in toward me. "You smoke hash?" he said in a loud whisper. "I will find some for cheap price!"

"I don't want to smoke hash," I said. "I know something better."

In the heart of the Sultanahmet tourist area—not far from Emporer Justinian's 1,400-year-old Church of the Holy Wisdom—I'd recently discovered a back alley water-pipe joint called the Enjoyer Café, which was run by a man who called himself Cici (pronounced like "G.G."). Though the café was wedged between Internet rooms and *kilim* vendors, Cici's homespun, adage-spewing charisma more than made up for the lack of authenticity. Thin, lazy-eyed and companionable, Cici would make his rounds as customers from every stripe of the tourist spectrum sat on cushions and pulled on the bubbling blue-glass pipes.

I'd first visited the Enjoyer Café (named for Cici's mantra: "Enjoy your life!") the night before, along with a few other clients from my postponed overland tour. Though my companions left when the tramlines closed, I stayed on the outdoor cushions and chatted with Cici about Islam and America until the café closed. Since Cici had sincerely asked me to come back, I'd decided to treat Ahmad to an afternoon at Cici's hookahs.

Ahmad looked dubious the moment he saw Cici's café. "Those are apple-smoke pipes," he said. "Apple smoke doesn't make you feel good. I will find some hash instead."

"The smoke is not important," I said. "I think it's just a good place to relax and talk."

"I am sorry. I must make an appointment with my brother. I can't smoke with you today. I will find you a girlfriend later, O.K.?"

"Whatever you say, Ahmad." I watched as the Senegalese teenager flopped off down the alley.

At the Enjoyer Café, Cici greeted me with a nervous smile. "I am glad you returned to talk to me," he said. "But I am sorry to worry. Maybe it's none of my business, but was that black boy your friend?"

"That was Ahmad. I wouldn't call him a friend, necessarily. He's just someone I know from walking around Sultanahmet. I just bought him a hamburger."

Cici looked at me like I was crazy. "You must be careful, my friend. He is a bad boy, I think. Many Africans are not honest people. They come here only to cheat and steal."

"I'm careful. Besides, I know Ahmad is a hustler, and Ahmad knows I know that. I think he's harmless."

"I am sorry. You are right. I only warn you to be careful because many people come to Turkey like blind men. Tourists, they come to take photos, but they don't see past their cameras. Businessmen, they come to Turkey to trade, but they are blind to everything that doesn't carry a price. Travelers, they look around, but they only see what is already in their mind. Do you know how you must come to Turkey, my friend?"

I already knew the answer (he'd given me a nearly-identical spiel in a different context the night before), but I didn't want to throw off his rhythm. "How's that?" I said.

"You must come to Turkey as a guest. Then you will look with your eyes and you will see. Not as a tourist with his camera or a traveler who looks and sees his own dreams. Be a guest of Turkey. A guest knows he is safe, because his hosts love him."

"I'll be your guest then, Cici. Do you have a pipe for me today?"

"Of course, my friend." Cici said something in Turkish to Mustafa, his sleepy-eyed assistant. When Mustafa had ducked into the small indoor hut to prepare a pipe, Cici shot me a sly grin. "Did you meet Mustafa yesterday?" he asked.

"Sure," I said. "But I didn't talk to him much."

Cici laughed cryptically. "Mustafa is too tired to talk. After the earthquake, he is afraid to go back to his apartment, so he sleeps here. None of his girlfriends want to sleep with him in the café, so he is very sad."

"Just how many girlfriends does Mustafa have?"

"Not very many, since his girlfriends cost 10 million lire for each night." Cici laughed heartily. "Mustafa is only twenty years old, so of course he is crazy for sex. Tell me, must Christians take a bath after the sexual act?"

"No, not that I'm aware of."

"Well in Islam, a man must wash after sex. If he dies before this bath, he will not be pure before Allah. So you see, when the earthquake hit Turkey in August, Mustafa was not pure; he had not yet washed."

"Had he been with one of his girlfriends?"

"No," Cici said. He grinned and made a wanking motion. "He was watching porno movies."

"Watching pornos counts as sex?"

"A man is impure whenever he, well, whenever he finishes." Cici made another dramatic wanking motion to underscore his point. "And Mustafa was impure, so when the earthquake came, he did not know whether to run outside and be safe, or to first take a bath. Because, you see, if he was killed trying to run outside, he would not be pure before Allah."

As Cici told me this, Mustafa came out and placed a blue-glass hookah before us. I watched as Cici spooned a few hot coals into the small brass bowl. The damp apple tobacco let off a curl of smoke. Mustafa took a seat beside me and handed me the pipe's wooden mouthpiece.

"So what happened?" I asked, choking a bit on the thin, sweet apple smoke.

"What do you mean, my friend?" Cici asked.

"What happened during the earthquake? The 'choice' you were talking about."

Cici laughed. "This is not a secret," he said. "You do not need to talk like a spy. In Turkey, there is no shame for men to talk about sex and purity. If you want to know what Mustafa did during the earthquake, ask Mustafa."

Mustafa gave me a puffy-gummed grin. "I ran outside," he said. "No bath." He blushed, then turned to Cici and asked something in Turkish.

"Mustafa wants to know something about America," Cici said. "He says he heard that in America, girls do not want money for sex. Is this true?"

I thought for a moment, thinking of the best way to phrase my answer. "In America, men and women are social equals," I said. "Sex is a free choice for both sexes."

Cici translated this for Mustafa, then laughed at the reply. "Mustafa says he will move to America, so girls will pay him for sex." Cici gave me a sardonic look. "I think he will never make any money."

I stayed at the Enjoyer Café with Mustafa and Cici for nearly two hours that afternoon. Mustafa asked me lots of baffling questions about sex in the West ("But what do you say to a woman to get sex if you have no money?"), and Cici preached for a bit on the values of Islam: how a gift to the poor is like a gift to the Creator; how everything in life beyond basic human needs is a matter of ego; how the Creator has ninety-nine nicknames, but only answers to Allah.

As I got ready to leave, Cici again warned me about Ahmad, the Senegalese boy. "I only mean to be careful around those black boys," he said. "I don't mean to worry about the future. Do you know why we must not worry about the future?"

"Why's that?"

"Because the future is the next moment. Who knows what will happen in the next moment? Who knows which of us is closer to death? This is why I say: enjoy your life."

That was the last time I would talk to Cici. Before that day was over, however, I would see both Mustafa and Ahmad again.

I left the Enjoyer Café at about half past three that afternoon. Unbeknownst to me at the time, I had only three waking hours left in my day.

II.

The simultaneous charm and risk of travel is it shakes up the paradigms and habits that help you simplify and interpret day-to-day life. Life on the road, for better or for worse, vivifies a muted aspect of reality: it makes you realize that random factors influence your life just as much as planned ones.

On page 80 of the *Lonely Planet Guide to Turkey*, there is a passage entitled "Turkish Knockout" that reads:

"Thieves befriend travelers, usually single men, and offer them drinks which contain powerful drugs which cause the victims to lose consciousness quickly. When the victims awake hours after, they have a terrible hangover and have been stripped of everything but their clothes. The perpetrators of this sort of crime, who are usually not Turkish, often work in pairs or trios."

Bad fortune tends to magnify and mythify these innocuous little details and oversights. That I never read page 80 of my guidebook during my first four days in Istanbul is one of a thousand factors which, in retrospect, seemingly conspired to leave me unconscious and penniless one night in the middle of the city.

A certain 101-level existentialist (Kierkegaard, I think) once suggested that life is lived forwards, but understood backwards. This in mind, I have recalled and re-recalled the three hours preceding my robbery so many times that, now, the event itself almost seems like a miracle—a divine shroud woven from 1,000 thin, perfectly-converging threads of chance.

Of all the factors that contributed to my demise in Istanbul, perhaps the most damaging variable was also the most innocuous: Shortly after purchasing a book of Middle Eastern myths at a shop near the Sultanahmet tram stop, I met up with a couple of Australians from my postponed overland truck trip. They informed me that our trip leader had finally turned up in Istanbul, and was due to arrive with the group in Sultanahmet at around seven that evening. Figuring this would be as good a time as any to register and pay my trip fees, I returned to my hotel and took my passport, traveler's checks, and $400 in petty cash from the lock-box.

Thus, for the first time since I'd arrived in Istanbul, I was personally carrying all of my money and identification at once.

I emerged from my hotel to find Mustafa, the sleepy-eyed assistant from Cici's café, waiting there for me. "I see you inside," he said. He pantomimed smoking a hookah. "You remember?"

"Of course," I said. "You're Mustafa, right?"

Mustafa nodded. "We eat now?" he said.

At the time, I wasn't sure why Mustafa had pegged me as a dining companion. Initially, I thought he was going to tout me to some expensive restaurant, but instead he took me to a street vendor for flatbread and meat-sauce. He briefly dug for pocket-change, but made no protest when I paid for the food myself. In an inspired flourish, I even stopped at a storefront market and bought two Efes-lager tallboys—one for each of us. Mustafa led me to a park bench near the Hippodrome, and we ate our meal in the late-day sun.

Since Mustafa wasn't much for conversation, I took out my Middle Eastern myth book and began to read. After a few minutes, Mustafa took the book from me and started to flip through the pages. Whenever he saw an illustration, he would ask me what it was. "I don't know," I would tell him each time. "I haven't read the book yet."

At some point during this charade, Ahmad flopped up out of nowhere and sat down beside us. "Mr. America!" he said, startling me a bit. "We go to McDonald's again?"

I looked over at the African teenager, who was already peering around for other tourists to hustle. "No, I think once a day is enough, Ahmad."

"You need a girl now?"

"Not right now. Maybe Mustafa wants one."

Mustafa looked up from the book, laughed and handed his beer to Ahmad. Ahmad took a polite sip, and the two of them paged through the illustrations in my myth book.

"What's this?" said Ahmad, pointing at a Babylonian drawing.

"He don't know," Mustafa said authoritatively.

For a moment, I felt perfectly happy to be perched on a park bench in Istanbul with a teenaged Senegalese pimp and a homeless Turkish onanist. Sitting there, basking in the first blush of my beer buzz, I felt like I'd rediscovered a couple of misfit little brothers.

After a few minutes, Mustafa made like he had to leave. "I work now," said, pantomiming a hookah again.

"Sure," I said. "No problem."

Mustafa held up the myth book. "You give to me?"

A part of me wanted to let Mustafa keep the book, but I'd just paid $13 for it and had barely read the first page. "Can you read English?" I asked.

"No."

"Then I think I'll keep it for myself," I said.

Mustafa stood up to leave. "You come?"

"No," I said. "I have to meet someone at seven. Maybe later tonight."

After Mustafa left, it didn't take long for Ahmad to get bored with both me and the myth book. "Will you stay here today?" he asked.

"Only for about forty more minutes," I said. "Why?"

"Because I will leave now. But maybe I will come back with a beautiful woman for Mr. America."

"Whatever you say, Ahmad."

Ahmad flopped off, leaving me alone on the park bench. Since the folks from the overland trip would be arriving on the tram, I moved fifty meters over to a bench within view of the tram stop. I wasn't there for five minutes before a round-faced, olive-skinned man came up and asked me if I would take a photo of him and his friend. I set down my beer and took a couple shots of them standing together. Even with their touristy hip-packs and sunglasses and cans of Efes, the pair looked awkward and out of place.

"Where are you guys from?" I asked.

"You try and guess!"

I've always been awful at guessing nationalities, but looked them both over. The round-faced man looked vaguely like an old Puerto Rican friend of mine. His friend, a skinny, brown-skinned fellow with intense eyes and smoke-stained teeth, looked Persian. I decided to place my guess somewhere in the middle. "Are you from Spain?" I said.

"Close: Morocco."

The Puerto Rican Moroccan introduced himself as Mohsin and said he ran a pizza parlor back home. The Persian Moroccan's name was Hasan, and he told me his parents were diplomats in Malaysia. They were on their way to visit Greece, and—since I'd recently arrived from Greece—I decided to offer a few travel tips. Paging through the maps in their French-language Greece guide, I gave them the kind of hearsay advice and half-digested guide-book information that travelers always share with one another when they cross paths: which mountains are supposedly good for hiking; which islands are supposedly good for partying; which historical sites are supposedly worth their while.

"This is great," Mohsin said as I briefed him on various attractions. "How do I thank you?"

"No worries; sharing travel secrets is a time-honored tradition."

"We are new to traveling, I guess." Mohsin held up his can of Efes. "Maybe you want a beer?"

"I already have one," I said, pointing to my own can.

"How about food? We can go to the waterfront and eat fish. Please. You are our first American friend."

"I don't much like fish," I said. "Besides, I really don't have time to eat. I'm meeting some people here in about thirty minutes.

Mohsin seemed distressed at the thought of me not liking fish. "You don't like fish only because you don't know fish!" he exclaimed. "Moroccans are the best fishermen in the world, and I know how to choose the best fish. I can look a fish in the eyes and know if he's a good fish or a bad fish. I can teach you!"

In the previous weeks, I'd had a Finnish girl teach me how to read palms and a pair of Hungarians instruct me on tasting wine. Learning how to size up a fish seemed almost too weird and charming to pass up. Still, I had other priorities. "I'm sorry," I said, "but I really can't miss my appointment."

"I will give you a ten-minute lesson to looking at fish. You will be back here before your friends, and when they arrive, you can teach them also about fish."

I pondered this for a moment. "We'd better hurry, then," I said.

I jammed my myth book into my back pocket as we trotted off toward the waterfront. Halfway across the Hippodrome, I spotted Ahmad chatting up a couple of unenthused-looking Germans. In good spirits, I yelled over to him: "Where's my girlfriend, Ahmad?"

Ahmad looked over at me distractedly. "Hello!" he said, as if trying to place me.

"Do you wanna learn how to buy fish?" I called to him.

A look of mortification came over Mohsin's face as I said this. "No!" he hissed. "Don't bring that boy with us."

"It's no problem," I said. "He's a friend."

"He's an African. Africans are cheaters and thieves."

"You're African too, Mohsin."

"Yes," he laughed. "But I'm not black!"

By this time, Ahmad had returned his attention to the Germans, so we kept walking. "You shouldn't judge people that way," I said to Mohsin. "You have to judge people as individuals. There are good and bad people everywhere you go. That's one of the things you learn when you travel."

"Americans are crazy," joked Hasan. "They like everyone."

Mohsin laughed and took a package of cream-sandwich cookies from his daypack. "Life is all we have." He popped a cookie into his mouth and handed another to Hasan. "Maybe it's good to like everyone."

Mohsin and Hasan had played their roles perfectly. When Mohsin tossed me one of the cream-sandwich cookies, I didn't even remotely suspect that it had been laced with (most likely) Rohypnol. I didn't think much of the slightly bitter taste as the cookie went down, nor did I think it suspicious when Hasan stopped to take a leak in the bushes near the waterfront. Mohsin suggested we sit on a park bench while Hasan did his business.

The last thing I recall that day is Hasan furtively poking around in the foliage along the old stone retaining wall that overlooks the Sea of Marmara. The very next instant in my memory is one of night and solitude—of me drugged and disoriented, momentarily trying to remember how to walk again.

Anyone who's been robbed-clean overseas will know that the days following your robbery provide a kind of masochistic therapy. Amidst the tedious hours of down time in various police stations, consulates and travelers-check offices, you have ample time to re-examine each individual thread of your demise.

To retrospectively pluck any one of these threads is to watch the robbery neatly unravel into some idealized parallel future. It's a torturous, yet irresistible exercise.

In time, this exercise of memory renders things relative: it makes you realize that things could have been much, much worse; it makes you realize that bad experiences, on the road or otherwise, help you appreciate good experiences otherwise forgotten. You come out, in the end, with a sense of wonder at all those other, unseen moments when the threads of chance fluttered—nearly connecting, but not—just past the periphery of your life.

And then—once you have replaced your passport and filed away the lessons-learned—you resume weaving.

Because you now know there is a certain holiness in the notion that those threads exist at all.

∾

ENDNOTES

1. **Page 84, paragraph 1:** *...drugged and dazed in the dim park, I strained to reconstruct what had just happened*: When this story was first published in *Salon*, I was amazed by how many people e-mailed to tell me I was a dumb ass for getting robbed. "I could see it coming the whole time," they'd write. "You were totally trusting the wrong people."

Well, duh. If you saw it coming the whole time, it's because *I describe how I'd been drugged and robbed in the very first section of the story.*

In essence, I recounted my Istanbul fiasco in the manner of a whodunit: I started at the end and kept coy about who had robbed me until I'd introduced everyone I'd met that day. This is an old genre-narrative framing device, and I half suspected readers would think I was being too obvious by planting such a pulpy hook at the beginning of a non-fiction story.

Instead they wrote in to tell me how lame I was for getting robbed—and after I got over my initial irritation I came to realize that it's quite the compliment when people forget how you're the one who structured their reading experience in the first place.

2. **Page 96, paragraph 5:** *...that the days following your robbery provide a kind of masochistic therapy*: Of all the frustrations I encountered in the wake of the robbery, one incident stands out for its sheer ironic absurdity.

Two days after I'd been robbed, I still hadn't received any emergency money from my family, since the banks had been closed for the weekend. Penniless, I'd wound up sleeping outdoors in the park-like expanse of the Istanbul Hippodrome. Dozens of Turkish families had been camped there since the earthquake, so this turned out to be safe—but I was hoping to come into some cash and move myself indoors.

There were plenty of tourists in the Sultanahmet area that day, but somehow I couldn't just go up and ask random people for money. I'm not sure why this was the case—maybe it was pride, maybe it was shame—but I've heard of other people who've been just as reluctant in similar situations.

Fortunately, I stumbled across three seemingly friendly Americans near the Blue Mosque. Standing on the street, they looked like something out of a Benneton ad: There was an Asian woman who looked about fifty, a white guy in his thirties, and a college-aged black guy. They told me they were evangelists from Tampa who'd come to Turkey to convert Muslims to Christianity. I told them I'd been robbed, and that I'd slept in the Hippodrome the night before.

At this point you'd think most anyone—particularly persons of faith—would have asked me if I needed any help. Instead, the Asian lady (who seemed to be the ringleader) told me that getting robbed was God's way of sending me a message. "For the wages of sin is death," she told me.

"But the gift of God is eternal life in Christ Jesus," I replied.

There was a long pause as the Floridians sized me up. Tickled at my own ability to finish Bible verses, I waited for them to help me out with some cash, or at least buy me lunch.

Finally, the Asian lady spoke again. "For God so loved the world—"

"That he sent you to Istanbul to float me $20!" I exclaimed.

Actually, I didn't say that (though, looking back, I wish I had). Instead I just stood there, befuddled, as the three freelance missionaries quoted Bible verses and urged me to accept Jesus Christ as my personal lord and savior.

Rarely do you meet folks so tone deaf to the essential teachings of the Gospel as self-identified evangelical Christians: I had literally told them I was homeless, and there they were trying to sell me fire insurance. Amid the knee-jerk proselytizing, not one of them offered me so much as a glass of water or a word of sympathy.

After a few minutes of this, I excused myself and resumed my wanderings around Sultanahmet.

To this day I'm not sure what those poor fools were thinking. Maybe, with my longish hair and unwashed appearance, they thought I was a drug-addict scam artist. Maybe they were waiting for me to ask their assistance directly.

Or maybe they were just a bunch of myopic holy-roller fuck-wits who honestly thought they were doing me a favor that would last an eternity.

Whatever the case, I later ran into a young Israeli guy named Dan, whom I'd met on the train from Greece the week before. The instant he heard my plight he gave me $50 and insisted on buying me dinner. As we ate our falafel, I told Dan that he was truly a Good Samaritan. Since he was Jewish I wasn't sure if he'd get the reference, but he chuckled in recognition. "It's funny you should say that," he said. "I come from a family of Levites."

If I ever see those Tampa Christians again, I might just tell them about Dan's kindness, though I doubt they'll grasp its significance.

After all, any good fundamentalist reading of the Bible will tell you that Levites leave the robbery victim to rot.

PART TWO

I'm a Tourist, You're a Tourist

❧ 7 ❧

Tantric Sex for Dilettantes

I. THE GIRL

You spot The Girl on your first afternoon in Rishikesh. She is long-limbed and graceful, and she walks carefully along the path, as if not to disturb the dirt beneath her bare feet. She wears loose cotton pants, and tiny bells in her hair. She is smiling. Her stomach is browned and taut; the tiny hairs on her arms are bleached from the sun. When she spots a cow in her path, she stops to stroke its neck and whisper into its ear. You watch, and you wish you were that cow.

You think to yourself: *If I have come here to learn Tantric sex, I want that woman to be my partner.*

II. THE HOLY PLACE

Rishikesh straddles the Ganges just below the point where the sacred river comes roaring out from the mountains. The water here is clean and cold: In the morning, Hindu pilgrims tip offerings of fresh milk from the riverside ghats; in the afternoon, helmeted tourists—Indian and foreign alike—bump through the current in rubber whitewater rafts. Monkeys chatter in the trees along the shore.

You did not initially come here to learn Tantric sex. Rather, you stopped here en route to the Himalayas, on the recommendation of a yoga-obsessed friend. You are not much into yoga, but one charm of travel is that it frees you to be a dilettante. Just as you tried scuba diving in Thailand and windsurfing in Galilee, you intend to try yoga in Rishikesh and decide later if you really want to make it an active part of your life.

Your guidebook says there are over fifty yoga ashrams in Rishikesh, and most of them are on the far side of the river, in an area known as Swarg Ashram. This enclave has been popular with travelers ever since the Beatles journeyed here to seek enlightenment in 1968. Moreover, most of the Swarg Ashram yogis have learned to speak English, and motor traffic here has been banned, imbuing the place with an uncommon sense of calm. Cassette-tape shops play sitar music; sacred cows wander the streets, garlanded with marigolds. A banner along Swarg Ashram's main avenue reads: "International Yoga Festival, with Mr. Andrew Cohen: Group discussions. Campfires. Simple appetizing yogic diet. Campfires!"

You are staying in a two-dollar hotel in the heart of Swarg Ashram. There is a restaurant on the roof, and travelers gather there to discuss yoga, Hindu philosophy, and where to find the street vendor who sells the bran muffins. As in other holy places in India, the dread-locked *sadhus* near the river do a steady side-business posing for tourist photographs. Middle-aged Indian men stroll the alleys, offering you marijuana in the same chirpy, unconcerned voice one might use in offering snack pellets to a pet gerbil. Kids here tug on your sleeve and ask you for ballpoint pens.

Advertisements for yogis are pasted everywhere in Swarg Ashram, and you sometimes stop to read them. Your favorite comes from a certain Swami Vivekananda (whose credentials, you notice, include Mensa membership and a gold medal in the Physics Olympics). "I mix the rational understanding of the West with the mystical approach of the East," his flyer states. "I will not bother you with religious nonsense, weird rituals, dogmas, or superstitions. If you have expected to find here some laid-back stretching gymnastics or some hippie cocktail of drugs with Oriental religions, you are in for a big surprise!"

The true selling point, however, is printed at the bottom. It says: "WEEKLY: A step-by-step approach to the oral secret tradition of the Tantric schools of India and Tibet."

You don't know a lot about Tantra, but you're pretty sure it's a technique that allows you to have sex for hours and hours at a stretch. You elect to pay Swami Vivekananda's ashram a visit.

III. THE SWAMI

You are met with two initial disappointments at Swami Vivekananda's ashram. First, you discover that—while standard yoga is available daily—Tantra class does not start for another four days. Second, Swami Vivekananda himself is not from India, but Romania. He is tall, bulky, and bespectacled, and he quotes Hindu scripture with vague Count Dracula inflections, pausing occasionally to brush a shock of brown hair from his eyes. At the beginning of class, he distributes photocopied instructional handouts, which read: "This information belongs to a secret spiritual tradition, and together with the oral instruction makes up a unique revelation concerning yoga, man, and the universe we live in." In his lectures, he quotes Lenny Bruce and Obi-wan Kenobi as readily as he references the Upanishads or the Bhagavad Gita. There are no Indians in his class.

Despite the seeming lack of authenticity, however, you are happy to discover that The Girl is taking the class. She sits in the back with her legs crossed—quiet and graceful, smiling at the birds outside, not seeming to pay much attention to what is being said. You steal glances back at her as Swami Vivekananda speaks, and resolve to stay out the week.

Thus, Swami Vivekananda's ashram becomes a structured part of your daily routine in Rishikesh: yoga in the morning and evening (usually taught by one of the swami's Israeli or Australian assistants), and lectures at night. Because your limbs are not very flexible, you prefer the lectures.

Moreover, you come to like Swami Vivekananda, if nothing else for giving you the impression that one merely need to read a lot of books and collect esoteric perspectives to be a guru. You like that he illustrates his points with allusions to forwarded e-mail jokes, or the Sermon on the Mount, or *The Blair Witch Project.* You like the way his overviews of Eastern philosophy are rooted in practical analogies. You like that the twenty or so other students in the class are young, curious, irreverent, and well traveled— much like you imagine yourself to be. Some of them pass notes to one another during the lecture; others ask off-topic questions about Ayurvedic medicine, or the life of the Buddha, or the movie *Gladiator.*

Occasionally, the swami returns to his central litany: "Nobody can drink a cup of tea," he'll say. "You may be drinking, but you are really someplace else. The mind can be a crazy monkey that is always trying to escape from the moment. Your goal must be to find and experience the present."

As you listen, you nod and take notes. You peek back at The Girl and think: "I want to learn how to have sex for hours and hours at a stretch."

IV. THE ROOFTOP RESTAURANT

Your two-dollar hotel is just down the hill from Swami Vivekananda's ashram. Your room is small and bare, but you like its ascetic vibe. Sometimes you hear elementary Vedic chants coming up through the pipes in the bathroom. Other times, the pipes emit snoring noises, or the tinny whine of your downstairs neighbor complaining about his diarrhea. The showers run cold, but a boy at the front desk will bring you a bucket of hot water at no extra cost.

The rooftop restaurant serves Italian food. The lasagna is sub-par, but the view of the Ganges attracts a steady stream of diners. Pink-faced rhesus monkeys infest the surrounding buildings, and sometimes they leap across to steal leftover garlic bread, or fight one another over bowls of tea sugar. The waiters chase them away, but they always come back.

You spend entire afternoons on this roof, sipping tea and staring at the river, eavesdropping on other travelers. You love that India constantly gives people something to talk about—yoga, music, dysentery, holy cattle. One man sits down with a newspaper and offhandedly recaps bizarre deaths for his girlfriend: a woman eaten by a crocodile in Kerala; a man strangled by his barber in Rajasthan; a busload of pilgrims careening into a canyon in Himachal Pradesh.

Though you have yet to see The Girl on the roof of your hotel, you do meet various other people from Swami Vivekananda's class. They say things like, "Yeah, yoga till Friday, then I go rafting" or "I'm just getting my yin and yang in order, getting a little exercise; it can't hurt." Some of your more earnest classmates explain to you how the seven chakras correspond to the seven planets, or how it's hard to travel in Cuba if you're a vegetarian.

Scott, a young guy from New Zealand, has also noticed The Girl. He tells you he thinks she's from Latvia, and that she is probably gaining positive karmic energy from your infatuation. "Mae West was actually one of the first Westerners to be aware of karmic energy, back in the 1930s," Scott tells you. "She took all that lustful male energy that was directed at her, and she cultivated it like a garden. It made her into a stronger person." The more you consider this, the more you enjoy the idea that—even if you have not yet mustered the courage to speak to The Girl—you are at least making her into a stronger person.

You also do a lot of reading on the roof of your hotel. You find the Penguin Classics edition of the Upanishads particularly accessible and engrossing ("And they say in truth that a man is made of desire; as his desire is, so is his faith; as his faith is, so are his works; as his works are, so he becomes."). For sheer entertainment, however, it's hard to beat Sir Richard Burton's translation of the *Kama Sutra*. This book is not just an index of sexual positions; it's an all-around lifestyle guide for fourth-century Hindu males. Among other things, the *Kama Sutra* suggests that the reader eat corn on the cob, learn how to make decorative parrots from yarn, use pigment from charred camel bones as an erotic stimulant, and avoid sexual congress with women whose breath smells like excrement.

In the early evenings, before you attend Swami Vivekananda's lectures, you leave the rooftop and go for hikes in the forest outside Swarg Ashram. The black-faced langur monkeys that live in the trees there are gentle and graceful and shy. Unlike the rhesus monkeys that haunt the hotel rooftop, they do not squabble, bare their teeth at you, or try to get at your food. If you stand silent among the trees, they will walk out on their branches and stare down at you with calm curiosity.

V. THE TANTRA CLASS

As with church or professional football games, Swami Vivekananda's Tantra class is held on Sunday. The turnout is three times larger than his other lectures, and you are slightly disappointed to discover that men and women must take the class separately. Before your lecture begins, the male travelers casually compare notes on things like yogic diet and chakra energy (though you suspect this is just their way of saying, "I want to learn how to have sex for hours and hours at a stretch").

Swami Vivekananda quiets the class and gets down to business. He explains that it is difficult to get beyond a certain point of spiritual awareness unless you learn to redirect your sexual energy. He outlines the concept of *brachmacharya*, wherein a man deliberately holds back his semen, recycling his sexual essence as an offering to God. Within the discipline of *brachmacharya*, he says, there are two schools of practice: ascetic and Tantric. The swami briefly talks about the wandering *sadhus* and monks who practice abstinence-based ascetic *brachmacharya*, then he steers the lecture back to the reason you're all here.

"Tantric practitioners do not abstain from sex," he notes in his slight Dracula lilt. "Rather, they seek to reverse the Pavlovian connection between orgasm and ejaculation. Ejaculation is in-built for species reproduction, but it interferes with the true spiritual nature of orgasm."

This declaration yields a flurry of questions. Does a Tantric orgasm feel like a regular orgasm? "It does not." Does a Tantric orgasm still originate in the genitals? "Not exactly. It is not even purely physical; it is a spiritual orgasm." Is a spiritual orgasm really better than a physical orgasm? "Yes," the swami says, losing patience. "And a man who has tasted honey doesn't want to eat shit any more."

Continuing in this culinary vein, Swami Vivekananda suggests that developing a Tantric awareness of sex is akin to cultivating a refined taste for food—turning it into a spiritual act instead of a mere pleasure-survival reflex. The kissing, biting and massaging encouraged by the *Kama Sutra*, he explains, is not mere sexual foreplay, but part of a recipe for deeper spiritual awareness (which, from your reading of the ancient Hindu sex-guide, must also benefit from yarn-parrots and corn on the cob).

"Sexuality is not of the body, but of the mind," the swami concludes, "and it is through the mind that we wage war with the ingrained reflexes of the body. Tantric masters learn to keep their physical instincts behind the point of no return, and this yields sexual and spiritual rewards."

Again, the class buzzes with questions. How exactly do you stay behind the point of no return? "Self-discipline is not a part-time job; it must be strengthened over time." But how? "By pulling your sexual energy into your mind and your chakras." But how do you actually do that while you're having sex? "You learn new ways to overcome your instincts; it's like training an animal by using a carrot." So is the carrot, like, counting backwards from a thousand or something? "No! Tantra is about mindfulness, not distraction."

Eventually, Swami Vivekananda becomes exasperated with ejaculation questions. "Look," he says, "there are some pelvic muscles that can help control ejaculation, and the best way to strengthen them is to urinate in short, start-stop bursts instead of one continuous stream. But please. Let us stick to spiritual matters."

As he says this, a palpable sense of relief fills the room. The swami continues to explain the mystical essence of Tantric discipline, but nobody thinks to ask any more questions.

VI. The Girl, Part II

The following day, as if by holy miracle, The Girl shows up on the roof of your hotel. When her tea arrives, she stretches her long arms up above her head, and you watch the graceful curve of her torso, the flat ripple of her stomach. She opens her shoulder bag, takes out a bran muffin, and places it on her table next to the tea.

You watch this, gathering up your nerve, and you think: *Tantra is about mindfulness.*

Before you can approach her, however, a rhesus monkey hops down from a nearby roof and climbs onto her table. The Girl's smile brightens. Whispering something you cannot hear, she slides a hand forward and begins to stroke the yellow-brown fur on the monkey's leg. You watch, and you wish you were that monkey.

Then, suddenly, the little pink-faced creature rears back and swats the teacup off the table. As The Girl flinches, the monkey grabs her muffin and leaps up onto an adjacent roof.

For a moment, everything on the rooftop is still. The Girl stares down at the streaks of tea on her shirt. The monkey clutches the muffin and stares down at The Girl. Conversations stop, and everyone at the restaurant silently waits to see what will happen next.

You fully expect The Girl to whisper up at the monkey—to coax it down, cradle it into her arms, and walk off peacefully to share the muffin on the shores of the holy Ganges. Instead, her face reddens, and she snatches a tin of tea sugar. Curling her thin, lovely lips, she screams, "COCK-SUCKING FUCKING MONKEY!"

The sugar-tin whangs off the roof and explodes into a grainy white cloud. The monkey blinks coquettishly at The Girl, and begins to nibble at the bran muffin. The Girl seizes a white plastic dining chair, and—in what you now recognize as a California accent—bellows: "COME HERE, YOU STUPID LITTLE FUCKER!"

Before The Girl can hurl the chair, an Indian waiter rushes over and places his hands on her shoulders. In what appears to be a weary and well-practiced routine, he tells her to please calm down—that everything will be O.K., that the monkey did not mean her any harm, and that he will be happy to clean up the mess and fetch her another tea.

Roughly shaking off the waiter's touch, The Girl drops the chair and bursts into tears. She snatches her bag and runs out of the restaurant. Everyone on the roof smirks and turns back to their tea or lasagna.

You flag the waiter, pay your bill and head for the forest.

VII. THE HOLY PLACE, PART II

As you walk through the trees, you keep quiet and look for langur monkeys.

You're coming to realize that travel anywhere is often a matter of exploring half-understood desires. Sometimes, those desires lead you in new and wonderful directions; other times, you wind up trying to understand just what it was you desired in the first place. And, as often as not, you find yourself playing the role of charlatan as you explore the hazy frontier between where you are, who you are, and who it is you might want to be.

Before long, you sense motion in the trees, and drop to a crouch. After a minute or so, a langur walks out onto a branch, gray-furred and dignified, his tail curved up over his head for balance. As he stares down at you, you realize how privileged you are to be in Rishikesh.

Later, when you return to your hotel room, you hear a strange, intermittent gurgling noise coming up from the bathroom pipes. For a moment, you can't place it; then, you smile at the sheer optimism of the sound.

It's your downstairs neighbor. He is urinating in short, start-stop bursts.

∽

ENDNOTES

1. **Page 103, paragraph 1:** *You spot The Girl on your first afternoon in Rishikesh*: Despite all the memorable details from the experience, I had trouble writing about my Rishikesh Tantra class until a few years after it happened. My breakthrough came when I found the following line in my notebook: "Yoga girl pets cow but loses her composure when monkey steals her muffin."

At a practical level this lovely young woman didn't figure much in my Swarg Ashram experience (I didn't even speak with her, after all)—but I eventually came to realize she symbolized the impetuousness that underpinned all of my desires in Rishikesh. She certainly wasn't the only girl I pined for in India (Eastern spiritual scenes are invariably crawling with attractive women), but the intensity of both her beauty and her emotional meltdown made her a perfect framing device for a story about the impulsive longings that seize you when you travel to new places.

2. **Page 103, paragraph 2:** *You think to yourself: If I have come here to learn Tantric sex*: I wrote the story in second-person voice after reading Lorrie Moore's delightfully experimental short-story collection *Self-Help*. This narrative approach not only afforded me the ironic distance to humorously examine my obsession with The Girl—it also allowed me

to implicate the reader in my half-baked flirtation with alternate futures (a time-honored tourist indulgence which, while frequently silly, is part of the joy of travel).

Novel as it was, this narrative experiment tended to confuse travel editors who weren't used to seeing second-person voice in nonfiction. After several months of submissions and rejections, *Perceptive Travel* published it online; Tim Cahill later selected it for inclusion in *The Best American Travel Writing 2006*.

3. **Page 104, paragraph 2: ...*popular with travelers ever since the Beatles journeyed here to seek enlightenment in 1968*:** The Beatles and their entourage came to Rishikesh to meditate with Maharishi Mahesh Yogi, but their visit ended in disillusionment when the yogi seemed disproportionately interested in money and allegedly tried to seduce Mia Farrow. Two songs from the *White Album* refer to the experience: "Dear Prudence" (which refers to Farrow's sister, who later became a Transcendental Meditation teacher) and "Sexy Sadie" (which criticizes the Maharishi's foibles).

4. **Page 105, paragraph 4: ...*two initial disappointments at Swami Vivekananda's ashram*:** Not unlike Maharishi Mahesh Yogi, Swami Vivekananda had a reputation for trying to seduce his female students. This was hardly surprising, given that his marquee class revolved around Tantra—but it still scandalized some of the travelers I met there.

Seduction aside, the Romanian yogi was popular with the backpacker crowd because his classes were inexpensive, he welcomed drop-in visitors, and he taught in the media-saturated vernacular of a younger generation of Western seekers. Some of the more cynical travelers in Rishikesh referred to his class as "McYoga."

5. **Page 107, paragraph 3: ...*Yeah, yoga till Friday, then I go rafting*:** To be honest, I'm not sure how many of these quotes came from people I spoke with directly, and how many were just fragments of conversation I overheard while I was writing in my journal on the roof of my hotel. In full context I'm sure these yoga-vacationers' conversations were perfectly

reasonable—but overheard in snippets they could be quite peculiar. Here are a few outtakes from my notebook that never made it into the story:

"When you think about it, shit isn't a dirty thing at all. It's actually a very clean and efficient way to purge the body of impurities."

"I can't say I've met anyone as famous as Janaki Jivan Sharan, but in San Francisco I used to live next door to this Chinese guy who got his ass kicked by Bruce Lee."

"I'll set you up with a teacher in Varanasi. He was the captain of the Uttar Pradesh yoga team. Actually, I'm not sure how they judge the competitions; I think it's a contest to see who can hold their poses the longest."

"Yeah, there were some Hindu nationalists protesting Valentine's Day. And when you think about it, Valentine's Day really is cultural imperialism."

"You've never heard of Amar Barati? He's a *sadhu* who's been holding his right arm up in the air since 1977. He's like the Michael Jordan of *urdhvabahu* mortification."

ᴄ 8 ᴄ

The Barbecue Jesus and Other Epiphanies

ᴍʏ last and perhaps most redemptive act as a tourist in the Vietnamese central highlands was to visit the Montagnard church in Kontum. There, perched innocuously on the back wall of the parish office, was a large painted-ceramic crucifix unlike any I had seen before.

Whereas most images of the crucifixion depict a Jesus agonized and exhausted by the pain of the world's sins, the Montagnard Jesus looked downright chipper—his hair feathered back in the manner of a 1970s rock star, his mouth spread into a huge, toothy grin, his hands (which had somehow pulled loose from the cross-bars) stretched out in a gesture of neighborly goodwill.

"Never mind the stigmata," the Montagnard Jesus seemed to be saying. "Let's have a barbecue!"

For devout believers, the notion of a Jesus so distracted and nonchalant in the face of his own crucifixion would seem a tad blasphemous. But for me—after a rather bewildering experience in the central highlands of Vietnam—the sight of Barbecue Jesus came as a kind of relief.

"Forget about your expectations," Barbecue Jesus seemed to tell me. "Forget about what you think you're supposed to do. Look at me. Run your hands over my ceramic finish and you'll see: I am just as real as you are."

My trip to the central highlands of Vietnam had started on a note of euphoric optimism on Route 13, around the same time half the people on my bus started vomiting.

Granted, watching a bunch of motion-sick Vietnamese farmers puke into plastic bags wasn't all that pleasant, but I enjoyed the quirky feeling of otherness, as I was the only foreigner there. I was intrigued by the details of the experience: how the women dabbed a green salve under their nostrils to ward off the stench of gastric acid; how the men squatted on small plastic stools in the aisles to compensate for overcrowding; how everyone shared water from a grimy Mickey Mouse cup that floated in a jug at the driver's feet; how the rounded corners and metal vent windows made our small bus look like an ice cream truck.

Route 13 is the main road through the central highlands, and I have since learned that it gained distinction as being the home of some of the heaviest fighting in the waning days of the Vietnam War. Portions of the road, which to this day are virtually impassable to anything bigger than a motorcycle, were once part of the Ho Chi Minh Trail supply route from the Laotian frontier.

In retrospect, the sole reason I had for traveling Vietnam Route 13 was because it wasn't Vietnam Highway 1. The sole reason I was headed to the highland town of Kontum was because it wasn't the highland town of Dalat. And the sole reason I wanted to travel a potentially dangerous stretch of the Ho Chi Minh Trail was because it wasn't part of the Circuit.

In Southeast Asia, every country has a standard (though largely unspoken) Budget Travel Circuit. In Thailand, the Circuit involves any combination of southern islands and northern hilltribe treks, with a few intermediary days in Bangkok. In Laos, the overland Circuit almost always includes stops in Luang Prabang,

Vang Vieng and Vientiane. In Cambodia, no Circuit is complete without stops in Angkor Wat, Phnom Penh and Sihanoukville.

Vietnam's Circuit roughly follows Highway 1 between Ho Chi Minh City and Hanoi. This largely coastal route features comfortable and convenient transportation, plentiful tourist facilities (from cheap motels to moped rentals) and sightseeing stop-offs from Haiphong to Hue to Hoi An. The problem with this, of course, is that so many travelers frequent this route that a person can go for weeks on the Circuit without having any legitimate interaction with the locals.

Perhaps no place illustrates this better than Nha Trang—a southern coastal city whose most famous citizen in backpacker circles is a small, visor-wearing woman named Mama Hahn. For about $7, Mama Hahn takes foreigners on all-day boat cruises that feature sightseeing, snorkeling, a nearly limitless supply of cheap beer and a floating lunch that features a man in a rowboat handing out marijuana cigarettes. Mama Hahn's cruise has proven so popular with backpack travelers that she has already spawned a couple of imitators (one of whom, confusingly, also calls herself Mama Hahn).

I joined Mama Hahn's boat trip one day after arriving in Nha Trang on the Circuit from Ho Chi Minh City. My seven Canadian boatmates (all of them friends, traveling together) were gregarious and funny—and the cruise through the bay was enjoyable enough—but I lost all sense of being in Asia within minutes of leaving the shore. It didn't help that Mama Hanh carried a loudspeaker, and continually used it to squawk such non-traditional Vietnamese aphorisms as "Let's party!" and "Who's ready to get fucked up?"

As usually happens when travelers get together, the Canadians and I shared our road tales. Various members of the Canadian crew had been to places like Tibet, Goa, Samarkand and Tanzania. I hadn't been to any of those places, but my

Southeast Asian experiences seemed to meet with their approval. "I could tell when I met you that you were a seasoned traveler," one of the Canucks confided at one point.

The thing is, sitting on Mama Hahn's boat, I didn't feel like a traveler at all—let alone a seasoned one. And—considering that my companions' travel experiences seemed to center around sampling drugs in various far-flung corners of the earth—I began to wonder just what defined a "seasoned traveler."

I came ashore from my Nha Trang boat excursion with a sunburn, a mid-afternoon hangover and the vague feeling that I could have experienced the exact same thing in Ontario.

Suddenly filled with the urge to do something different, I visited my guesthouse travel office and scanned the map, looking for a southern region that was as far from the Circuit as possible. I put my finger on an area near the Laotian border. "I want to go here," I said to the Vietnamese woman who ran the office.

"That's the central highlands," she told me. "A very wonderful place. We can get you a ticket to Dalat for tomorrow."

I knew plenty about Dalat. Dalat was a Niagra Falls-style highland resort town that boasted waterfalls, swan-shaped paddleboats on the local lake and a "minority village" that featured a giant concrete chicken. Dalat—on kitsch value alone—was already a part of the Circuit. "I don't want to go to Dalat," I told the tour woman. I tapped my finger on the northern stretch of Route 13. "What's on this road?"

She thought for a moment. "Buon Ma Thot, Pleiku—but those places aren't so interesting. Kontum is good. It's like Dalat—lots of nature and hill tribes. But the road after Kontum is very bad. It's only for motorcycles, or maybe army trucks. Nobody ever goes that way. Kontum is kind of a headache. I think Dalat is better."

The next morning I went to the Nha Trang inter-city bus station and headed for Kontum.

It took me two days to get there—one day on a crowded, lumbering DeSoto bus bound for Buon Ma Thot, and one day on the ice cream truck vomitorium to Kontum. By the time I reached my destination, fresh air and legroom seemed like glorious, decadent luxuries.

After checking into a cheap hotel near the bus depot, I set off down the side streets of Kontum, hoping to find some place— such as a market—where I could mix in with the local folks. Not far from my hotel, I stopped to hold a storefront door open for a young man overloaded with boxes. A minute later, he came jogging up to me on the sidewalk and handed me a plastic sack filled with coffee beans.

"Is this for me?" I asked. At the time, I had temporarily forgotten that asking a yes/no question to someone who doesn't understand English is possibly the most pinheaded mistake a traveler can make in Asia. Still smiling, the Vietnamese guy nodded.

I had no use for a big bag of coffee beans, but I was nonetheless touched by this seemingly generous gesture. Wanting to express my appreciation, I took out my Vietnamese phrase book and tried to make conversation. This proved to be a slow process, since spoken Vietnamese is a tonal language, and difficult for beginners. I mostly just communicated by pointing to words. It took me fifteen minutes to establish that my friend's name was Tran, he wasn't married and his hobby was singing. I threw in a few personal bits about myself and showed him some pictures of my family.

As I made to end the conversation and leave, Tran seized the phrase book and flipped through the pages for a few moments. He stopped at the numbers page, pointed to "20" and looked at me quizzically.

"Twenty," I told him. "That's twenty."

"Twenty," Tran repeated in English.

"Is that how old you are?" I asked, still oblivious to the yes/no rule.

Tran nodded. "Twenty," he said. "O.K.!"

"Great," I said. "I'm twenty-eight."

"Twenty!"

I pointed to myself. "Twenty-eight."

Tran pointed to the coffee beans. "Twenty!" he said.

I suddenly realized, after all this time spent endearing myself to Tran, that he'd never intended to give me the coffee. He'd merely been attempting to sell it to me. Figuring it a cheap enough way to save face, I took 20,000 dong (about $1.50) from my pocket and held it out to him. Tran scowled and pushed away the Vietnamese money. He dug into his pocket and pulled out a dollar bill. "Twenty!" he said.

I shook my head and handed the coffee back, but it was too late: Tran was convinced I wanted the coffee. By the time I gave up trying to say no and started to walk away, the price was down to $12. Tran pursued me, dropping the price to $10, then $8, where it hovered for a good ten minutes as Tran backpedaled in front of me, waving the coffee in front of my face.

On paper, ten minutes doesn't seem like much, but when it's spent trying to wave off an absurdly aggressive coffee salesman, ten minutes is a maddening eternity. Finally, I broke. "No, Tran!" I yelled, coming to a halt on the sidewalk. "How many times do you want me to say it? No! No! No!"

Tran sneered and shoved the bag of coffee beans right up under my nose. Without thinking, I smacked it out of his hands. This sent Tran into a fury, screaming what I can only assume were the choicest of Vietnamese curses. I took it as my cue to leave when he spun around and kicked over a parked bicycle.

I never did find the market that night. I ended up weaving through the streets for upwards of an hour, trying to remember my way home.

It was after dark by the time I'd found my hotel. As I walked through the lobby, I noticed two little Vietnamese girls sitting on the couch, watching television. The older one looked to be about six years old, and the younger one couldn't have been any older than three. They were both clutching orange sodas.

"Hello!" the older one cried as I walked past.

"Hello," I said. "How are you?"

"What is your name?" she replied.

"My name is Rolf. What is your name?"

"What is your name?" she said.

"I said my name is Rolf. But what's your name?"

The girl gave me a confused look. "What is your name?" she said, a bit uncertain this time.

I squatted down by the couch and gave her a friendly smile. "We know my name. What's your name?" I playfully wiggled my finger at her. Her face went blank. I pointed again. "Not my name," I said brightly. "Your name!" The girl looked at me as if I'd just said I was going to hit her on the head with a hammer.

Worried about the direction our conversation was heading, I stood up and tried to look as cheery and non-threatening as possible. "Time for me to say goodnight!" I said. "Can you say goodnight?"

At this, the younger girl suddenly burst into tears.

I went to bed that night feeling like some kind of tragically misunderstood cartoon monster.

The following day I rented a clunky one-speed bicycle (a chore in itself; I won't divulge how much I ended up paying for it), and rode out of the city in search of Montagnard ethnic minority villages. Following random roads out of town, I bicycled into a stunning landscape of river valleys, coffee plantations, huge white clouds and far-off purple mountains. The roads were lined with broad fields of maroon soil, smoking brick kilns, cement graves painted mustard yellow, and mud-walled longhouses. In packed-dirt yards along the roadside, little girls coasted precariously on adult-sized bicycles while little boys ran around trying to urinate on each other. Tiny babies buzzed past on 100cc motorcycles, stoically perched on their fathers' laps.

After about three hours of pedaling, I arrived at a rural minority village that looked suitably remote and authentic. I decided to stop and check things out.

In a way, I've always been a bit confused about the purpose of hill-tribe tourism, which has become a travel fad in places like Thailand and Vietnam. I guess the rural treks are meant to expose travelers to an exotic way of life and provide contrast to the modernized ways of places like Bangkok and Ho Chi Minh City—but I suspect that such treks largely serve to validate the sentimental standard of foreign exoticism set by *National Geographic* magazine.

My most immediate challenge upon arriving was simply trying to figure out what to do. In my mind's eye, I envisioned a grand entry, replete with tribal dancing, pigs butchered in my honor and a hearty round of toasts with some ill-tasting fermented beverage. In reality, I found the town largely deserted at midday. The few dark-skinned locals I did see were wearing western clothes (with occasional ethnic flourishes, such as a woven sash or a porkpie hat) and didn't take much interest in me, even when I pulled out the phrase book and tried to make conversation.

After twenty or so awkward minutes of skulking around the village, I managed to insinuate myself into a group of teenaged boys, who were standing in a circle and kicking a chicken-feather birdie into the air. My rusty soccer skills were good enough to keep up with the boys, and we'd just managed to get a good volley going when a boozy, toothless old man wheeled my bike up and indicated that he wanted me to get on it and leave. The boys shouted angrily at the old man; the old man pointed at me and shouted back.

Then, without warning, the tallest boy cuffed the old drunk on the side of the head. As the old man reeled backwards, a second boy pushed him to the ground. When he tried to stand up, the tall boy kicked him in the rump. The others jeered and laughed. When the old man had scampered away, the tall boy looked over at me, smiled and gave a thumbs-up.

Not comfortable with the notion that my new companions had just shown their hospitality by beating the bejesus out of the town drunk, I excused myself at the first opportunity and—after a few more halfhearted attempts at interaction with the locals—pedaled back to Kontum.

Independent travel is often an act of hope—an optimistic attempt to blur the line between cultures through somewhat random interactions. By my second night in Kontum, however, I felt more like an outsider than ever. I decided to make a play at salvaging my trip by moving on.

The next morning I managed to hire (again, at a price I will opt not to share) a battered green '70s era Dodge van to take me to Phuoc Son along the Ho Chi Minh Trail portion of Route 13. The driver was a high-strung wheeler-dealer type, and by the time we left the blacktop at Dac Glei, he had managed to fill the remaining seats in the van with a motley assortment of Vietnamese farmers. Despite my protests, I ended up having to share the shotgun seat with a parcel-laden old woman. I noticed, with a bit of dread, that she was carrying a bottle of green salve.

Thirty minutes into our creep down a rutted stretch of the road, the driver brought us to a rough and sudden halt. An overloaded white transport truck had rolled over in the middle of the road and burst like a sausage, jettisoning torn bags of rice and smashed boxes of clothes in its wake. Our driver cursed and stubbornly honked his horn, but there was no way around it. Angrily, he threw the van into reverse and managed to get us mired in the gravelly mud on the side of the road. After several minutes of flooring the accelerator, he yelled at everyone to get out. The farmers made for the side of the road and began to take out their food, looking like they expected to be there for a while. The driver remained in the van, cursing and stomping on the accelerator.

At that moment, with the back wheels of the Dodge sending chunks of gravel thumping off into the trees, I suddenly realized that I had no good reason for being there. I had gone to a remote corner of Vietnam with no sense of the language or culture—with no host or guide or guidebook, and no specific ideas about what to find there. The decision that brought me there was not a savvy act of independent travel, but an insipid act of negation—a ritual of avoiding other travelers, as if this in itself was somehow significant.

Wearily resolved, I shouldered my pack and started walking back up the road. After an hour or so, I hitched a ride on a flatbed lorry and made it back to Kontum by late afternoon. Since no buses back down to the coast were available until the next day, I checked back into my hotel and went for an aimless walk that eventually landed me in the Montagnard church.

There I offered up my confusion to Barbecue Jesus.

There is no such thing as a seasoned traveler, because travel is an ongoing experience of the unfamiliar. Regardless of how many stamps you have in your passport, you eventually find yourself in a place like Kontum, Vietnam, inadvertently making small children cry, hopelessly trying to deal with people who see you as nothing more than a consumer and haplessly walking in concentric circles until you can find something that resembles your hotel.

Sometimes, the Circuit is not a physical route, but a largely unavoidable state of mind that regulates your expectations. I had gone to the highlands looking for Vietnamese authenticity, but perhaps I was just looking for a generic affirmation experience—something superficial and positive to make me think I wasn't just passing through like a ghost.

Ironically, the utter lack of affirmation and positive interaction I found was—in its own, frustrating way—bluntly authentic. All too often, the random workings of reality simply don't match up with your reverent, idealized hopes.

Hanging there before me—strange, grinning, half-crucified—Barbecue Jesus seemed to understand.

~~~

ENDNOTES

1. **Page 115, paragraph 3: …*Montagnard Jesus seemed to be saying, "Let's have a barbecue!"*:** Since this Vietnam tale essentially recounts a string of travel frustrations and failures, it took me a while to realize it was worth writing about. After leaving Vietnam, I largely forgot about the experience: I traveled overland to Laos, where I contracted cholera (a story in itself); I evacuated to Thailand and flew to South Korea, where I spent a couple of weeks recovering; I continued to Beijing and took the Trans-Siberian train across Mongolia and Russia.

It was in Moscow, nearly three months after I'd left Vietnam, that I re-read my notes and noticed the recurring theme of stymied expectations and misperceived authenticity. Using the Montagnard Jesus to frame the story, I wrote every word of it in the Russian State Library near the Kremlin.

2. **Page 117, paragraph 2: …*weeks on the Circuit without having any legitimate interaction with the locals*:** Granted, I'd met plenty of Vietnamese people in places like Saigon and Nha Trang, but each interaction ultimately boiled down to what, as a tourist, I might be willing to pay for. When a Nha Trang cyclo driver asked me to sign a memento book full of messages from previous customers, it was really just a pretext to bully me into paying an inflated fare; when I struck up a conversation with a teenaged boy in Saigon's Van Hoa Park, he walked me several blocks to what turned out to be a gay bar—then got angry when I didn't go inside (thus costing him his commission).

To an extent this kind of thing happens along every tourist route in the world, but I've never seen it practiced so aggressively as I did in Vietnam. In no other country, for example, have I had a winsome eight-year-old girl call me a "cocksucker" when I declined to buy her postcards (as happened to me on my first day in Saigon).

3. **Page 120, paragraph 6: *I took it as my cue to leave when he spun around and kicked over a parked bicycle*:** It's because of encounters like this that I usually cite Vietnam when people ask me to name my least-

favorite travel country. Whereas in a place like Thailand the rote routines of dealing with tourists are always cloaked in a smile (which can be genuine or cynical, depending upon the situation), most Vietnamese had little patience for pretending a given encounter was anything other than a transaction.

Anthropologist Kalervo Oberg noted that when you suffer from culture shock, "you talk as if the difficulties you experience are more or less created by the people of the host country for your special discomfort." Since I frequently felt as if I were being singled out as a walking dollar sign in Vietnam, my lingering distaste for the country may well be the residue of culture shock.

Or maybe I was just there during a bad week.

4. **Page 121, paragraph 10:** *I went to bed that night feeling like some kind of tragically misunderstood cartoon monster.* I might add that I barely slept that night, since several drunken Vietnamese businessmen were downstairs at the hotel bar singing karaoke until the wee hours of the morning. I wasn't taking notes at the time, but I could swear they sang each and every song from *The Eagles Greatest Hits 1971-1975*.

Hence I had the strange misfortune of living most of the events I describe above with a reverb-heavy version of "Tequila Sunrise" stuck in my head.

❧ 9 ❧

Going Native in the Australian Outback

I. THE PITJANTJATJARA WORD FOR TOURISTS AND ANTS IS ONE AND THE SAME

Here's some advice for anyone hoping to capture the contradictions of Australian outback tourism within a single snapshot: Bring your camera to the base of Uluru—the massive orange-red monolith smack in the center of the Australian continent—and aim the lower half of your viewfinder at the large sign near the hiking trailhead. This sign, which was erected by the local Pitjantjatjara people, solemnly requests that you don't climb up the face of a rock that they consider sacred. Aim your camera at a certain angle, however, and the top half of your viewfinder will capture the knots of tourists who've decided to climb the rock anyway (aided by a safety chain designated by the Australian National Park Service for that very purpose).

The Pitjantjatjara euphemism for tourists in their homeland is *minga tjuta*—"ants"—and from this angle you can see why: Looking up from the base of Uluru, the tidy lines of people inching up the climbing trail look like insects on a mound.

I, too, have come to central Australia as a *minga tjuta*, though I'm not here to scale the slopes of Uluru. Rather, I have resolved to spend the next week looking for a meaningful experience of Australian aboriginal culture. My guide for today, a Pitjantjatjara man named Wally Jacob, is late—so I've been killing time by taking photos of central Australia's iconic sandstone landmark and the dusty red desert that surrounds it.

I've always prided myself on traveling independently in unfamiliar cultures, but joining a guided tour of aboriginal Uluru is something of a necessity: Indigenous people in this part of Australia are famously averse to the notion of random backpackers wandering onto tribal land without a formal welcome, and anthropologists have noted that Aborigines generally prefer busloads of superficial tourists (who buy a lot of souvenirs and are quickly gone) to more earnest seekers, who unwittingly traipse through ceremonial lands, make themselves at home, and ask a lot of intrusive questions. This cultural distaste for drop-in visitors goes back to the earliest interactions with Europeans in Australia. The first aboriginal phrase recorded by eighteenth-century British convict-settlers was *warra-warra* ("go away"), and Captain James Cook noted in his 1770 expedition journal that, in spite of his attempts to interact with indigenous Australians, "all they seemed to want was for us to be gone."

Since it has become unrealistic for outsiders to "be gone" from this Australian landscape, local Aborigines have used organized tours as a way of retaining control over how visitors see their ancestral homeland. Besides competition from non-aboriginal tours—including camel treks and helicopter flyovers—local control is certainly not all-encompassing: Because of functional compromises in regaining legal ownership of Uluru from the Australian government in the 1980s, climbing the rock was never formally outlawed. And, given that 250,000 or so tourists ascend the sacred site each year in defiance of Pitjantjatjara wishes, it's safe to assume that many visitors are more interested in the scenic pleasures of the monolith than the aboriginal culture that surrounds it. During the tourist high season, the nearby hotel complex swells to become the fourth-most-populous settlement in Australia's Northern Territory—and more people pass by Uluru in a single week than Pitjantjatjara people of previous generations saw in a lifetime.

When Wally arrives—dressed in flip-flop sandals, dirty brown pants, and a crisp blue oxford shirt that reads "Anangu Tours"—he barely notices the crowds of tourists. Instead, he grins and points to a spot twenty feet away from us. "*Ngintaka,*" he says.

I look to Keiran Lusk, the tall, salt-and-pepper bearded Australian who serves as Wally's interpreter. "Perentie lizard," he says. A couple of seconds pass before I see the wrinkly, long-necked reptile—a four-foot-long creature that has probably been sitting there since I first arrived. "No worries," Keiran confides. "I didn't see him, either."

Now that the *ngintaka* has been spotted, a knot of tourists gathers. Several cameras flash at once, and the lizard flees. Wally shrugs, tugs a brown Billabong ball cap onto his head, and leads us down the hiking trail.

As we skirt the base of Uluru, I chat indirectly with the gray-haired Pitjantjatjara guide, asking my questions via Keiran. Wally tells me that he was born in the bush fifty-three years ago, then taken by his mother to a Lutheran mission, where he was given his European name. He tells me that he's tired today, because he was busy collecting spear-wood the night before. He tells me about his efforts to teach old traditions to Pitjantjatjara teenagers, who often prefer video games or hip-hop music to spear hunting and bush-craft. These young people, he says with a weary giggle, are like tourists: It's hard to hold their attention for very long.

Keiran adds details and clarifications as he translates for Wally. "Modern improvements have had mixed results in aboriginal Australia," he says. "The younger generation is living on TV and junk food. They're losing a part of themselves because they've lost their connection to the land. Some of them are dying before their parents because of alcoholism or diabetes."

As he says this, Keiran keeps an eye on people in other tour groups, and he casually steps into the line of sight whenever someone tries to take Wally's picture. When I ask him why he does this, Keiran tells me it's not just an issue of respect, but also business integrity. "Tourists love to have aboriginals in their pictures of Uluru. It makes the photos seem more authentic. But if we let every random person take Wally's picture, people would lose an incentive for taking our tours. Plus, we'd never get anything done."

Wally leads us to a cave at the base of Uluru that is associated with the *mala tjukurpa*, or "hare wallaby dreaming," which describes an event in Pitjantjatjara prehistory. Such mythic stories of "dreamtime"—epic tales wherein snakes walk, wallabies throw spears, and mulga seeds seek revenge—are central to aboriginal religious and ethical beliefs, describing in detail the creation of the world and humankind's role in it. Celebrated in classic travel books like Bruce Chatwin's *The Songlines*, these dreamtime stories are one of the most intriguing aspects of indigenous Australian culture.

The stories are also one of the most misunderstood aspects of indigenous culture. One hundred years ago, for example, European anthropologists believed that a central dreamtime story for the Pitjantjatjara involved the *pungkalungu*—giant, flesh-eating ogres who exacted revenge for misdeeds. As it turned out, *pungkalungu* stories were merely informal Pitjantjatjara folk tales—a local variation of the bogeyman, used to scare naughty children.

"'Dreamtime' is an imperfect translation," Keiran tells me. "*Tjukurpa*, as the Pitjantjatjara understand it, is no dream. There's no good equivalent word in English; it's a kind of traditional law, which describes history, geography, and morality. Researchers estimate humans have lived near Uluru for 22,000 years, but the Pitjantjatjara believe that they have always been here, that *tjukurpa* is part of an ongoing condition, not a mythic past. This oral tradition is accumulated through years of ceremonial initiation and life experience, and it's one of the most technically and legally complex religious systems in the world."

Keiran goes on to relate the dreamtime story of mythic hare-wallabies who visited Uluru and unwittingly found themselves in a feud with the mulga-seed men, the *wintalka*. The vengeful *wintalka* created a dog monster to destroy the ceremonial camp of the hare-wallaby men, and signs of the struggle are evident in the lumps and notches of Uluru's furrowed red slopes.

As stories go, the *mala tjukurpa* isn't particularly spellbinding, but Keiran tells me the purpose of *tjukurpa* is not to entertain but to teach lessons about respecting ceremonial rules or finding food. "Besides," he says, "you're only getting a small fragment of the story, which itself is connected with other stories. To fully understand the *tjukurpa*, you'd have to live close to the land for many years. Even then, tradition dictates what you can and cannot know. Wally may be a male elder, but that doesn't mean he has access to female stories and ceremonies."

I notice Wally has wandered off and is now rolling a cigarette under a tree near the Kantju Gorge water hole. "*Piiwi*," he says, as Keiran and I approach him. He points up at the tree, but it's several moments before I spot a pair of owl-like tawny frogmouths—mother and hatchling—perched on a branch. Their coloring is so similar to the tree bark that I can just barely make them out. "She's moved," Wally says to Keiran. "She used to live in a different place. I've never seen her here before. And I never knew she'd had babies."

As Wally puffs on his cigarette and grins up at the *piiwi*, I realize that his very strength as a tour guide is that he doesn't really give a crap about tourists. Instead of trying to deliver standardized cultural information, the Pitjantjatjara elder is merely offering me the chance to tag along as he enjoys a stroll in his homeland. And, while a morning tour of Uluru can hardly do aboriginal heritage justice, Wally's keen eye for the land hints at a richer cultural story. His story is, in fact, the tale of the oldest continuous culture in the world—stretching well into the Pleistocene Age, when people lived with no permanent possessions, no food preservation, and no distinction between labor and leisure. It's a tale of the first continent in human history to be settled by sea travel, 60,000 years ago—and the intimate knowledge of climate, animal habits, plant cycles, and insect life necessary to subsist in a harsh land.

It's also a story that gets muddled by the noise of the modern world—though modernity seems to be popularizing Pitjantjatjara culture as much as it compromises it. Indeed, even though resort restaurants, camel treks, and tour buses would seem to diminish the aboriginal presence here, the constant stream of visitors creates an inevitable market of fascination in the local culture. Among the hundreds of historically distinct indigenous societies within Australia, mass tourism has transformed the Pitjantjatjara into an antipodean equivalent of the Navajo—a culture that is celebrated and romanticized by the same public consciousness that threatens to dilute it.

When our morning trek concludes, Keiran mentions that I can buy into a more in-depth Pitjantjatjara tour tomorrow, where I'll be able to dine on witchety grubs, identify bush fruits, and learn how to throw a spear.

I decline—not because I don't want to do these things, but because of that old tourist irony: To get a proper taste of aboriginal culture, I feel I need to find a landscape that isn't so overrun by other tourists.

Bidding my Uluru guides farewell, I fire up my rental car and head east on the Lasseter Highway.

II. If It's Tuesday, This Must Be Arrernte Country

Travelers wanting to catch a glimpse of an aboriginal dance performance near the tidy Australian outback town of Alice Springs are usually pointed to the Red Centre Dreaming show, which includes a three-course buffet dinner and all the sparkling wine you can drink. Since the local Arrernte Aborigines don't feel comfortable sharing their ceremonial dances in front of a paying audience, the Red Centre Dreaming performers are brought in from the state of Queensland, hundreds of miles away. In cultural terms, watching Queensland aboriginal dances in Alice Springs is kind of like going to Denmark to watch a flamenco performance—but the tourists here don't seem to mind.

Though I'm trying my best to understand the cultural intricacies of indigenous Australian society, at times it can be hard to keep up with all the new information. Yesterday, while visiting Uluru National Park, I managed to learn a number of Pitjantjatjara aboriginal words, such as *kapi*, which means "water," and *tjala*, which means "honey ant." Today, having driven five hours to Alice Springs—a small increment on any map of Australia—I've discovered that these words are now useless. Here, in the local Arrernte language, "water" is *kwatye*; "honey ant" is *yerrampe*. For travelers hoping to learn about aboriginal culture while seeing the sights of central Australia, this can be somewhat befuddling—kind of like the "If it's Tuesday, this must be Belgium" phenomenon of Western European package tourism, but without any easily identifiable frontiers.

Before the arrival of European interlopers, indigenous Australian societies spoke around 250 languages and 700 dialects. Though all these aboriginal subcultures shared a land-based nomadic lifestyle, similar religious practices, and some forms of intertribal trade, they never developed a collective sense of "aboriginal" identity, and broad cultural variations existed across relatively short distances. British settlers in the late eighteenth century, for example, noted that Aborigines on the north side of Sydney Harbor spoke a different language from those living on the south side. To this day, most indigenous Australians identify more with their historical kinship group than a general "aboriginal" identity, and the closest thing to a cultural lingua franca is English.

Thus, a visit to Alice Springs can be confusing, since the town functions as an administrative center that attracts people from all parts of central Australia. Tourists browsing the souvenir shops and indigenous-art galleries along the Todd Street Mall might assume that the groups of aboriginal people dozing along the walkway are all hard-luck locals—an outback variation of the urban homeless—when, in fact, there's a good chance those aboriginal folks are themselves tourists to Alice Springs. One group lounging along Todd Mall, for example, might be a family of Pintupi speakers in town for a daughter's softball tournament; another might be Kaytetye women who've hitched in for land-rights hearings; a third group might be young Alyawarr men indulging in a one-week bender, since their elders don't allow alcohol on indigenous land. And, since more than 20 percent of Alice Springs' 30,000 permanent residents are of aboriginal heritage, all these visitors might have trouble relating to indigenous locals, who are known to drive Land Cruisers, live in suburban bungalows, and feel more comfortable speaking English than their traditional languages.

My guide here in Alice Springs, a handsome, forty-six-year-old Arrernte man named Bob Taylor, speaks almost no Arrernte. This is because, at age eight, he was forcibly taken from his Arrernte mother and—with the approval of the Australian government—sent to a home for "half-caste" aboriginal children in South Australia, where, for the next nine years, he was allowed to speak only English. More than 100,000 indigenous children, collectively called the "Stolen Generation," suffered this practice of enforced assimilation between 1910 and 1970. Unhappily trapped between cultures as a young man, Bob eventually found his calling as a chef and wandered his way to Europe, where he landed work at various five-star hotel restaurants in Holland. Ask him about this experience, and he'll tell you about the idiosyncrasies of his Dutch ex-girlfriends with the same affection and enthusiasm he uses to describe his Arrernte cousins.

Bob started his tour operation two years ago, as a way of embracing his heritage and taking a break from the boozy trappings of restaurant culture. His business, RT Tours, has one twelve-person bus; he is the only employee. Since this is low season for tourists, I am his lone client. Today we are driving fifty miles out of Alice Springs to West MacDonnell National Park, where Bob plans to grill kangaroo filets and teach me how to find bush food. I notice he's packed a didgeridoo—a long, wooden, tube-like aboriginal instrument famous for its growling, ethereal sound. From my research, I know that the Arrernte people didn't historically use the didgeridoo, but I don't mention this to Bob.

As we drive, the landscape outside our bus is spectacular: prickly yellow spinifex grass clumped in the dark orange soil; furrowed ridges of dusty purple rock; broad blue horizons. Twice the size of California, Northern Territory is home to just over 200,000 people (most of whom live in Darwin, on the northern coast), and the sense of dry, sprawling emptiness is visceral and humbling. Leathery kangaroo carcasses—road kill, from the looks of it—fringe the roadside.

I ask Bob how it feels to be a child of the Stolen Generation, but he doesn't seem to want to dwell on it. Instead, he steers the conversation to his business and how he feels he's in a unique position to bridge two cultures. "Tourism is a great opportunity for aboriginal people to share their culture and create economic opportunities," he says. "The biggest problem is that we're not really driven by the dollar. Most aboriginal businesspeople are more interested in living close to the land, getting off welfare, and preserving traditions for future generations. I like to think that my business is an example of the opportunities that are out there."

"What kinds of people usually come on your tours?"

"Europeans. A lot of Germans, plus some Italians and French. For some reason, these people are interested in indigenous cultures from all over the world. That means my main competition isn't Sydney or the Great Barrier Reef, but places like Nepal and Peru. Aboriginal tour operators are trying to get the word out, trying to convince people that our culture is as old and interesting as you'll find anywhere. I just wish we could get more of you Americans to come out."

"You don't get many Americans?"

"American tourists out here tend to be older folks, who don't like hiking around and getting dirty. They're happy to see a dance or listen to a didgeridoo at their hotel, then fly back to Sydney. But if you want to understand aboriginal Australia, you have to come here for the land itself. If you don't experience the flies and the heat and the long distances, you're going to miss the point."

When we arrive at MacDonnell National Park, Bob dons a broad-brimmed felt hat and leads me on a two-hour hike along the steep, red-rock chasms. Here, we spot rock wallabies along the cliffs, examine the sandy foxholes made by kangaroos digging for water, and scan the landscape for bush food. Since plants don't grow much in the searing heat of the Australian summer, Bob breaks out a Tupperware jar containing fruits he's collected on other journeys. I can't keep up with the Arrernte words for all the food, but Bob points out that each fruit has an English nickname: bush fig, bush cucumber, bush banana, bush orange. As I sample the foods, I find that these names are somewhat arbitrary: The bush coconut, for example, is sweet and fleshy, but it resembles a tree gall; the bush tomato has an acidic, raisiny taste. Bob tells me that over thirty edible bush fruits are known to aboriginals in central Australia and that the European explorers who famously starved to death here in the nineteenth century died in a land where indigenous people had prospered for 20,000 years.

Leading me back out of the canyons, Bob sets up kitchen gear at a picnic area and cooks me a tasty lunch of seared kangaroo filets and bread dipped in bush spices. As I eat, he takes out the didgeridoo and begins to play, showing me how he circulates air through his nose to make a continuous breath. As much as I enjoy the spooky, reverberating music, I can't contain my curiosity. "I've read that the didgeridoo doesn't come from central Australia," I say when he's finished.

"You're right," he says. "It comes from the north, in Arnhem Land. But I've found that tourists want to hear aboriginals play the didgeridoo, regardless of where it comes from. When you run a business like mine, that's the trick: balancing people's expectations of aboriginal culture with the real thing. That's why a town like Alice Springs has galleries full of paintings from a culture that never had houses to hang them in."

"You mean all that aboriginal art isn't authentic?"

"It depends on what you mean by authentic. But yeah: If you want to see how tourist demand changes local traditions, look at the aboriginal art business."

The following day, I head into Alice Springs to do just that.

III. A VISIT TO THE ARTISTIC HILLBILLIES OF UTOPIA

Driving along the desolate and gorgeous Sandover Highway northeast of Alice Springs, there are only two sure indicators that life exists in this parched red-orange landscape. One is the curious ubiquity of pink cockatoos, which dart out of the bush and swoop over the Land Cruiser, occasionally exploding into the grill in a suicidal puff of pastel feathers. The other is an abundance of junked cars—sun-bleached Ford Falcons and rusty station wagons that have been abandoned at the side of the road by Aborigines going to or coming from their isolated homes in the outback. In the heat of the afternoon, when the horizon shudders like a mirage and towering dust devils swirl across the highway, this place can feel like the end of the world. Perhaps seized by irony or optimism, the German immigrants who tried to settle this area in the 1920s named it Utopia.

I'm traveling along this barren Utopian byway with Dale Jennings, a twenty-four-year-old Australian woman who works as a field research manager for the Mbantua Gallery in Alice Springs.

Our goal for the day is to collect and document new paintings from the aboriginal artists who live out here. We're also going to investigate a mystery concerning the Dixon clan of Tomahawk Camp—a promising group of female artists whose intricately detailed dot paintings declined in quality when the gallery began to pay them more money. Dale can't understand how a pay increase could result in shoddier dot work, so she's packed a box of reading glasses and prepared a pep talk in the hope that the women's work will return to its previous standard.

For the past couple of decades, paintings and folkcraft have been the most vibrant—and marketable—expression of Australia's indigenous culture. Tied to the intricacies of dream-time spiritual law, aboriginal rock art and body painting is said to be the oldest ongoing artistic legacy in the world, stretching back at least 40,000 years. Despite such ancient traditions, however, Aborigines have been selling paintings to outsiders for only a lit-tle over half a century. Albert Namatjira, a pioneering Arrernte watercolor artist, was the first indigenous person to be granted citizenship by the Australian government, in 1957. (Average Aborigines didn't get this privilege for another ten years.) In the early 1970s, a teacher named Geoffrey Bardon encouraged artists in the Western Desert community of Papunya to re-create their sand-art designs on canvas, using synthetic paints. Initially con-troversial (some Aborigines considered their art to be sacred and private), the symbolic, dreamtime-inspired "dot" paintings of the Papunya community soon proved a hit with tourists and collec-tors. Other indigenous communities around Australia began to render their dreamtime stories on canvas, and aboriginal painting centers sprang up around Australia. At least fifty such art collec-tives now operate in the Northern Territory alone.

Thanks to this indigenous renaissance, Australia has more working artists per capita than any country in the world—and the Alice Springs area has more art galleries per capita than any place in Australia. Of the four H's said to motivate indigenous tourism worldwide (habitat, heritage, and history included), handcrafts are by far the most sought-after aspect of aboriginal Australian life. A souvenir dot painting is as close as many tourists to central Australia come to actual contact with indigenous culture—and this is usually no accident, since aboriginal communities tend to protect their privacy. To gain entry into the far-flung communities of Utopia, in fact, I had to shed the tourist mantle in Alice Springs and brandish my press credentials in the Mbantua Gallery. Hoping to make the most of my last-minute intrusion, Dale Jennings has deputized me to hand out paints and take photos while she collects and documents the new paintings.

Turning off the Sandover Highway, past a large sign decreeing a liquor ban on aboriginal land, Dale steers the Land Cruiser over a series of rutted dirt roads that take us into the heart of Utopia. Nearly the size of Luxembourg, this area includes more than a dozen remote communities, where the primary languages are Anmatyerr and Alyawarr, dialects vaguely similar to the Arrernte spoken in the Alice Springs area. Despite its isolation, Utopia is one of the most renowned art regions in Australia, made famous in the 1990s by the stylistic innovations of the late Emily Kngwarreye and Gloria Petyarre, whose paintings now sell worldwide for tens of thousands of dollars. The Utopia scene is female-dominated and derives its most distinctive canvas techniques from the ceremonial body painting used by generations of Anmatyerr and Alyawarr women. Of the two thousand or so people who live in the Utopia region, more than 250 artists sell their work through the Mbantua Gallery, representatives of which make a 350-mile round-trip journey to collect paintings twice each month. Dale is the second generation of Jenningses to make this biweekly excursion; her father, Tim Jennings, founded the art gallery in 1992, after two decades of working in Utopia as a policeman and shopkeeper.

Our first stop is Rocket Range (named for the shape of the local water tower), where I quickly learn why tourists aren't encouraged to come here. Simply put, the settlement is filthy: Smashed soda cans and broken glass glitter in the dust; plastic grocery bags float in the breeze; festering dogs cower in the shadows. Children sit in the dirt, half-naked, snuffling amid clouds of bush flies. The concrete houses resemble military barracks long since given over to squatters; beds with soiled mattresses lie in dirt yards. In one slow, 360-degree gaze, I am able to count over thirty junked cars sitting tire-less on the sun-baked soil.

Having grown up visiting the area, Dale is unfazed by the squalor. Spreading fresh canvases and paintbrushes out on the Land Cruiser tailgate, she greets the white-haired old ladies by name as they dodder over to show off their new artwork. Abstract, colorful, and richly detailed, each of these women's paintings corresponds to a unique dreamtime story (often involving food, such as bush plums or bush tomatoes). Speaking a combination of pidgin English and Alyawarr, Dale updates her files on each artist, logging new acquisitions, passing out fresh art supplies, and asking each artist to sign the paintings she intends to buy. Mostly illiterate, the elderly artists sign their names in big block letters. For each painting Dale collects, my job is to take a photo of the artist with the handiwork. In addition to creating a personal keepsake for the potential art buyer, these photographs are meant to serve as a badge of authenticity, since aboriginal-style art is now widely forged in places like Vietnam and China. With Rocket Range artists like Queenie Kemarre creating canvases that sell for upward of $2,000 each, proving authenticity is becoming increasingly important.

After collecting art, dispensing supplies, taking photos, and handing out payments, Dale and I continue on to other Utopia settlements, where we repeat our routine. As we travel from camp to camp, I'm amazed by the local art variations: It's as if each camp of a dozen or so Utopia artists has its own signature style. Whereas the Rocket Range artists paint large and colorful canvases, with lots of impressionistic abstractions, the painters at Mosquito Bore have held to the traditional method of tightly grouped dots, occasionally accenting their work with linear details. The chatty women at Camel Camp use white paint to create a bright and dreamy mood in their paintings, while the stoic male artists of Mulga Bore stick to earth-based ocher hues (yellow, red, and black) and traditional symbols derived from sand art.

Amid the artistic diversity, the only thing these aboriginal artists seem to have in common is the fact that they all live like hillbillies. At every camp we visit, the scene is the same: trashed cars, mangy dogs, dilapidated houses, piles of garbage swirling in the wind, entire families lolling in the shade. Most startling is Jeannie's Camp, where a half-dozen families have centered their lifestyle in and around twenty or so broken-down sedans and station wagons, which they use for shelter. There are no houses here, just dead cars, dusty clumps of trash, a few shade-hutches made from sticks and dirty blankets, and one sickly calf tied to a tree. When Dale and I first arrive, we pass a sleepy-eyed man patiently driving a car with four flat tires.

Though years of political prejudice and territorial disenfranchisement have led Aborigines here to live this way, cultural choice is also a factor. Three years ago, the residents of Jeannie's Camp lived in concrete houses in a nearby settlement, before aboriginal funeral rites (known in pidgin English as "sorry business") required them to move to a new location. Unlike Western funerals, sorry business can last for months—and after relocating to this dusty knot of old cars, most of the families in Jeannie's Camp enigmatically elected to stay, even after the mourning period had finished.

Considering that some of these artists can make thousands of dollars a month from their paintings (in addition to hundreds of dollars in welfare benefits), it can be hard to understand why they'd choose to spend their days living in such primitive settlements. One easy assumption is that middlemen and art dealers are exploiting their isolation.

"We hear that quite often," Dale tells me, as she collects paintings from the Jeannie's Camp artists. "About once a week someone will come into the gallery and accuse us of taking advantage of the artists. All we can say is that we've been working with the Utopia communities for years, and we've gone to great trouble to make their interests a priority. We can pay the artists a generous compensation, but we can't force them to move into town and live a middle-class life."

A thousand generations of nomadic heritage is undoubtedly part of the problem. In his book *Collapse*, biologist Jared Diamond notes that "the values to which people cling most stubbornly under inappropriate conditions are those values that were previously the source of their greatest triumphs over adversity." Diamond was referring to fifteenth-century Norse settlers using inappropriate farming methods in Greenland, but this notion could just as easily apply to indigenous Australians facing the modern world. For 40,000 years, the accumulation of possessions was considered an impediment to a lifestyle that required constant mobility within a harsh climate. Surplus food was used or destroyed, and refusal to share resources with the community (a cautionary motif in many aboriginal dreamtime stories) could result in violent punishment. Life was lived in the mythic moment; most aboriginal languages didn't have specific words for "yesterday" or "tomorrow." To this day, most of the Aborigines living in Utopia spend or share their money as soon as they receive it. White Australians run all the outback supply shops, since indigenous proprietors would be culturally obliged to give away their goods for free. For the same reason, aboriginal auto mechanics are virtually nonexistent—hence the abundance of dead cars.

In many ways, the social complexities of aboriginal culture (from extensive, memorized traditional laws to an intricate kinship system meant to eliminate inbreeding) were rendered functionally obsolete when globalization and modernity arrived with

European settlers, beginning in 1788. And, while all humans lived with hunter-gatherer values before the advent of agriculture, most world cultures have had eight thousand or so years to adapt to the idiosyncrasies of settled life. Cultures like the Anmatyerr and Alyawarr of Utopia, on the other hand, have been aware of this new worldview for less than a century—which could explain why cosmetic garbage disposal (an absurd concept to nomadic people) has yet to catch on here.

As Aborigines across Australia struggle to sustain nomadic traditions within the abundance and abstractions of modern life, many of their communities have suffered. Unemployment among Aborigines is four times the national average, infant death three times more likely. In remote communities, bush foods have given way to carbonated drinks and tinned meat purchased with welfare money. Alcoholism and obesity are rampant, and aboriginal life expectancy is 20 percent shorter than that of mainstream Australia.

Still, there are signs of improvement, and—despite the impoverished appearance of places like Jeannie's Camp—the Utopia communities are actually a comparative success story. Thanks to the financial and moral successes of the decade-long art movement, heart disease and smoking are on the decline in Utopia; obesity is virtually nonexistent, and life expectancy is significantly longer than in neighboring Northern Territory aboriginal communities.

The final settlement we visit on our Utopia art run is Tomahawk Camp, where Dale hopes she can inspire the Dixon ladies to return to their previous standards of artistic excellence. Even famous artists like Emily Kngwarreye were notoriously inconsistent in their craft, for reasons the gallery curators of Alice Springs have yet to fully understand.

As it turns out, Dale's pep talk is not necessary: Today, after two months of progressively inferior work, Thelma, Lorna, and Maggie Dixon show up bearing vibrantly colored canvases filled with detailed dot work. Dale seems equally delighted and perplexed with the quality of the new paintings. "*Morrengre*," she says to the elderly sisters. "These are beautiful." Perhaps for good measure, she gives the old ladies reading glasses anyway.

It would appear as if the artistic anomalies of the Dixon clan have been resolved for now—yet I can tell from the look on Dale's face that the whole episode is still very much a mystery.

IV. Cowboys, Indians, and Noble Savages

One night, while sipping beers in an Alice Springs tourist pub called Bojangles, I befriended a florid-faced, fifty-five-year-old marketing rep named Richard, who had just flown in from Adelaide. Richard proved a happy-go-lucky drinking companion until I mentioned that I'd come to Australia to experience aboriginal culture.

"Aboriginal culture?" he scoffed. "You mean going bush and eating bugs? Throwing spears, that kinda rot?"

"Maybe," I offered.

"Bollocks, mate. A bunch of Disneyland bollocks, that is. You wanna experience real aboriginal culture? Try cashing a welfare check and going on the piss for two weeks. Get into a punch up, huff some petrol, pass out in the Todd River. Maybe steal a car and drive it bush, use it as a house until your next welfare check arrives. That's aboriginal culture, mate, not some spear-chucking, Garden of Eden horseshit."

At the time, I found Richard's rant off-putting, but the next morning I learned to appreciate its honesty when I met an auburn-haired twenty-seven-year-old named Cynthia in an Internet café. A Sydneysider visiting Alice Springs for the first time, Cynthia made my acquaintance when she overheard me using the word "tribe" to describe the Arrernte people.

"We don't use the word 'tribe'," she said. "Aboriginals don't consider themselves 'tribes.' So, when you use that word, you're just showcasing your ignorance."

Since any journey to a new land is an ongoing encounter with one's own ignorance, I could only agree with her. "So, what word am I supposed to use?" I asked.

Cynthia never did tell me exactly. "Western ideas and assumptions have poisoned indigenous culture," she said. "Look around. There's a bloody KFC up the street, and it's full of aboriginals. How is that supposed to make their lives better? These people lived in perfect harmony with nature for thousands of years, and now we have them drinking bloody Pepsi and eating fat-fried chicken wings."

"Well, nobody's forcing anyone to—"

"Fifty years ago, aboriginals weren't even considered citizens," she said, holding up her palm as if to shush me. "All we've taught them since is how to love junk food and drink themselves to death. Most of them don't even have ownership rights to their traditional land, so they're stuck in shantytowns instead of living next to nature. Did you know that for 150 years white Australians could kill aboriginals without fear of justice? That the state could take their children away and force them to speak English? That we've destroyed the very environment that gave aboriginals their livelihood?"

I was indeed aware of this information—a brief reading of modern aboriginal history forces one to ponder such sobering facts—but the more Cynthia talked about the destruction of aboriginal culture, the less I was convinced she had much interest in real-life aboriginals. Though I'm sure she meant well, Cynthia had never spent much time in aboriginal communities, nor had she studied any indigenous languages. She'd never witnessed any initiation ceremonies, and her knowledge of "dreamtime" (another incorrect word, she informed me) seemed suspiciously limited to what a tourist might learn after a couple of days at Uluru.

Moreover, Cynthia seemed to be less interested in realistic solutions than in spreading the blame for aboriginal woes as broadly as possible. (Apparently, I'm part of the problem, since I hail from the nation that invented Kentucky Fried Chicken.) By implying that Aborigines won't be happy until they've reverted to munching witchety grubs and wearing loincloths—by assuming that indigenous Australians are little more than simpering victims under the heel of white oppression—Cynthia's bleeding-heart paternalism felt as racist as Richard's bile.

After a week of informal chats with Australians of all political stripes, in fact, I was left with the sense that Aborigines themselves are the only ones with any realistic chance of solving aboriginal problems. Considering that indigenous societies spent 40,000 years demonstrating an innate brilliance for adaptation in harsh settings, I'm optimistic that they will, in time, find ways of better integrating a globalized worldview into their culture.

In saying this, I realize I'm contradicting the very impulse that brought me here. I did not, after all, come to the outback to hang with latte-sipping, Xbox-playing aboriginal accountants who've uploaded their dreamtime songs to iTunes; I've journeyed here with the specific hope of witnessing a way of life that is utterly foreign to me. Such is the irony of indigenous tourism: In seeking out a culture based on its difference from our own, we risk confusing "authenticity" with our idealized expectations of what that authenticity is supposed to look like. This could be why the self-ghettoizing brand of tour-bus-and-dinner-show tourism is so popular: It offers visitors a seamless product—didgeridoo performances, dot paintings, gift-shop boomerangs—that flatters expectations without raising any complicated questions.

In a way, travel anywhere can easily turn into an exercise in fantasy, as I learned when I made an afternoon journey to Ooraminna Homestead, an old cattle station twenty miles south of Alice Springs.

Ooraminna has no aboriginal connection—quite the opposite: It celebrates the heritage of white Australian settlers in the outback—but I hope a visit here will earn me a useful perspective. First settled by William and Mary Hayes in 1884 (and still owned by their descendants), the Ooraminna operation consists of 5,000 head of Hereford cattle scattered across 450,000 acres of outback. A decade ago, when droughts were taking a heavy toll on the cattle industry, the Hayes family introduced tourist farm-stays as a way of diversifying their income. After a film-production company built a replica pioneer township on the property in 1998, the family incorporated the new buildings into their tourism venture. The scenic cattle station now hosts weddings, corporate events, and a steady stream of overnight tourists yearning to experience the Australian outback.

Sal Hurn, a barrel-chested Hayes son-in-law, takes me around the Ooraminna property in his Ford F-250. As we drive across the cattle station checking windmills and water tanks, I can see why this setting caught the attention of movie producers: Sprawling and craggy, with sandy red soil and kangaroos lounging in the shadows, the landscape seems lifted from a postcard. When I marvel at the setting, Sal tells me that hosting visitors has helped him appreciate the beauty of his own land but that he's still getting used to balancing his calling as a rancher with his duties as a tour guide. "I know how to chase cattle," he tells me. "I don't always know how to chase people."

In attempting to sustain a traditional way of living by letting tourists experience it in small doses, Sal shares many similarities with the indigenous tour guides I've met. Since cattlemen and Aborigines would seem to be at odds over land issues, however, I ask Sal how he gets along with his indigenous neighbors. "We have mutual respect for each other," he says. "Blackfellas have worked with us as trackers for over a hundred years. They've always lived close to the land; they appreciate it the same as we do."

"What about the people who'd say that cattle stations have destroyed the indigenous way of life?"

"Some of the most successful aboriginals in Australia own cattle stations," he says. "There's a lot of sad history in this country that can't be taken back, but you have to spend time out here before you make judgments about what goes on. Australia is the most urbanized country in the world; 95 percent of the population lives in cities on the coast. The loudest opinions on aboriginal issues usually come from people who haven't spent much time outside the city."

"Do they change their minds when they come here to visit?"

"I couldn't say, but I hope they at least come to appreciate how we live. When you've spent your whole life in the city, you can learn a lot from a few days in the outback. I've lost count of how many guests have told me they were happy to finally experience the 'real' Australia."

Of course, the "real" Australia can be a slippery concept, as I discover when Sal drives me back to the homestead, where a conference group of sixty Australian travel agents are several cocktails into a noisy al-fresco banquet. Most of the celebrants, I note, have dressed up for the occasion in pioneer costumes—broadbrimmed hats, blue jeans, pointy-toed boots—but something seems a little off-kilter about the whole affair. It isn't until I'm forking a kangaroo steak onto my buffet plate that I realize what's wrong: In addition to cowboys and saloon wenches, a number of the celebrants have come dressed as Plains Indians and serapedraped Mexicans.

By all appearances, these travel agents have chosen to throw a banquet at Ooraminna not because it reminds them of their Australian heritage, but because it reminds them of a Hollywood Western set.

"You think this is odd, you shoulda been here last month," Sal tells me. "We had a *Mad Max* party and a *Priscilla Queen of the Desert* party at the same time. What can you say? Some people come here to learn our history and see how we live. Others just want to have a good time."

V. IF ZEUS AND MOSES LIVED IN YOUR BACKYARD

The people of the Arrernte Corkwood Dreaming in central Australia have a story about the first time man discovered he had urges beyond his ever-present struggle for survival.

This tale of dreamtime law—or *altyerre*, as it in known in the Arrernte language—begins in the days of the first happenings, when catlike marsupials called *achilpe* transformed into men. Delighting in their new form, like butterflies loosed from their chrysalises, these men thrived amid a land where corkwood nectar dripped in abundance, until finally the nectar flowed so fast that the land flooded, and most of the men were drowned. The survivors regrouped and learned how to hunt for survival.

One day, a lone man—a *chilba*, or hunter—was stalking a bush turkey when he heard an amazing sound coming from beyond a grove of trees. It was a noise that no animal had ever made before, and he was entranced by its haunting rhythm. Gathering up his nerve, the hunter crept closer and closer to the sound, and soon he spied the most beautiful beings he'd ever seen. Sitting in a circle, these creatures resembled his fellow hunters, but with lovely curves and more delicate limbs. Mesmerized by the songs and the brightly painted bodies of these strange beings—these women—the *chilba* man touched himself. Then, ever so gently, he took his spear and touched the women, one by one. When he saw that they did not fear him, he seized the singing damsels and ran off with them to a distant waterfall.

When the man did not return to the camp that evening, his fellow hunters set off to find him. In the fading light, they tracked his footprints until they heard the singing of the women. Following this song to the waterfall, they saw the *chilba* man cavorting with the women—and neglecting his hunting duties—so they dragged him off and punished him severely.

How exactly they punished him I can't say, since Magdalene Lynch is too embarrassed to go into details. "I'd prefer not to talk about that section of the story," she tells me.

Magdalene, a heavyset Arrernte grandmother, is the tradition-al landowner of her ancestral homeland—a flat, dusty stretch of outback colloquially known as Black Tank, one hour north of Alice Springs. Unlike the trash-strewn settlements of Utopia, Black Tank is a neatly maintained homestead; a sign at the front gate proudly announces that it won the "Territory Tidy Town" award in 2004.

Dressed in running shoes and a maroon polo shirt, Magdalene has been walking me along the dreaming trails of her property, which she is developing into an indigenous cultural camp for tourists and school groups. Her hope, she tells me, is that the camp will generate income and keep her grandchildren close to the land. Since her dot-painting classrooms and shaded rest-pavilions are still under construction, she has primarily been telling me the local creation stories. "We never believed our terri-tory existed within borders," she tells me. "We belong to *altyerre,* our dreamtime law, which stretches over the land like lines. We may live here, but our dreamtime stories go as far south as Port Augusta, one thousand miles away. If we went there and did our ceremonial dances, we would be welcomed like next-door neigh-bors. Their elders know our songs, as we know theirs."

I look out across the landscape and try to imagine how this physically unremarkable stretch of countryside could be so full of mythic history. As with all aboriginal territory, the Black Tank property is densely strung with landmarks of deep religious sig-nificance—Arrernte Meccas, Delphis, and Golgothas spread out amid the dust and the mulga trees. For someone like Magdalene, a three-mile stroll from the backyard to a neighboring settlement might be a de facto pilgrimage across territory distinguished by epic feats of a local Zeus or Moses.

On an intellectualized level, these aboriginal dreamtime tales played a practical role in nomadic survival, using their rich details to teach lessons about sharing resources or avoiding dangers. Given the stories I've just learned (and which I rephrased here in an admittedly impressionistic and Western manner), one might conclude that the tale of the corkwood-nectar flood is an admonition against complacency in the face of abundance, or the story of the *chilba* a cautionary tale about getting your freak on when you should be out hunting.

Magdalene, however, is not so scientific in speaking about her heritage: When she tells me about the mythic kangaroos that crossed her land bearing ceremonial shields, leaving watering holes in their giant footprints, she speaks in an offhand manner, as if it happened yesterday. "We teach our children to be aware of the spirit world," she says, "and not be frightened. If they listen to the spirits, and respect the laws of the land, the spirits will give them what they need from life."

As a tour guide, Magdalene is charmingly prone to distraction—interrupting the kangaroo story, for example, to brandish a stick and thrash a tree for ten minutes until a single bush banana falls out (as it turns out, the fruit is too fibrous and overripe for us to eat). Since she had a Catholic education in Alice Springs and speaks prim, precise English, I ask Magdalene if she plans to add a modern perspective when she shares her culture with students and tourists. "Of course," she says. "People can only understand our culture if they can relate parts of their life to ours. The stories of the *altyerre* were never separate from day-to-day life; I often describe them in terms of education. On a given day, mathematics might have involved finding the right mulga stick for a spear and straightening it in the fire; social studies could have been learning the dreamtime song to a place you would never visit."

"And you can still live by these traditions, even when you drive a car and live in a house?"

"Traditions were always meant to serve the present," she says. "We may not be fully nomadic, as we were in the past, but we still travel to visit family, or pay respects, or attend initiation ceremonies. Hunting is still hunting, even if our men use rifles and Land Cruisers. Our culture doesn't teach us to hide from new things, and in many ways modern life is easier and less violent than our old ways. But that doesn't mean the *altyerre* is any less important or sacred to us."

As I listen to Magdalene, I have a small epiphany that puts my entire journey here into perspective: As much as my visit to indigenous Australia has been an implicit quest for cultural novelty, true aboriginal authenticity was never mine to discover. This is because authenticity anywhere is an internal dialogue within a culture as it synthesizes its past with the present, hoping to better navigate a changing world. The job of the traveler, I reckon, is to slow down and listen so that he can hear snippets of that conversation.

Before I can do this in earnest, however, I have one matter of clarification for Magdalene. "About the *chilba* man," I say. "How did the other hunters punish him?"

"I'll just say that they did something that suited his crime. Something that made him unable to do it again."

"You mean they chopped off his penis?"

Magdalene purses her lips, her eyes wavering just slightly before she turns to continue my tour of her homeland.

Taking this as a "yes," I follow behind, trying to envision singing maidens and lakes of nectar where I might previously have seen just scrub grass.

ENDNOTES

1. **Page 129, paragraph 6: *Keiran adds details and clarifications as he translates for Wally.*** Some months after this story first appeared in *Slate*, I noticed that Keiran had commented about my article on his blog. "Whilst Mr. Potts seems to have caught on to the general ideas and concepts of Anangu culture and Uluru," he wrote, "I must point out that some of the quoted statements attributed to myself were definitely not word-for-word from my mouth."

Keiran brings up an interesting point about travel writing (and, I'd reckon, most nonfiction narrative in general): Short of walking around with a tape recorder all the time, it's almost impossible to fill your stories with word-for-word quotes from the people you meet. In the case of Keiran, I'd reconstructed his quotes from the scribbles I'd made in my notebook while I was taking Wally's tour. Since I was essentially using Keiran as a conduit for communicating facts about Pitjantjatjara folklore, I bolstered his presumed real-life quotes with after-the-fact research about the culture. No doubt there wound up being a hazy line between what he'd actually said and what I'd found in books weeks later.

In this way, it's inevitable that assorted real-life people are going to wind up as mere informational or dramatic pawns within a given travel tale. It's nothing personal; it's just that there's no room in a given story to detail every aspect of a person's life and personality. In this way, Keiran is doomed to exist as an encyclopedia of Pitjantjatjara folklore in this story, just like Mr. Singh and Mr. Gupta were doomed to exist as porn-loving drunks in Chapter 5, and Mohammed and Sayeed will be doomed to exist as dorky teenagers in Chapter 17. Any one of these guys would probably be less than thrilled by the angle at which I hold a mirror to their existence—especially since, as an itinerant writer, I only knew them for a matter of hours.

Other travel writers have wrestled with this reality before. In his semi-fictional 1996 book *My Other Life*, Paul Theroux describes an encounter with a woman he'd written about unfavorably in a previous book. "You think people are insects to catch and exhibit," she tells him. "…And the most bloody arrogant thing about you is that you think that once you've written about them they're yours—they belong to you, because you've stuck them on the page."

In a sense, this is true. But, short of editorial word-count (and reader patience) that would allow for full biographies on everyone who traipses through the story, writers of narrative nonfiction are pretty much stuck with painting subjective portraits.

2. **Page 130, paragraph 2:** *Celebrated in classic travel books like* **Bruce Chatwin's** *The Songlines:* While I was researching portions of this story in Alice Springs, I stopped into a place called the Arunta Art Gallery and Book Shop, which was run by a woman named Iris Harvey.

Within minutes I was convinced I'd walked into Chapter 6 of *The Songlines*, where Chatwin introduces Enid Lacey, "an Old Territorian in her late sixties," who runs the "Desert Bookstore and Art Gallery."

Since Chatwin's book had been written a good two decades earlier, I wasn't sure if this could be same woman. Picking up a copy of *The Songlines* from the bookshelf, I casually asked Iris if the book was fiction or nonfiction. "It's fact," she replied.

"But some people say Chatwin made parts of it up," I said.

"It's fact," Iris repeated. "I should know: I'm in it."

As it turned out, the woman Chatwin had dubbed Enid Lacey was just short of her ninetieth birthday, and she'd given audience to British naturalist David Attenborough that very morning. ("He was here to film some new program," she'd told me. "He always pays me a visit when he's in Alice Springs.")

Iris was quite proud of her appearance in *The Songlines*. She pointed out where Chatwin had sat when he'd interviewed her twenty years earlier, noting that novelist Salman Rushdie had been with him at the time. Until then I'd never known Rushdie had traveled with Chatwin in Australia, since one finds no mention of him in the pages of *The Songlines*.

That said, I'm not surprised Rushdie didn't make the cut in Chatwin's book, since I rarely manage to complete a travel tale without omitting the mention of someone who traveled with me. In my own Australian Outback story, for instance, my account of Wally's Uluru tour falls technically short of reality by four German women—and in the Black Tank scene I managed to pull off the entire exchange with Magdalene Lynch without mentioning I'd been accompanied by a Northern Territories Tourism representative (who'd given me the ride out there, since Magdalene's operation wasn't officially opened for business yet).

Iris Harvey never made it into the story because I didn't set any scenes in Alice Springs (though I'm happy to report she still sends me Christmas cards).

3. **Page 139, paragraph 1:** ...*shed the tourist mantle in Alice Springs and brandish my press credentials*: In truth, I don't have any formal "credentials" to brandish; usually I just offer a business card, or mention my author website (rolfpotts.com). Years ago, when I was first working as a travel writer, I bought a fake press pass on Khao San Road in

Bangkok. The little laminated card looked utterly convincing, but I found I never needed to use it (and I ended up losing it amid the events of chapter 6). With the ubiquity of the Internet worldwide, I'd reckon formal press credentials are increasingly irrelevant; it's easier to confirm the validity of a travel writer by Googling his name.

Identifying myself as a journalist was simple in central Australia, since I'd already been in touch with the Northern Territories tourist board for help with story leads in the Alice Springs area. Tourism NT did, in fact, sponsor my journey to Ooraminna Homestead (and I'll touch more on the issue of subsidized "press trips" in the endnotes to chapters 12 and 13).

4. **Page 142, paragraph 2:** *In his book* **Collapse,** *biologist Jared Diamond notes*: Of all the stories in the book, this one required the most research, since any seemingly casual reference to Australian Aboriginal issues can quickly become contentious (as my interactions with Richard and Cynthia in part IV show). Not wanting to litter the story with naïve assumptions and conclusions, I spent the better part of two months doing research when I got home from Australia. In addition to travel guidebooks, tourism-anthropology papers, and online Aboriginal-studies databases, I read a number of book-length historical narratives, including Geoffrey Blainey's *Triumph of the Nomads* and Robert Hughes's *The Fatal Shore*. In addition to *The Songlines*, I dipped into Outback-themed travel narratives by the likes of Bill Bryson, Robyn Davidson, Tony Horwitz, and Paul Theroux. All of this research helped me familiarize myself with the world of my story (though, as Pico Iyer pointed out in *Video Night in Kathmandu*, itinerant writers can never claim true authority about the places they visit; at best their research simply informs and balances their subjective experience).

As for the Jared Diamond quote, it doesn't come from research specific to Australia; I took it from a massive file of quotes and annotations I've been compiling on everything I've read since around 1995. The Walker Percy quotes in chapter 1 come from this file, as do the details from Herodotus in chapter 10, and the observations about Columbus's "mermaids" in chapter 14. I try to avoid quote anthologies for this kind of information, since individual quotes can be misleading if you haven't familiarized yourself with their context.

ᘓ 10 ᘖ

Backpackers' Ball at
the Sultan Hotel

Y first instinct upon arriving in Cairo is to fear the pyramids.

This is not a fear of existential belittlement in the presence of the ancient megaliths, nor do I fear some presumed Pharaonic curse. Rather, I fear letdown. I fear I won't see the grand old monuments with the proper degree of awe or historical perspective. I fear that in the process of comparing reputation with reality, I will be disappointed. I fear that the pyramids—which have been perused, praised and plundered for thousands of years—will prove, in experience, to be little more than a static tourist cartoon, devoid of genuine inspiration or beauty.

The most irritating part of this pyramid phobia is that I will ultimately be forced to confront it. After all, going to Cairo without seeing the pyramids is like a marriage without consummation: You can try it, but ultimately the obsession with what you're missing will get the best of you.

I can procrastinate, however—and that's what I've resolved to do. Taking a taxi from the Cairo airport to Orabi Square at midday, I unsling my pack at a park bench, do a bit of reading and let the city soak in before I look for a place to stay.

My literary companion in Cairo is Gustave Flaubert, who, before penning *Madame Bovary,* traveled to Egypt in 1849 and recorded his impressions in a series of letters to his friends. Like me, the twenty-eight-year-old Flaubert was indecisive in his opinion of the ancient Pharaonic ruins. At times, he regarded the old tombs and temples with humble awe, but at other times he expressed disappointment at the realities of his tourist itinerary. "The Egyptian temples bore me profoundly," he wrote home at one point. "Oh necessity! To do what you are supposed to do; to be always, according to the circumstances (and despite the aversion of the moment), what a young man, or a tourist, or an artist is supposed to be!"

In keeping with the age-old traveler's instinct to seek on the road what one enjoys at home, Flaubert eased his tourist angst in Egypt by frequenting the local whorehouses. Not only did this activity provide his journal with some memorable passages ("Coup with Little Sophie: She is very corrupt and writhing, extremely voluptuous—I stain the divan"), but it also gave him the impetus to stray from his luxury hotels and riverboats into the seedier parts of town. Here, Flaubert found the depraved exoticism he'd hoped for. "There is one new element which I hadn't expected to see and which is tremendous here," he wrote to a friend shortly after arriving in Cairo. "And that is the grotesque. All the old comic business of the cudgeled slave, of the coarse trafficker in women, of the thieving merchant—it's all very fresh here, very genuine and charming. In the streets, in the houses, on any and all occasions, there is a merry proliferation of beatings right and left."

Sitting on my bench, paging through Flaubert's memoirs, I take in the sights of Orabi Square. Around me, a brown smog hangs low over the buildings as Egyptians in jeans, dresses or djellaba robes crowd the sidewalks. Children wrestle with each other at curbside, and round-faced Berber women sell tissues on the corner. Colored pyramids of fruit stretch back into alleyways;

purple slabs of meat swing in doorways. Teenage boys bicycle through the crowds with crates of bread balanced on their heads; old men wearing checkered kaffiyeh scarves stop to ask me where I'm from. Idle businessmen haunt the teahouses to smoke their sheesha water pipes and play dominoes. Out in the street, stalled taxis blast their horns uselessly.

From what I can see, Cairo is noisy, crowded, chaotic and friendly, but by no means grotesque in Flaubert's sense of the word. If first impressions mean anything, I would have to conclude that this city has tamed a bit in the past 150 years.

But then, I've only been here for an hour.

When Flaubert visited Cairo, he passed his days at the Hotel du Nil, a comfortable and lavish place where "desert robes brush against all kinds of things that civilization sends here as supposedly the last word in Parisianism." There, he was waited upon at dinner by a team of silk-jacketed Nubians, one of whom had the sole assignment of waving away flies with a feather duster. Since my means are considerably humbler than those of the nineteenth-century French aristocracy, I shop around for accommodation among the grotty backpacker dives adjacent to Orabi Square.

I eventually settle on a place called the Sultan Hotel, which charges eight Egyptian pounds (about $2.35) for a bed in a dorm room. I am attracted to the place not because of its facilities (the showers are leaky, the halls stained, the elevator dusty and disused) but because of its lobby, which is the epitome of jolly international chaos. There, under kitschy day-glo wall paintings of Pharaonic gods and camels, street hustlers and fruit vendors from the alley have come inside to practice their English with a motley mix of Western travelers, who—not to be outdone—are throwing out phrases of Arabic. Half-understood insults and ironic declarations of love converge into a disorienting swirl of fractured English and pidgin Arabic. A Swiss teenager, draped in a red-checkered kaffiyeh, packs honey tobacco into a sheesha pipe in the middle of the room. Arabic pop music crackles from a boom box at the reception desk; a black-and-white 1950s Egyptian musical shimmers, ignored, on a TV in the corner.

I soon discover that the de facto ringleader amid this afternoon madness is Tom Bourbon, a wild-haired aspiring playwright from Toledo, Ohio, who has been slumming at the Sultan ever since he arrived in Egypt two months ago. At six foot eight, with steel-rimmed spectacles and a patchy beard, Tom looks like an ebullient cross between Gustav Mahler and former L.A. Laker Kurt Rambis. By the time I've moved into my room, showered and put on fresh clothes, Tom has persuaded a dozen or so fellow travelers to crash a local performance of Gioacchino Rossini's *Il Signor Bruschino*. Inspired, a gaggle of Belgian, Canadian, German and Japanese travelers fuss their hair, rummage through backpacks for clean clothes and otherwise try to make themselves presentable enough to pass the standards of the Cairo opera.

Figuring this kind of experience is simply too charming to pass up, I tag along. As we walk to the opera house, I meet a few of my new companions: Kathleen, a German teen who has been working as a camel wrangler at a kibbutz in Israel; Don, a forty-five-year-old Canadian who had planned to motorcycle around the world, but was forced to improvise when he wrecked his bike before he got out of Canada; Stefie, a willowy Belgian whose parents first met at a Rossini opera; and Stu, a recent Harvard grad who seems inordinately proud of his high school wrestling career.

By the time we settle into our seats at the Al-Gomhouria Theater—most of us clutching $1.50 student tickets—we've received more than a few baleful stares from the high-class Egyptians and European expatriates in the audience. No doubt, in our hiking boots, kaffiyehs, assorted facial piercings, rumpled t-shirts and stained khakis, we look like the boorish epitome of youthful irreverence. Fortunately, the opera, which Rossini wrote for the Venice carnival season at age twenty-one, is as youthful and irreverent as any of the teens or post-teens in our group. A credulous, slapstick tale of romance and mistaken identity, *Il Signor Bruschino* is as much a blueprint for the '80s sitcom *Three's Company* as it is a precursor to *William Tell*. We leave the opera in high spirits and retire to the Sultan Hotel lobby for beer, whiskey and half-baked post-curtain analysis.

Inspired by our brief taste of Cairo high culture, Tom disappears into his dorm room and returns with some of the duty-free liquor he says he has been hoarding in the hopes of (and he says this with a straight face) starting a speakeasy. Mixing slugs of Four Roses whiskey with Coke, he fills me in on the idiosyncrasies of the Sultan Hotel.

"We always have a pretty interesting crowd here," he tells me. "Especially in the six-pound [$1.75] rooms on the third floor. Up there, you're never really sure why or how long people are going to stay. Just last week we had a transvestite from France: nice legs, a full collection of sequined miniskirts and a five o'clock shadow. He—or she—didn't last long. On the other hand, we have a Sudanese Christian up there who first checked in a year and a half ago. She tells people she's an opera singer."

"Why are you staying here?"

"Lots of reasons," Tom says, absently pulling at his beard with long fingers. "Right now I'm learning Arabic. Plus, I'm trying to pull some strings and get an Egyptian passport."

"Why would you want an Egyptian passport?"

Tom looks at me as if the answer should be obvious. "So I can go to Iraq," he says.

As the whiskey makes its way around the room, people start telling travel stories, all of them outrageous, most of them third hand: the Norwegian guys who sold a bottle of Chivas Regal for $1,000 in Saudi Arabia; the British teen who bought a camel in Daraw, Egypt, and supposedly rode it to the Sinai; the Japanese trekking group who lost their jungle guide to a land mine in Laos. Hassan, the Sultan's charismatic night clerk, puts some Arabic pop tapes into the boom box, and the Swiss kid unwraps his honey tobacco and primes some more sheesha coals on the kitchen stove.

As the lobby conversations reach a boozy crescendo, I wonder to myself whether Flaubert would have felt at home here. On one hand, the flophouse atmosphere—$2.35 beds and bad plumbing—combined with our middle-class goofiness might have caused the patrician French novelist to sniff with disdain. On the other hand, this far-flung international cast, with its freewheeling late-night discourse, harks back to social rituals that were much more common in Flaubert's day. Indeed, the scene here in the Sultan Hotel lobby is in its own way reminiscent less of commodified twenty-first-century electronic culture than it is of ritualized nineteenth-century parlor culture.

As the night wears on, Tom breaks out a few more choice bottles from his speakeasy stash. The conversation becomes less coherent, and our post-opera soiree dwindles to a handful of sleepy-eyed stalwarts.

On the TV in the corner, an Egyptian man in a cardigan sweater and black horn-rimmed glasses sings a ten-minute love song to a corpulent woman in a headscarf.

My second day in Cairo begins at two in the afternoon, which is when I wake up. Encouraged by the fact that it is far too late to try to see the pyramids, I wander down to the Sultan lobby in search of diversion. There I find the towering Tom, who tells me that he plans to lead an excursion to the Palmyra belly-dancing club later in the evening. Thrilled by the excursion's exotic implications, I tell him to count me in.

When Flaubert visited Egypt 150 years ago, he took particular interest in belly dancing. In all likelihood, this had more to do with the fact that most dancers doubled as prostitutes than with the dancing itself. In Esna, Flaubert saw the performance of a dancer named Kuchuk Hanem, who performed "The Bee"—a striptease reputedly so erotic that the musicians had to be blindfolded.

Flaubert's descriptions of his extracurricular activities with Hanem ("Effect of her necklace between my teeth; her cunt like rolls of velvet as she made me come: I felt like a tiger") and various other Egyptian performers ("and there was another, on top of whom I enjoyed myself immensely, and who smelled of rancid butter") seem to underscore Europe's erotic obsession with "the Orient" at the time.

However, erotic stereotypes in Egypt long predate Flaubert— as even Herodotus's description of the Nile Valley in the fifth century B.C. is full of sexual footnotes. When describing Egyptian customs, for instance, Herodotus noted a spring festival wherein women carried puppets with huge, hinged penises that were pulled up and down by strings. "There is some sort of religious significance to the size of the genitals," Herodotus noted dryly, "and the fact that they are the only part of the puppet's body which is made to move."

As it turns out, belly-dancing performances in Cairo don't start until after midnight, so I have a full evening to anticipate the sensual delights that await.

I ultimately discover, however, that anticipation doesn't always mesh with reality.

The best belly dancing in Egypt, it is said, costs $50 a show and can be found at five-star hotels like the Meridien Le Caire or the Parisienne. At the Palmyra club, which is within walking distance of the Sultan Hotel, admission is about $1.50. The performance value (I suspect) is calibrated accordingly.

When our disheveled traveler posse arrives from the Sultan to take a table in the back of the Palmyra, a man in a djellaba and two women in chadôrs are happily shaking their moneymakers on the dance floor. At first I think this is a prelude to some kind of Islamic-themed striptease, until I realize that these people are just overzealous customers. The real dancer—a big-haired, large-breasted girl in a faux snakeskin jumpsuit—is at the back of the stage, idly joking with the accordion player. As my eyes get used to the darkness, I take in the surroundings. The club features tall ceilings and textured rock walls, accessorized with red curtains. If the lighting were improved and the velvety curtains replaced with, say, country knickknacks, this place could easily pass for a family restaurant in Minnetonka, Minnesota.

The crowd, however, is decidedly non-Middle America: Bedouins in red-checkered kaffiyehs and long gowns wave five-pound notes (each about $1.45) at the edge of the dance floor; Egyptian office stiffs with wrinkled neckties leap up from their tables to clap along with the music; fat men with thin mustaches sit alone in corners, sweat stains growing out from their armpits. The band looks straight out of a David Lynch movie: the melancholy lute player who blinks and stares at the floor as he strums; the grinning, leather-faced bongo drummer who wears brown pants over white, patent-leather shoes; the keyboardist who stops playing in the middle of the song to light a cigarette. The music is rhythmic, dissonant, deafening.

Eventually, the girl in the snakeskin jumpsuit starts to dance again, humming to the music into a cordless mike. After thirty minutes of this, she yields the stage to a dull-eyed blonde with feathered hair and a sequined evening gown. This new dancer is so amorphously plump that her rear end seems to start just below her neck. As she dances, the slightest wiggle sends her sequined extremities into a gelatinous fury of motion. For those of us at the Sultan table, the effect is mesmerizing and somewhat disturbing. The Egyptian men, however, go nuts, shouting along to the music and periodically jumping onto the stage to bust a few dance moves and shower the blonde with one-pound (thirty-cent) notes.

By 3 A.M. we can take no more of this, so we return to the Sultan Hotel lobby to discuss the merits of the performance. Since Tom's duty-free booze stash was nearly wiped out the previous night, Don the Canadian brings out a bottle of Egyptian whiskey—a Johnnie Walker Black Label knockoff called (literally) "Johnny Wadie Black Tabel." We sip the medicinal-tasting

Egyptian spirit and grimace as we debate the dubious erotic merits of the belly-dancing performance.

We have nearly exhausted this topic when a previously taciturn Canadian girl suddenly begins to instruct everyone on her preferred methods of attaining orgasm. All conversation pauses momentarily, and before long everyone is merrily debating the merits and challenges of clitoral vs. vaginal stimulation. The more we delve into this topic, however, the more Orgasm Girl seems disappointed. Her purpose, it seems, was not to initiate an objective debate on the physiology of erotic climax but to create a personal mystique—to pique any romantic attentions that might have been dulled by the belly-dancing fiasco.

Unfortunately for would-be Cleopatras and Mark Antonys, the physical realities of the Sultan Hotel pretty much preclude amorous intrigue. Within the entire complex—which spans three floors of a run-down building in downtown Cairo—there is not a single place wherein one can fornicate with any sense of dignity. The kitchen and lobby are always otherwise in use, the roof is home to a small community of Egyptian squatters and the back stairwells are swamped in years of accumulated garbage and grime. Coitus is technically possible (for the well coordinated) in the cramped shower/toilet stalls, but there is the ever-present danger of slipping on soap scum or impaling oneself on the unspeakably soiled copper bidet hoses that curve out from the toilet bowls.

This leaves only the dorm rooms themselves, which, in addition to being officially gender segregated, are crowded enough to discourage sexual dalliance. Thus, whereas cleaner and roomier backpacker dives on the travel trail can resonate with romantic maneuverings in the boozy wee hours, the sexual currents in the Sultan are for the most part friendly, theoretical and platonic. After a few more drinks and some pulls on the sheesha pipe, the sex chitchat gives way to talk of Sudanese visas and Israeli border stamps, of Arabic history, of where to score weed.

Perhaps chagrined at losing her spotlight, Orgasm Girl goes to bed early. Flaubert, no doubt, would have shared her irritation.

By my fourth day in Cairo, avoiding the pyramids has taken on a comfortable sort of rhythm. I have fallen into the indolent habit of waking up past noon, stumbling down to the market for oranges and falafel, then wandering into the city for afternoon sightseeing. The fewer goals I set for this activity, the more Cairo seems to bloom out from its strange corners. My favorite activity is to buy a ticket for the Metro, get off at random, walk until I'm lost, then ask directions back to the station.

In this manner, I have collected sights like souvenirs: men in alleys building lattices, baking bread, butchering chickens; a herd of goats toddling through a public plaza; Berbers in donkey carts stuck in traffic jams. I have seen the incense man swing his censer through a fruit market, collecting ten-piaster tips; I have seen women in full ninja-style burqa dive onto speeding buses; I have seen pious Muslim men selling vegetables, their foreheads black with welts from praying to Mecca. I have seen garbage choking rooftops and raw sewage flowing through the medieval gate of Islamic Cairo. The call of the muezzin from the mosques—at first a strange, haunting cry—has now blended into the music of my day.

Gustave Flaubert was equally impressed by the random mundane in Cairo. "I am scarcely over the initial bedazzlement," he wrote. "It's like being hurled while still asleep into the midst of a Beethoven symphony, with the brasses at their most ear-splitting, the basses rumbling, and the flutes sighing away; each detail reaches out to grab you; it pinches you; and the more you concentrate on it the less you grasp the whole.... It is such a bewildering chaos of colors that your poor imagination is dazzled as though by continuous fireworks as you go about staring at minarets thick with white storks, at tired slaves stretched out in the sun on house terraces, at the patterns of sycamore branches against walls, with camel bells ringing in your ears and great herds of black goats bleating in the streets amidst the horses and the donkeys and the peddlers."

As with Flaubert, these details captivate my imagination: I go for hours at a time without feeling the slightest twinge of pyramid anxiety.

Today I return from my afternoon wanderings to find out what kind of absurdity towering Tom Bourbon has cooked up for the evening. Yesterday, he and Don the Canadian went off to find a foreign wife for a neighborhood kid they've dubbed (because of his eponymous t-shirt) Rolling Thunder Boy. Rolling Thunder Boy's main impetus for finding a foreign wife is to avoid conscription into the Egyptian army—a ruse that goes back at least a couple of hundred years (in Flaubert's day, young men were known to gouge out an eye to avoid hated conscription; the viceroy of Egypt finally circumvented this stratagem by creating a special one-eyed army regiment). Tom and Don's solution to Rolling Thunder Boy's dilemma was not to find him an American bride (as perhaps was hoped), but to go to the Internet café and enroll his name in a half-dozen mail-order marriage services based in the Philippines. On the basis of socioeconomic guesswork alone, I don't think I'll hold my breath for Rolling Thunder Boy's chances, but Tom and Don remain optimistic.

Tonight, Tom suggests that—in a culinary attempt to "go native"—we visit the market, find a live animal and cook it for dinner. Last week, apparently, he and a few other members of Team Sultan failed to cook a pigeon ("we never could find any meat on it," he explains ruefully), so tonight he wants to try to boil a rabbit or two. About half a dozen Sultanites are up for this, but this number quickly dwindles the moment the market vendor starts pulling bunnies out of the split-reed cages and sizing them up for us. By the time our two rabbits' throats have been slit and the butcher has begun to peel off the fur, Tom and I are the only takers left. Undaunted, Tom buys a sack of vegetables, and we go upstairs to start in on the rabbit stew.

This activity proves to be an interesting study in the psychology of eating meat: After we slowly boil the rabbit along with vegetables and aromatic spices for two hours, half a dozen new Sultanites hungrily volunteer to join us for dinner. Those who saw the rabbits when they were alive, on the other hand, keep a grim distance from the kitchen.

We decide to cap off Rabbit Night by walking down Talaat Harb Street to catch an Egyptian flick at the Metro Cinema. None of us is good enough at Arabic to fully understand the dialogue, but that's half the reason for going: The task of trying to discern the plot will add a bit of mystery and challenge to the experience. Tonight, the Metro is showing a film called *Hello America*, a comedy about an Egyptian man who travels to New York in search of the American dream.

In its portrayal of American stereotypes alone, *Hello America* provides a fascinating example of Egyptian filmmaking. From the moment the movie starts, however, I notice a strange detail: Almost all of the American-looking characters—gang members, bodyguards, cops and homosexuals alike—look a bit unkempt and vaguely emaciated. Tom eventually explains this detail: Since film work in Cairo pays a pittance, the only foreigners consistently willing to work as extras are backpackers. Over the course of the movie, Tom spots three minor characters—a robber, a crossdresser and a homeless person—who are portrayed by current or former occupants of the Sultan Hotel.

What the film lacks in authenticity and artistic value, it makes up for in quirky moments of satire. When the main character joins what he thinks is a "freedom march," for instance, it turns out to be a gay pride rally; when he shows affection for his young American nephew, he is accused of being a pedophile; when he relaxes in his room with a late-day sheesha, the fire marshal kicks in the door and hoses him down. Although there are a few scenes that take digs at Egyptians (when the main character is stopped at the airport for suspicious-looking luggage, he declares, "It's O.K., I'm an Arab!" and the other passengers flee screaming), the movie is certainly a reinforcement of traditional Egyptian values. Relationships take precedence over rules, individualism is suspect and family is more important than money.

When we return to the Sultan Hotel, our obligatory post-film discussion turns into a heated argument between Stu the Wrestler and Orgasm Girl about American imperialism. Relishing their roles as agitators, the two North Americans lay into each other— Stu citing statistics and examples of how America is a benevolent superpower, Orgasm Girl quoting stats and examples of how America is a bullying neocolonizer. Not up for the Patented America Debate (an endless polemic that invariably surfaces whenever strong-minded Americans share hostel space with strong-minded near Americans), I go to bed early.

As I drift off to sleep, I realize—with a twinge of trepidation—that I've run out of original, legitimate reasons to avoid the pyramids.

To travel the historical sights of Egypt is to invite information overload. Whereas less than 5 percent of Egyptian land is arable and the local oil output is a mere drop compared with Egypt's cousins in the Persian Gulf, this old Pharaonic land has repeatedly proved to be an inexhaustible source of ancient relics.

Just last year, for example, 200 new mummies (thought to be part of a necropolis that held as many as 10,000 preserved human remains), some of them wearing golden burial masks, were discovered in the western desert. A mere four months ago, ancient symbols carved into a limestone cliff—believed to be part of the earliest known alphabet—were discovered west of Luxor. Also near Luxor, the temple precinct near Akhmim, which is still being excavated, might well join Angkor Wat and the Vatican as one of the world's biggest religious complexes.

Someday these discoveries may find a special place in the Egyptian tourist canon, but for now, none of them comes close to rivaling the popularity and allure of Giza, Saqqara and Dahshur. Cowing to the inevitable, I arrange a trip to the pyramids on the morning of my fifth day in Cairo.

When Flaubert went to see the pyramids of Giza and Saqqara, he traveled by horseback and slept in the desert. These days, Cairo's urban sprawl has turned these sites into virtual suburbs. Hoping to catch all the sites in one efficient trip, I hire Hussein (the Sultan Hotel night clerk) to drive me around for the day. Stefie the Belgian, her friend Nele and a Japanese fellow named Yoshito join me; Tom, who has already been to the pyramids three times, elects to stay in Cairo.

We strike out from the Sultan early in the morning. Hussein's driving style is a blend of good intentions and bad technique; we sputter through the stop-start Cairo traffic in second gear. At one point, when I ask Hussein the name of a towering mosque, a chubby Egyptian adolescent goes bouncing off the front fender. Fortunately, Cairo traffic is generally slow enough to preclude physical injury in this type of situation: The kid flamboyantly curses Hussein, but seems otherwise unharmed; I make a point of not asking any more questions while Hussein is driving.

Our first Pharaonic destination is Saqqara, which lies south of Cairo's sprawl. As we leave the Nile Valley, a pale tan desert drops out from beyond the palms and canals; mud-brick houses crumble in the sun. A sign near the monument admission booth reads "Good life, immortality and happiness can be found in Egypt."

At Saqqara, the tombs and pyramids of Teti exude a quiet, plundered grandeur. As I walk through the dusty chambers and corridors, I try to imagine these places as they might have been in their original splendor, but my brief reveries of ancient Egypt keep getting pushed aside by remembered images of the Luxor Casino in Las Vegas. This proves to be a disconcertingly persistent association, so eventually I just give in and allow my mind to wander—blending personal memories and spontaneous feelings with historical speculation. At Zoser's step pyramid, my thoughts are interrupted by a fresh carving in the limestone near the bottom: "Edward, 1/1/2000," it reads. And beneath that, "Fuck you."

Such thoughtless defacement of the ancient here in Egypt is certainly nothing new. When Flaubert explored the Giza pyramids, he expressed shock at all the recent graffiti. "One is irritated by the number of imbeciles' names written everywhere," he wrote. "On top of the Great Pyramid there is the name of a certain Buffard, 79 Rue Saint-Martin, wallpaper manufacturer, in black letters; an English fan of Jenny Lind's has written her name; there is also a pear, representing Louis-Philippe."

I return to the car and tell Hussein about the scrawl on Zoser's pyramid, but he doesn't seem all that shocked. As I've seen in so many other countries, the flagship phrase of English profanity doesn't resonate much with Egyptians. As with Nike or McDonald's, perhaps "fuck you" has simply become another Western trademark—a standardized mantra that tough guys say in American movies.

"You know," I say to Hussein, "I think someone should build a huge limestone monument that says 'fuck you,' just so people will have to think of something different to carve on it."

Hussein nods over at the pyramids of Zoser and Userkef. "Maybe that's what they mean already."

"How's that?"

"The pyramids," he says. "Maybe they're Egyptian for 'fuck you.'"

Hussein grins to show he's joking, but for a moment I see the pyramids in an unexpected and brilliant new light.

After a stop at Dahshur, we finish our day at Giza. There, I discover all the tourist madness I'd originally hoped to avoid, but now it seems novel in its own weird way. As I walk up to the ticket booth, swarms of pasty-faced Scandinavians pour out from pink tour buses to jostle me on the walkway; touts bully me with offers of camel rides or painted papyrus. A demoralizingly long line stretches out from the Pyramid of Cheops; Cairo's skyscrapers tower in the distance. In front of the Sphinx, a ragged band of German hippies bangs on drums and bows in prayer; in front of the adjacent Pizza Hut, Mexican backpackers pose for photos. For some reason, this all seems perfect: I pay my ticket and see what I'm supposed to see.

"You ask me whether Egypt is up to what I'd imagined it to be," Flaubert wrote to his mother after having been in Cairo for five weeks. "Yes, it is; and more than that, it extends far beyond the narrow idea I had of it. I have found, clearly delineated, everything that was hazy in my mind. Facts have taken the place of suppositions—so excellently so that it is often as though I were suddenly coming upon old forgotten dreams."

At sunset, black-uniformed guards chase us out of the pyramid complex, and Stefie, Nele, Yoshito and I pile into Hussein's car and ride back into the living heart of Cairo.

ENDNOTES

1. **Page 157, paragraph 1:** *My literary companion in Cairo is Gustave Flaubert:* The book in question is *Flaubert in Egypt: A Sensibility on Tour,* a collection of diaries, letters and travel notes published by Penguin Classics. I picked up a copy at the American University bookstore in Cairo a few days after arriving in Egypt.

Compare this book-purchase timeline to the actual beats of the story, and you'll realize that the scene where I'm engrossed in Flaubert one hour after arriving in Cairo is a contrivance unique to the "footsteps" genre of travel writing. Indeed, whenever a travel writer depicts himself primly sitting on some exotic park bench engrossed in the book that is purportedly guiding his journey, there's a good chance this is a purely hypothetical flourish. During my own Cairo sojourn, in fact, I read most of *Flaubert in Egypt* after the five-day sequence I describe in the story—and my own belly-dancing, hotel, and pyramid experiences transpired before I knew of Flaubert's parallel adventures. In effect, Flaubert became an inspiration for my Cairo hijinks retroactively (though in the story I never claim to be following his example; I just make a few colorful comparisons).

Footsteps and narrative sleight-of-hand notwithstanding, reading locally relevant novels, travel literature, and history books invariably adds a new dimension to your travels, especially if you plan on writing about them. Indeed, while the whimsical premise of this book is that I didn't follow in the footsteps of Marco Polo, I'll confess that reading his *Travels* has enriched my own (just as Marco's travels were enriched by reading *The Alexander Romance*, and Alexander's travels were enriched by reading Homer's *Iliad*).

2. **Page 158, paragraph 4: *...I shop around for accommodation among the grotty backpacker dives adjacent to Orabi Square*:** I framed this story with allusions to Flaubert's travels and Pyramid angst—but re-reading it after all these years makes me realize it was at heart a warts-and-all celebration of backpacker culture.

For some reason, major media outlets see fit to ridicule backpackers at regular intervals in the news cycle. Around the same time my Sultan tale was published in *Salon*, one could find articles in *Time* and *The New York Times* bemoaning how watered-down independent travel had become. The template for these articles was quite predictable: *Foreign-desk correspondent visits backpacker ghetto in Thailand (or India, or Guatemala) and observes information-age ironies and/or party scene; reporter then evokes supposed independent-travel ideals of the 1960s and notes how today's backpackers don't live up to said ideals; reporter proceeds to quote Lonely Planet founder Tony Wheeler, cite tourism statistics, summarize perceived backpacker hypocrisies, and grandly declare independent travel to be irrelevant (or consumerist, or stone-cold dead).*

This kind of story is the travel equivalent of those perennial op-ed pieces that use the latest demographic survey to conclude that young people are stupid, or morally lacking, or destined to destroy civilization. And, just as "kids-these-days" op-eds are meant to convince older generations of their own virtue, "death-of-travel" articles essentially serve to reassure working stiffs that they aren't missing anything by staying at home.

In truth, backpacker culture is far more dynamic than reporters assume when they visit Goa or Panajachel to shake down stoners for usable quotes. Outside of the predictable traveler ghettos (which themselves aren't as insipid as these articles let on), independent travelers distinguish themselves by their willingness to travel solo, to go slowly, to embrace the unexpected and break out from the comfort-economy that isolates more well-heeled vacationers and expats. Sure, backpackers are themselves a manifestation of mass tourism—and they have their own self-satisfied clichés—but they are generally going through a more life-affecting process than one would find on a standard travel holiday.

My experience at the Sultan is a good example. At one level my companions and I were indolent and impulsive in Cairo, skimming the surface of a culture as we cooked rabbits, ogled belly dancers, and swilled duty-free booze. But most of us also studied Arabic and learned the rhythms of the neighborhood around Orabi Square; we attended Sunni mosques and Coptic churches; we lingered in teashops and made Egyptian friends. Moreover, the Sultan Hotel (like many backpacker haunts) was a curiously class-free environment, where a Melbourne construction worker could hang out with a Pennsylvania Ivy Leaguer and an Egyptian fruit vendor in a spirit of mutual respect and curiosity. Hassan the night clerk had trained as a lawyer, but he wasn't bitter about working a lesser job while he waited for the slow wheels of Egyptian bureaucracy to provide him with a law position. For him, the Sultan was an international education in itself (not to mention a far-reaching networking opportunity).

It's been eight years now since I stayed at the Sultan, and I've probably kept in touch with as many of the friends I made there as I have friends from high school. A few of them are still traveling; most of them went home and became teachers, lawyers, carpenters, city planners, park rangers, social workers, and graphic designers. Tom Bourbon is on his way to becoming a college professor in Montana; Stefie the Belgian (who I briefly dated a year later) designs jewelry in Brussels. Sultanites Dan

Neely and Paul McNeil, who didn't even merit a mention in my story, now count as two of my most reliable friends; I've attended both their weddings, and I've traveled with them (backpacker-style, of course) in places like the Sinai, Thailand, France, Brazil, and Louisiana.

All of which is to say that backpacker culture is far more diverse and engaged than its layabout stereotype would imply. Along with a stint as an expatriate, there are few other activities that—if approached mindfully—can sharpen the senses and tweak the perspective of someone who intends to leave home and experience the world.

ꙮ 11 ꙮ

Death of an Adventure Traveler

ATTHEW, the small Burmese Kayin man who worked the front desk at the Lotus Guesthouse, was the first one to suggest that Mr. Benny might be dead. "Benny went back to Burma so he could die near his family," he told me, his eyes fixed on the TV set as flickering Shiites danced in the streets of Iraq. "He was too sick to live in Thailand any more."

I had just returned to the rainy border town of Ranong, Thailand after an absence of five months. It was April 9, 2003, the day U.S. tanks rolled into central Baghdad. Matthew had been squatting in the guesthouse lobby, translating BBC commentary for the other hotel workers—all of them illegal migrant workers from Burma. Deciphering the images from Iraq proved to be a difficult process, since even the BBC commentators didn't seem to know what was going on. Had Baghdad fallen or not? Were the U.S. soldiers welcomed or reviled? Nobody knew for sure, but when a soldier on the TV flung an American flag over the head of the Saddam Hussein statue in Firdos Square, the Burmese workers had let out a cheer, as if Rangoon's junta would be next.

When the BBC cut to a commercial, Matthew finally looked over at me. "How did you know Benny?" he asked. Matthew's eyes were dark, fringed by faint yellow; he wore a crisp oxford shirt, and his black hair was just beginning to show gray. A devout Baptist like many ethnic Kayin, he was painfully earnest in his beliefs—a quality that would eventually get him fired from the guesthouse.

"Mr. Benny was my barber," I said. Benny had also been my best friend in Ranong, and one of the most remarkable men I'd ever met. He'd evaded death so many times in his life that I found it hard to believe that he would submit to a quiet end back in Burma. "Are you sure he's dead?"

Matthew shrugged. "I didn't even know him. You should talk to Phiman. He'll know if Benny is still alive."

Phiman was a Thai man who owned the dusty little TV repair shop where Mr. Benny slept at night. Since I didn't speak enough Thai for Phiman to understand me, this meant I had to get translation help from Ezio, a barrel-chested Italian who lived with his Thai wife on the other side of Ranong. Since I'd sold my motorcycle when I'd last left Thailand, I headed off to Ezio's place on foot, skirting the hot, murky puddles that choked the streets after heavy rains.

Of all the places in the world where I'd lived for more than a couple months, Ranong was by far the most obscure. A frumpy border town of thirty-thousand people in the rainiest part of Thailand's isthmus, it held little appeal for tourists—apart from its proximity to the southern tip of Burma, where backpackers enamored with Thailand's meditation retreats and full-moon parties could get a cheap re-entry visa in a couple of hours. Besides fishing and tin mining, timber poaching and ampheta-mine smuggling seemed to be Ranong's principal industries, and scores of refugees from Burma's repressive dictatorship lived in squalid huts at the edges of town. Heavy rains resulted in power blackouts that could last for days, and the sour-fresh scent of rain-forest competed with the fishy smell of the port. Though just four hours by motorcycle from the tourist resort of Phuket—and ten hours by bus from the modern hum of Bangkok—Ranong felt years away from the rest of Thailand.

I'd first arrived in Ranong two years earlier, while writing an article about the Moken sea gypsies who lived in the islands on the Burmese side of the sea-border. I'd been trying to build my career as an adventure-travel writer, and a Major American Luxury-Travel Magazine had underwritten my journey to investigate recent tourism ventures into Moken territory. I didn't have a permanent address at the time, so I'd rented a studio room at the Lotus Guesthouse to write the sea gypsy article. When it was finished I decided to stay in the sleepy town to work on my first book, a philosophical how-to primer about long-term travel.

Writing my book required long stretches of isolation, and I didn't socialize much during my stint in Ranong. I tried to get out of my room to explore the town from time to time, but even six months into my tenure, Thai kids who lived just a few blocks away from my guesthouse would shout "*farang!*" at me as I walked past, as if I was just another random backpacker in town for a visa run. The word, which means "foreigner," was a reminder of how little I really knew about the daily workings of Ranong, or of Thailand in general.

The only person I saw regularly when I lived in Ranong was Mr. Benny a thin, sexagenarian Burmese émigré who worked at a humid storefront barbershop in the center of town. His haircuts cost forty baht (about $0.90 at the time), and afterwards he'd invite me to a dim café next door and spend most of his fee on coffee thickened with condensed milk. As we sipped from dented aluminum cups, he would tell me stories about his younger years, when he would make ends meet for his family by smuggling tin to Malaysia, or diving for pearls off the coast of Burma. Sometimes he'd invite me to join him for Sunday services at the local Catholic chapel; other times, he'd ask me to meet him at his cramped bunkroom in the TV repair shop to practice English vocabulary.

When he learned that I hailed from the prairies of North America, he told me that his favorite English-language book was an old cowboy novel called *The Big Sky*. I'd found a used copy of the novel when I was back in the U.S. on my book tour, and one reason I'd returned to Ranong was so I could present *The Big Sky* to Mr. Benny.

I'd also returned to Ranong to find some isolation so I could finish a magazine article that was weeks overdue. The adventure stories I'd written two years earlier for the Major American Luxury-Travel Magazine had attracted the attention of a Major American Adventure-Travel Magazine, and I'd been discussing possible assignments with an editor for months. Unfortunately, no story I proposed—exploring fishing villages along the upper Cambodian Mekong, mountaineering in Turkish Kurdistan, visiting the isolated tribesmen of the Andaman Islands—seemed quite right for him. We'd finally settled on a how-to feature about "classic adventures" in Asia. I'd spent much of the previous three years adventuring through the distant corners of the Asian continent, but this experience had put me at a weird disadvantage in reporting the story. "You're giving us too much geography," my editor would tell me every time I submitted a new list of destination summaries. Readers of Major American Adventure-Travel Magazines, he told me, didn't want to read about journeys that were obscure or complicated; they wanted exotic challenges wherein they might test—or, at least, imagine themselves testing—the extremes of human experience.

For weeks, I had trouble understanding exactly what this meant—and my increasingly irritated editor returned my story drafts marked with comments like "Is there a helicopter service that can get you there faster?" and "Would you recommend some cutting-edge outerwear for this kind of trek?" and "Can you think of any celebrities who've visited the region recently?" In time, I discerned that adventure itself was far less important to the magazine than creating a romanticized *sense* of adventure—preferably with recommendations on where to buy a cappuccino and a Swedish massage afterwards. The Major American Adventure-Travel Magazine, it seemed, wanted me to create a tantalizing recipe for the exotic and the unexpected—but only the kind of "unexpected" that could be planned in advance and completed in less than three weeks.

It took me less than half an hour to walk the damp streets to Ezio's house. Pong, his slim, shy Thai wife answered the door. At twenty-three, she was exactly half his age; he'd met her when she was still a student in a country village across the isthmus in Chumphon Province. Before Pong, Ezio had a previous Thai wife—an ex-bargirl who had borne him two daughters and twice tried to kill him before their marriage ended. Once she had stabbed him in the back with a kitchen knife; another time she'd dumped poison in his soup. He had recovered unshaken both times, but their marriage fell apart after a few years, and he rarely saw his daughters anymore. Newly remarried, Ezio was teaching Pong how to help him with his website-design business, and they were successful enough to employ two Burmese girls to cook and clean for them.

Ezio teased me about my latest magazine assignment as he stood in the kitchen, his hulking mass bent over a tiny espresso pot. "These American magazines don't even know what adventure is," he said. "They want you to write about camping toys and sports vacations. They want you to make people think adventure is something that costs $8,000 and lasts as long as a Christmas holiday. They want you to make rich people feel good for being rich."

I didn't argue with him. Twenty-five years ago Ezio had left Rome for a winter holiday in North Africa, and he'd never returned. He'd taught himself Arabic in Algeria, learned to live in the desert, bought a few camels, made a living as a tour guide. Intrigued by wars, he eventually wandered on to Uganda, and then Lebanon, and then Sri Lanka, picking up languages as he needed them. He eventually landed in Southeast Asia, where he fell in love with Thai women—all of them, from the way he described it—and he'd been based in Thailand for over ten years now. What Ezio had done with his life was unusual, but not unique. Every out-of-the-way province in Southeast Asia, it seemed, had a few guys like him—aging expats who'd lived remarkable lives, enjoyed their anonymity, and had no plans of going home. Whenever I talked to Ezio I was reminded of how the storied travelers of history invariably discovered they were not alone in their wanderings—how William of Rubrouck arrived in Karakorum to find Ukrainian carpenters, Greek doctors, and Parisian goldsmiths; how Marco Polo encountered Lombards, Germans and Frenchmen in the streets of Cambaluc. These people's stories were never told because they never went home.

I took my espresso and moved on to the living room. Ezio brought out a package of cigars he'd bought during his latest run to Burma. We lit up, and Ezio caught me up on the local gossip—how local gangsters were turning the island of Koh Samui into the Sicily of Thailand; how an influx of Burmese girls had turned Ranong into one of the cheapest places in the country to buy a prostitute. When Ezio ran out of news, I asked him about Mr. Benny.

"I didn't know him; Pong cuts my hair. Did you ask at the barbershop?"

"He had to stop working there," I said. "He was getting sick, and his hands were too shaky. Last time I saw him he was helping Phiman at the TV repair shop."

Repairing televisions and cutting hair were just two of Mr. Benny's many callings in life. Born to a Portuguese-Kayin mother, who met his Chinese-Thai father in southern Burma during the Japanese occupation of Ranong in World War II, young Benny was trained in English by Irish priests at the local mission school. When finances got tight for his family, his unique language skills led to his first job at age fourteen: fighting communists with a regrouped Chinese Kuomintang army in northeastern Burma. At a time when the average daily income for a Burmese soldier was 15 kyat, Benny made 150 kyat a day carrying ammunition belts and translating intelligence information for American CIA advisors.

Mr. Benny deserted the Kuomintang army when the CIA funding dried up, and he returned to the Burmese south convinced that risking danger was the most efficient way to make a living. Against his mother's protestations, he crossed the border and used his newfound skills to detonate explosive charges in an illegal tin mine owned by a Thai general who was said to have twenty-two wives. When his father forced him to return home, Benny found a job diving for oysters in the Mergui Archipelago, each day donning a weight belt and a hose-fed air-helmet to the bottom of the sea ("you couldn't just bend over and get the shells," he'd told me, "or else you could fall out of your helmet and drown; you had to squat and feel for the oysters with your hands").

Marriage to a local girl took Mr. Benny out of the sea and into a barbershop, but the arrival of children left him in need of a better income, so he took up an offer from a group of wealthy Taiwanese men who needed a guide and translator for a rhino-poaching excursion in the Burmese jungle. Dodging the Burmese army along the Thai borderlands, the expedition party dragged on for six months, surviving on deer and monkey meat before they managed to bag a rhino; Benny came home with his hair "long, like an Indian," and his young children didn't recognize him.

After the Burmese military coup in 1961 English was officially regarded as a "slave language," and Mr. Benny was forced to toss out his books, including his favorite, A.B. Guthrie's *The Big Sky*. The local economy nose-dived, and Benny increasingly found it necessary to cross into Thailand and do construction work to keep his family fed. For a while he managed to make as much as

800 baht a day smuggling tin across the sea border to Malaysia—until one winter day a group of pirates posing as policemen seized his boat and tossed him overboard. Mr. Benny swam the three miles back to shore and returned to cutting hair. On the side, he taught himself how to fix radios, and, later, TVs. It was a skill he returned to in his old age.

Ezio seemed skeptical that a man who was too sick to cut hair could work on televisions. "You can't do that kind of thing with shaky hands," he said.

"Mr. Benny used to joke that without steady hands he was just a nurse in the TV shop," I said. "He would locate the illness, and Phiman would do the surgery."

Ezio chuckled and stubbed out his cigar. "Let's go and see what Phiman knows," he said.

As I rode into central Ranong on the back of Ezio's motorcycle, it occurred to me that I didn't even know the exact nature of Mr. Benny's sickness. His shaky hands implied Parkinson's Disease, but he also had increasing trouble keeping his food down. On a couple occasions I suggested that he visit a doctor, but he always waved me off. "This is just what happens to old men," he said.

Mr. Benny didn't like talking about his health, and it was only at my urging that he elaborated his memories of Malay pirates and Kuomintang mercenaries. To him, smuggling tin or tracking rhinos were merely jobs—better paid, but not entirely dissimilar to cutting hair or pouring concrete. Usually, he would steer our conversation to the small, charmed moments he remembered from his life, like the first time he learned what garbage was ("before, everything was reused or fed to the animals"). One of his favorite memories was the time a fisherman brought him a bottle containing an English-language letter from a seven-year-old Dutch boy named Donald, who became Mr. Benny's pen-pal for the next five years. He also loved to recall his friend's failed attempt to make an airplane using wood planks and a 120-horsepower motorcycle engine. He asked me countless questions about what it was like to live on the American plains; in his mind, I think, my home was inseparable from pages of *The Big Sky.*

The last week I saw him, all Mr. Benny could talk about was an article he'd read about Sudan's "Lost Boys." He kept telling me how forty years of war and repression had left Burma with countless refugees of its own, and that maybe Americans would care more about Burma if he could think of a name as clever as "Lost Boys."

Ezio and I found Phiman in the back of his shop, his white hair tousled, his glasses hanging on the end of his nose as he soldered a wire into the back of a television. He frowned as Ezio spoke to him in Thai, then set down his soldering iron. "Mr. Benny left two months ago," he said, Ezio translating. "He's in Rangoon now, with his wife and grandkids. It's better for him to die there."

"But are you sure he was going to die?" I asked.

"Yes. But if he comes back, I'll be the first to know; I still owe him some money." Phiman laughed soberly. "He was good at fixing TVs, you know. That even saved his life once."

"How's that?"

"Sometime in 1979 Benny got word that you could make a lot of money getting gems in western Cambodian and taking them across the border to sell. Back then that area was mostly lawless, except for the Khmer Rouge. He camped out there for a couple of months, digging for rubies, and trading food for raw stones from Cambodians. One day a Khmer Rouge patrol found him, took him back to their camp, beat him up a little, took his rubies. They probably would have killed him, too, but he heard them complaining about how they missed their Thai soap operas. He fixed their TV, and they let him go. They kept his rubies, of course—but they let him go."

Phiman picked up his soldering iron and resumed his work. "Come back in a week," he said. "I'll let you know if I've heard anything new."

I went back a week later—and the week after that—but Phiman had no new news about Mr. Benny.

I stayed on at the Lotus Guesthouse and struggled with my article for the Major American Adventure-Travel Magazine. Every time I researched some upscale mountain trek in the Nepal Himalayas or two-week scuba diving excursion off the coast of Papua New Guinea, I couldn't help but ponder how pointless it all was. I began to e-mail my editor pointed questions about how one should define the "extremes of human experience." How was kayaking a remote Chinese river, I asked, more notable than surviving on its shores for a lifetime? How did risking frostbite on a helicopter-supported journey to arctic Siberia constitute more of an "adventure" than risking frostbite on a winter road-crew in Upper Peninsula Michigan? Did anyone else think it was telling that bored British aristocrats—not the peoples of the Himalayas—were the ones who first deemed it important to climb Mount Everest? My editor's replies were understandably terse.

Things changed as Ranong slipped further into the rainy season. Ezio and Pong decided the power blackouts were bad for their Internet business, so they moved upcountry to Chiang Rai. At the guesthouse, Matthew made the repeated mistake of assuming Western backpackers were as excited about the fall of Baghdad as he was. It didn't help that he was an unrepentant Baptist, given to salting his conversations with cheery Gospel references. More than once this led to bizarre scenes in the lobby, where sunburned Germans and Canadians and Californians angrily lectured Matthew about the pacifistic merits of Buddhism while the Kayin desk clerk tremblingly tried to explain how Burmese Buddhists had murdered his brothers. It was as if the backpackers didn't know what to do with this meek little brown man who, with his professed love of Jesus and affinity for George Bush, didn't follow accepted narrative of how Southeast Asians were supposed to act. Less than a month after he translated the defeat of Saddam Hussein for his coworkers, Matthew was fired and replaced with another Burmese migrant—a serious young Buddhist kid who fetched keys, kept his mouth shut, and garnered no complaints.

Eventually I finished the last rewrite of my article for the Major American Adventure-Travel Magazine. I e-mailed it to my editor, requesting that it run without my byline.

After checking out of the Lotus Guesthouse, I slipped a self-addressed envelope into my copy of *The Big Sky* and left it with Phiman in the hope that Mr. Benny might one day come back.

Then I did something Mr. Benny never had the option of doing: I headed back across the ocean, to a place where "adventure travel" was not a way of getting by in life, but a whimsical, self-induced abstraction—a way of testing our limits so that we can more keenly feel our comforts.

ↄ

ENDNOTES

1. **Page 175, paragraph 1:** ...*Benny went back to Burma so he could die near his family.* Because of my emotional closeness to this story, I didn't attempt to write it until three years after it happened. I initially wrote it as fiction, with a world-weary, Graham Greene-style journalist taking the place of me. I wasn't happy with the result, so I set it aside until an editor at *The Smart Set* sent out a call for nonfiction essays. Ditching the Graham Greene conceit, I rewrote the story in the first-person, scrapping a couple of ineffective subplots and adding Matthew as a character. The result was a simpler, more evocative story—and the non-fictional inclusion of Matthew underscored my theme more effectively than any of my previous, fictional subplots.

By nature, most narrative nonfiction utilizes the same organizational elements as fiction, including character, foreshadowing and flashback. As my colleague Tom Bissell has noted, "Travel writing is, of any genre of nonfiction save memoir, the most similar to fiction. You have an experience that is both intensely personal and, usually, frustratingly unformed, and you have to turn it into a narrative."

Though all the stories in this book implement various fiction-style techniques to shape and focus the nonfiction narrative, this story contains the most directly fictional elements. Except for Mr. Benny, all the names, including that of my guesthouse, have been changed (primarily to protect the identity of Matthew, who was technically a Burmese dissident; chapters 5, 14, 15, and 19 of this book also contain name changes where it seemed appropriate to honor the privacy of certain people I portrayed). I also altered some of the information from the e-mail exchanges with my editor at the "Major American Adventure-Travel Magazine" to keep it all concise and on-theme (although I did stay true to the spirit of the correspondence). Moreover, I never finished the article itself; it was "killed" (canceled, with compensation) by the editor not long after I suggested I didn't want to put my name on it. Since an explanation of this editorial procedure would have detracted from the story's resonance so near the end of the narrative, I fudged the detail about the article's completion.

2. **Page 177, paragraph 4: *The only person I saw regularly when I lived in Ranong was Mr. Benny*:** This is a slightly misleading statement that I'll clarify in the endnotes to chapter 18 (which functions as a prequel to this story, since it details how I initially met Benny).

3. **Page 179, paragraph 4: *…Twenty-five years ago Ezio had left Rome*:** "Ezio" is actually Max Arcangeloni from chapter 3, and his inclusion in this story hints at how most of the tales in this book are interconnected in one way or another. Max and I became friends during our Laotian trek, and nearly a year after that journey he was the one who recommended the "Lotus Guesthouse" when I was looking for a place to live in Ranong. (Note that Max doesn't show up in chapter 18 because he was still living with Pong in Chumphon Province at that

time; Matthew is absent from chapter 18 because the Lotus Guesthouse hadn't hired him yet).

On a side note, "Ezio" is actually the name that shows up on Max's passport, though nobody has called him that since he lived in Italy.

4. **Page 178, paragraph 2: ...*Major American Luxury-Travel Magazine...Major American Adventure-Travel Magazine*:** The "Major American Luxury-Travel Magazine" in question is *Condé Nast Traveler*. My article about the Moken "sea-gypsies" of Burma appeared in the July 2002 issue and was nominated for (but not included in) *The Best American Travel Writing 2003*.

As for the "Major American Adventure-Travel Magazine," I'll leave it anonymous for reasons of tact—though I will note that its editorial priorities aren't all that different from other glossy travel magazines. If you don't believe me, go to any newsstand and compare the adventure-recreation articles and "celebrity travel" profiles to the stories about migrant and/or refugee wanderers. There is no comparison, because people like Mr. Benny don't exist in consumer travel magazines. To expect otherwise would be (as the Buddha observed) as silly as "suffering because a banana tree will not bear mangoes."

Does this all mean that we, as First World wanderers, should feel guilty every time we pack our bags and take a journey? I don't think so. But it certainly can't hurt to retain a sense of perspective as we indulge ourselves in haughty little pissing contests over who qualifies as a "traveler" instead of a "tourist."

In truth, we are all tourists: Mr. Benny and his ilk confirm that.

PART THREE

The Dubious Thrill of Press Trips

ᘓ 12 ᘔ

Cycladian Rhythm

'M talking to Pavlo the Sailor in a back-alley Piraeus café, where mustachioed old men come each morning to sip Greek coffee under bluing Titanic posters and generic wall murals of the Acropolis. It's two days before I'm scheduled to sail the Greek islands, and this has proven my favorite way to kill time in Athens's old industrial port town. The harbor sits just three blocks away, and apart from the café, every shop in the alley sells buoys, rope, or life preservers.

Though he tells me he has plenty of experience at sea, Pavlo doesn't look much like a sailor: no wool cap, no bristly beard, no faded tattoos. His appearance is closer to that of a scientist: slight of build, clean-shaven, with graying hair and an intense gaze. When I tell him what I do for a living, he nods approvingly and lights a Marlboro. "If you're going to write an article about sailing in Greece," he says, "you must mention Odysseus."

"I don't want to write about myths," I tell him. "I want to see the Greek islands as they are today. Besides, Odysseus sailed to Ithaca; I'll be sailing in the Cyclades."

Pavlo puffs on his cigarette and thinks this over. "I have seen the Cyclades many times," he says. "Each visit to each island depends on when you go, who you go with, and how long you stay."

"Exactly," I say. "It's subjective. That's why Odysseus has nothing to do with me."

"Ah, but you're wrong." Pavlo's eyes glitter at me through a cloud of smoke. "That's why Odysseus has everything to do with you."

Three days later I find myself in eight-foot seas off the coast of Serifos Island, trying not to vomit as I wrap the mainsheet onto the winch of a fifty-five-foot sailboat. The boat's skipper, an unflappable thirty-three-year-old Californian named Max Fancher, comes over to assess my work. "You almost got it," he says diplomatically. "Only you should probably wrap it clockwise instead of counterclockwise, since the winch only goes in one direction."

Nodding at my own mistake—a blatant flub, vaguely akin to putting on underwear over the outside of your pants—I unwrap the winch and start over.

In spite of my seasickness and nautical ineptitude, I'm happy to be sailing into the heart of the Cyclades—a stunningly beautiful archipelago of two-dozen major islands spread across 5,000 square miles of the Aegean, south and east of the Greek mainland. Indeed, when most people envision Greek islands, the Cyclades are what they see: dramatic cliffs and golden beaches; ridges crowned with blue-domed churches; harbors clustered with whitewashed cubist houses. To glimpse these islands from the seat of a plane or the deck of a commercial ferry is no doubt a thrill, but I've resolved to explore them in the purest sense. Just as the Sahara is best seen by camel and Machu Picchu ideally approached by the Inca Trail, I'm wagering the Cyclades are best experienced from the deck of a sailboat.

The only problem with this plan is that I know very little about sailing—and that's why I've joined on with a six-boat flotilla organized by Berkeley-based OCSC Sailing. Our goal for the next two weeks is to island-hop through the Cyclades to the gorgeous volcanic crescent of Santorini, then loop our way back to Athens—a journey of nearly three hundred nautical miles. Most of the forty-six sailors in our flotilla are folks who have trained for months on San Francisco Bay specifically for this kind of experience; others, like Gar Dukes and Nicole Friend, who helm the *Dafne*, are sharpening their sailing skills in anticipation of buying their own boat and sailing it around the world.

My boat, the *Assos*, consists of Captain Max, his fiancée Maggie Holmes, a first mate, a photographer, and five female novices ranging in age from twenty-five to thirty-six. Like me, my fellow novices have come here to mix a hands-on vacation in the Greek islands with informal sailing instruction. Unlike the sailing lessons OCSC offers on San Francisco Bay, this experience does not involve book-study or comprehensive training. Rather, those who want to get a taste of sailing are invited to learn the ropes (which, Max informs me, are called "lines") by helping with the day-to-day operation of the boat. Amidst the learning, Max continually reminds us we're on vacation, and the atmosphere onboard the *Assos* is fun and relaxed. Most of my fellow boatmates are friends of Maggie's, and they all share her insouciant intelligence, a predilection for wearing bikinis, and the tendency to giggle whenever they hear the name *Assos*. I have a boyish crush on each and every one of them, despite the fact that most of them have thrown up at least once this afternoon.

Rewrapping the sheet, I grind the winch and adjust the mainsail. The *Assos* pitches in the waves, and sea spray whips across the cockpit. As we clear the lee of Serifos Island, the wind edges up past twenty-five knots, and Captain Max decides our crew has had enough drama for one day. Sheeting in the sails, we motor across the channel to the island of Sifnos, where we moor for the night.

We awaken the following morning to angry whitecaps churning the channel, and reports of sixty-knot gusts along the fifty-three-mile route to Santorini. Until these winds let up, Max tells us, we'll be marooned indefinitely on Sifnos.

Compared to the marquee islands of the Cyclades—Santorini, Ios, Mykonos—Sifnos doesn't have much of a reputation. According to Herodotus, the Classical Era gold and silver mines on this thirty-square-mile island made it the richest in the Aegean; a century later, Sifnos won notoriety as the site where the Spartans met with the Persians to plot against Alexander the Great. For the most, part, however, Sifnos has existed as a nondescript suburb of an island, with two thousand or so inhabitants, known more for its poets and pottery than political or geographical distinction. During Ottoman rule, the Turks never bothered sending a garrison to the island, and though pirates periodically haunted the Cyclades, the patron saint of Sifnos, Panaghia Chryssopighi, is best known for protecting the island against grasshoppers.

Despite such lack of distinction, however, the *Assos* (as my boat-mates and I have taken to calling one another) immediately fall in love with Sifnos. The tourist crowds have left with high season, and we have the island mostly to ourselves. Renting motorcycles, we cruise up intricately terraced valleys to the central plateau, where the houses of Apollonia town lay scattered like big white dice among blue-domed churches and olive groves. We wander out to the far coast and swim on empty beaches under ridges dotted with almond trees and clumps of wild juniper. We explore the mazelike alleyways in the hilltop fortress of Kastro, where bright pink bougainvillea creeps over shuttered windows, and stray cats blink in the sunlight. In the evening, we sit outdoors at wooden restaurant tables and dine on *tzatziki*, olives, stuffed peppers, lamb, and local white wine. After dark, we hike up to the empty monasteries overlooking the harbor, where we listen to the sound of the wind and the tinkling of goat bells. One day on Sifnos stretches into two in this manner, and two days stretch into three.

The longer we spend on the island, the less ambitious we get. By the third afternoon on Sifnos, we're spending most of our time swimming in a lovely turquoise cove under the cliffs of Kastro, and our talk of winds and weather has given way to sunbathing and cliff diving. As the sun goes down over the water, I swim slowly along the cliff's edge, watching schools of fish dart beneath me in big, watery beams of late-day sunlight.

I flip over onto my back and watch butterflies skim the water as doves dart in the sky above. If the lotus-eaters of Odysseus's day had it any better than this, I'd be surprised.

After three blissfully indolent days on Sifnos, Captain Max reports that the winds have calmed; we raise anchor, slip lines, and my crash-course in sailing resumes. As I practice tying soggy half hitches and sheet bends in a rainy stretch of sea near Folegandros Island, Max assures me that the willingness to make mistakes speeds the learning process. "Sometimes you learn best by just going out to sea and having things happen," he says.

The more time I spend aboard the *Assos*, the more I appreciate the way sailing connects me to the rhythms of the weather and the water. Away from land, moment-by-moment life is less of an abstraction, and the sea gradually reveals itself as an intricate and powerful wilderness. Moreover, I'm discovering that so many of the metaphors one uses to describe life on land originate from the rituals of the sea. Many times—when asking if we're "making headway," for instance, or offering to "batten down the hatches"—I find myself using correct sailing terminology entirely by accident. With each day at sea, through trial and error, I get more and more comfortable with my role on the boat.

Two days out of Sifnos, the rain clears, and we sail into the caldera of Santorini under brilliant blue skies.

Often associated with the lost city of Atlantis, this caldera dates back to 1,500 B.C., when the biggest volcanic eruption in recorded history collapsed the middle of the island and sent deadly tidal waves surging out across the Mediterranean. Three thousand five hundred years later, the dramatic, red-veined cliffs that rim the caldera are studded with elegant churches, flagstone paths, and pastel-hued houses. It's a singularly gorgeous sight, and we trim in our sails and drift around the thirty-two-square-mile caldera to take it all in.

Later, when my boat-mates and I dinghy in to the Santorini shore, we discover an island snarled with rental-car traffic jams, high-tension power lines, and billboards for places like "Señor Zorba's Mexican Restaurant." After the sleepy anonymity we enjoyed on Sifnos, this comes as a letdown. As we make our way to the cliff-top village of Oia, we see flyers advertising full-moon parties, tavernas touting all-day English breakfasts, and ubiquitous beachfront kiosks selling towels that bear the image of Bob Marley and Che Guevara.

Oia, with its twisting alleyways, cave houses, and grand Orthodox churches, feels more authentic, though visitors from places like Houston, Helsinki, and Hong Kong easily outnumber the five hundred or so locals. The time-honored tradition here is to photograph the sunset as it glitters over the waters of the caldera below, and the crew of the *Assos* is not to be left out. Brandishing our digital cameras, we position ourselves among hundreds of fellow tourists at cliff-side, each of us trying to catch the perfect angle of sunlight on the whitewashed mansions and church domes—without getting each other's arms and heads and cameras in the frame.

There's an element of postmodern farce here, to be sure, but I'd reckon this has become a nightly ritual at all the strange and beautiful landmarks of the world—from Angkor Wat, to Iguazu Falls, to the south rim of the Grand Canyon. At best, we'll all come home with images indistinguishable from what one could buy at a decent postcard stand, but somehow—as with high Mass, or a Buddhist kora—the ritual itself hints at a deeper reverence.

In the end, of course, Santorini was never the goal of our flotilla so much as it was a pivot point. After two nights anchored offshore of the volcanic crescent, we begin our journey back to Athens.

As we follow the winds home, each new island yields humble discoveries. On Sikinos, I dine on wild rabbit and hike at night under the stars; in the marble-studded mountains of Naxos, I talk politics and drink Nescafé with Greek shepherds; on Paros, I eat ice cream along the harbor while a film crew shoots fight scenes for a Greek soap opera. Not the stuff of Odysseus, perhaps, but I love the buzz of each little adventure.

On our final day at sea—the thirty-nine-mile leg from Kea to Athens—a pod of dolphins begins to flirt off our port bow. Enchanted, we fire up the engine and weave along with the elegant gray sea creatures for the good part of an hour before running out of fuel. In an instant, the dolphins are gone, and the *Assos* is left bobbing in the waters off the Greek coast.

We have only a hint of wind for our sails—and Athens is still over ten miles away—so Captain Max has us haul out a colorful spinnaker. With two weeks of sailing experience behind us, we rig the downwind sail with cheerful efficiency.

For a moment, we roll with the waves as the spinner hangs limp at the bow. Then, a slight breeze billows the sail, and we witness a phenomenon as elemental and bewitching as a bolt of lightning or a spark of fire: Wind and boat connect; lines go tight, and we surge forward.

As the slight breeze pulls us slowly into Athens, I again think back to Pavlo the Sailor. Nearly one hundred years ago, the Greek poet Constantine Cavafy also used the example of Odysseus to downplay the importance of one's final destination. "Don't expect Ithaca to give you riches," he wrote. "Ithaca has already given you this journey."

∾

ENDNOTES

1. **Page 192, paragraph 6:** *...and that's why I've joined on with a six-boat flotilla*: At a certain level I did indeed join the OCSC flotilla to sharpen my sailing skills and see the Greek Cyclades by sea. Just as significantly, however, I'd joined the flotilla because an editor at a popular adventure-sports magazine had asked me to write about it. Moreover, this Greece journey was technically a "press trip" funded by the sailing company that organized the flotilla.

Press trips are a source of controversy within the travel-writing milieu, since they create an obvious conflict of interest between the writer's presumed objectivity and the promotional interests of the company that financed the journey. Some magazines (such as *Condé Nast Traveler*) won't publish stories that have been funded by press trips, while other publications (such as *The New York Times*) refuse to work with writers who have a consistent track record of accepting such freebies. On the other hand, many newspaper travel sections (particularly in England) use press trips to fund most of their in-house assignments. In principle it should be possible to travel on a press trip and keep your objectivity, though obviously the business or tourist board that's sponsoring your journey has a vested interest in your subjective appreciation for whatever they're offering.

For the most part I've been able to sidestep the ethical dilemma by avoiding press trips altogether. This hasn't been purely a question of ethics: For the most part, I find press trips to be an insipid charade of tourist-department shuttle vans and awkward conversations with hospitality marketing managers (see the chapter 13 endnotes for details). Since I don't specialize in hotels, food, or package tours, press trips are of little use to me; I find I get better stories spending $12 of my own money to sleep in a local flophouse than spending $500 of someone else's money to stay in a five-star hotel. Nevertheless, I have on occasion accepted tourist-board assistance (my visit to Ooraminna Homestead in chapter 9 being an example), and in the mid-2000s some of the magazines I worked with started utilizing press trips to cut down on expenses during story assignments.

My sailing trip in Greece is an example of what can happen when press trips go right: I loved traveling by boat; I loved the islands I visited; I loved the people I traveled with. In terms of pure moment-by-moment enjoyment, it was one of the best trips I've taken anywhere (and early on I was nervous about how I would write it, since misadventures offer you more narrative grist than flawless journeys). Just re-reading the notes from this journey puts a smile on my face.

That said, a peek at the earlier pages of my Greece-travel notebook provides an interesting perspective, since I'd also visited the region that month to research a story about kayaking in Crete. This paddling journey (which had been assigned by a different travel magazine) was also an outfitter-funded press trip, and I didn't really enjoy it all that much.

Looking back, this had a lot to do with circumstances. While my sailing adventure had taken me past gorgeously empty Cycladian coves, my kayaking trip took me past beaches full of leathery old German nudists. Whereas the *Assos* was crewed by ebullient young women who'd shared my travel interests, my fellow kayaking clients were reticent married couples a good twenty years my senior. Where I'd sailed the Cyclades in perfect health, I'd spent most of my days in Crete fighting a fever I'd picked up on the flight in from New York. And, circumstances aside, the kayak guides exuded a perky enthusiasm that at times felt phony and condescending.

Does this mean I was obligated to write a downbeat story about kayaking in Crete? Actually, it wasn't as simple as that. Unlike the other clients on that kayaking excursion, I spent most months of each year gallivanting around as a travel writer, and hence I wasn't a typical customer. Whereas my ongoing world-wanderings had jaded me to travel experiences that felt the slightest bit canned or predictable, the other kayakers weren't nearly so picky. Like most of the people who subscribed to the magazine I represented, these folks only traveled a few weeks each year. Thus, they didn't share my fever-tinged disappointments in Crete; they just showed up and had a great time. Where I saw condescension in the kayak guides, they saw charm; where I considered the German nudists an eyesore, my fellow kayakers considered them hilariously exotic.

Hence the dilemma not just of outfitter-sponsored press trips, but of consumer travel writing in general: As an ethical person you want to reflect a degree of critical insight when writing about the experience, yet as a person who travels for a living your critical insight may be of limited use to the kind of people who actually plan to take these trips.

In the end, I struck a compromise when I wrote about Crete: Since nobody else on the excursion had shared my irritation with the paddling guides, I kept them in the background of the story. Instead, I focused my narrative on the aesthetic pleasures of kayaking in Greece, balancing the spectacle of German nudists with the more enjoyable encounters I had with Greeks in villages along the way.

As for Cyclades sailing story, I could have written another 2000 words without flagging in my enthusiasm for the happy languor of Sifnos, the rocky grandeur of Folegandros, and the simple thrill of harnessing the wind from island to island.

Thrills aside, however, I gained some leavening insight into this sailing experience during the five-month lag between the journey itself and my story's appearance in the magazine. Around month three, Captain Max sent me a nervous e-mail, pointing out how OCSC had spent a lot of money to send me to Greece, and he expected my coverage to be both timely and positive. It was a courteously worded message—and I could understand how he had a lot at stake in the article—but I'll confess it stole a slight edge of joy from my memory of the experience.

Even the most enjoyable press trips, he'd reminded me, are never created for the mere sake of enjoyment.

ᴄ 13 ᴦ

Seven (or So) Sins
on the Isle of Spice

ᴇʀᴇ's a hint for those wanting to embrace the tempo and culture of Grenada immediately upon arriving on the mountainous, southern Caribbean island: Lose something essential to the personal enjoyment of your vacation, then spend the first day of your visit trying to find a new one. By the time you've located this elusive object—be it a five-bladed vibrating razor or a tube of jasmine-scented SPF 3,000 sunscreen—you will have adapted to the unhurried pace of Caribbean island life, and made plenty of new Grenadian friends in the process.

In my case, the item in question was a pair of foam flip-flops, which were tucked away in a suitcase that was lost by the airlines en route from Miami. Admittedly, flip-flops aren't difficult for folks of average foot-span to replace, but I have size-thirteen feet, so my sandal-quest sent me from my hotel boutique at Grande Anse Beach to the streets of St. George's, Grenada's hilly, harborside capital town, where old churches and terracotta-roofed buildings slope up over the horseshoe-shaped waterfront.

Here, on narrow streets that twisted up past the tin-roofed market square, my initial queries yielded no leads on extra-large size flip-flops—though I did happen across a pleasant café called

Marvelous Marva's, where (perhaps out of consolation) an old Grenadian named Ronald sized me up and suggested that I try an aphrodisiac drink called "Under the Counter."

"Aphrodisiac?" I said, momentarily forgetting about sandals. "What exactly will it do to me?"

"It will give you lust," said Ronald. He cocked his head and gestured to the cloudy liquid that Dennis, the dark-skinned, floral-shirted bartender was pouring into a glass on the wooden bar in front of me. "It will increase your sexual desire."

The other bar patrons tittered with laughter as I took the glass and whiffed the drink's strong, rummy odor. Having just arrived on the island, I had yet to discern the subtleties of Grenadian laughter, so—unsure if I was being laughed with or laughed at—I looked to the bartender for help.

"This is *bois bande*," Dennis told me. "It's a local root, soaked in rum. It won't give you lust. Not exactly. It's more like Caribbean Viagra, if you know what I mean."

"And it works?"

"Some people say so," Dennis said. "It works best if you add cloves, cinnamon, some turtle meat, and maybe an earthworm or a little bit of deer horn. Of course, other people say it's all psychological." The bartender grinned at me. "There's one way to find out, yeah?"

Intrigued by the notion that my search for flip-flops might possibly result in increased sexual potency, I lifted the glass and gulped down the liquid. The barflies tittered cheerfully, and a warm tingle spread into my stomach.

Half an hour later I was back on the streets of Grenada's capital, absently wondering if the warm tingle in my stomach might spread to some other, more socially awkward extremity before I located a decent pair of sandals. On Dennis and Ronald's advice, I scoured the shops along St. George's bustling market-square. Half a dozen failed footwear queries led me down a small side-street into what appeared to be my last remaining hope—a dimly-lit storefront staffed by a pious Grenadian grandmother who kept her gray hair up, nun-like, in a blue scarf.

When I asked about flip-flops, Blue Nun nodded and took me to a dusty shelf that displayed hand towels, coffee mugs, toothpaste, toy racecars, sewing supplies, and one enormous pair of plastic-mesh shoes. Swathed in the green-yellow-red colors of Grenada's national flag, the shoes vaguely resembled "jellies," the mass-produced plastic footwear that went through a brief phase of popularity among fourteen-year-old girls in 1983.

"I don't think these would look too good on me," I said. "Don't you have something else?"

The old woman lifted an eyebrow. "Those shoes will keep your feet comfortable," she says. "What more do you need? Anything more is pride, and pride is a sin. Just try them on."

I took off my leather shoes and buckled the oversized jellies onto my feet. They made my feet look like a pair of Rastafarian water skis.

"Don't you think they're kind of ugly?" I offered.

"The only thing ugly in this world is sin," she said. "Everything else is beautiful."

Trumped, I handed the woman my money and headed back to the white sands and calm waters of Grand Anse Beach.

Back when this journey was still in the planning stages, my friends had asked why, of all the destinations in the Caribbean, I was going to Grenada. The best answer I could give them was sloth. My sincere travel goal, I'd told them, was to find a nice, quiet beach and do absolutely nothing for a full week.

Grenada, a tropical, mountainous island roughly twice the size of Washington, D.C.—but with a population comparable to that of Fargo, North Dakota seemed to fit the bill. Nearer to Caracas than Miami, Grenada's place in the popular imagination was not tied to beaches, but to a headline-grabbing 1983 U.S. military intervention, and the 2004 devastation wreaked by Hurricane

Ivan. In my experience, this kind of track record lent itself well toward empty beaches and blissful solitude.

After my quasi-successful quest for sandals, however, I'd come to realize that seeking mere sloth would be selling my Grenada experience short. Indeed, while my impromptu shopping excursion through the streets of St. George's had burned off the better part of an afternoon—technically a waste of vacation time—it had also taught me the Grenadian virtues of good cheer, patience, and making the best of your circumstances. Had I spent that whole afternoon idling solo on Grande Anse Beach, my instincts might have still been calibrated to the assumptions of home, where the temptation is to micromanage everything (even one's free time), and to become impatient when expectations aren't met.

Instead, drawn into the easygoing cadence of Grenada by a missing pair of flip-flops, I felt a new sense of mission. Having conquered pride with the help of the Blue Nun, and risked lust under the influence of *bois bande* root (which, perhaps lacking the proper dash of cinnamon or deer horn, never really kicked in), I felt that I couldn't truly appreciate Caribbean sloth until I'd braved a few more deadly sins.

Since Grenada is known as the Isle of Spice, I reasoned gluttony would be a good place to start. Thus, on the morning of my second full day on the island, I hired a van out of my hotel and set off to find something delectable.

Ever since the arrival of Christopher Columbus, who first sighted the island in 1498, the history of Grenada has been intertwined with the rivalries and idiosyncrasies of the spice trade. In truth, greed. Over time, the European passion for the transplanted flavors of the Orient (and sugar cane in particular) led to slave-labor plantation colonies across the Caribbean. After wiping out the local Amerindians, French and British interests sparred for control of Grenada throughout the seventeenth and eighteenth centuries. Slavery ended in 1838, and independence from Britain arrived in 1974, but the economy and culture of Grenada still bear the mark of colonial-era arrivals, from a population that largely traces its roots and traditions back to Africa, to a sloping landscape thick with spice plants indigenous to India (ginger), Sri Lanka (cinnamon), and Indonesia (cloves).

These crops, along with nutmeg—a spice so important to the economy that it appears on the Grenadian national flag—are central pillars of the island's economy, but the glutton in me was more interested in cocoa beans, which were reputedly processed into chocolate bars in a small factory on the north end of the island.

As we cruised north, my driver, Roger Augustine, an athletic thirty-one-year old with a passion for all things Grenadian, kept me informed with tidbits of national pride: how St. George's would host matches leading to the 2007 cricket World Cup; how, due to the local water, Carib beer bottled in Grenada tastes better than the Carib sold in other parts of the Caribbean; how, because of early migrations to Trinidad, calypso music is essentially a Grenadian art form. When a rousing calypso song called "Ivan the Messenger" came on over the radio, Roger turned it up and began to sing along.

"Is this a Grenadian song?" I asked.

"Of course. This is Croqueta. I know him."

"What, you mean you've been to his concerts?"

"I mean I know him," Roger laughed. "He was one of the teachers at my school when I was growing up. In this song, he says that Ivan wasn't a hurricane, but a messenger from God. The message says that we're doing a lot of wrong things, and that we need to change our ways."

If Ivan's fury was indeed a message from God, then our drive north was my encounter with the aftereffects of wrath. In St. George's, all the grand, old Catholic and Anglican cathedrals were still missing their roofs; in the foothills, rows and rows of nutmeg plants had been recently planted to replace a crop that was 80 percent destroyed by the hurricane. Climbing inland, past misty waterfalls and up into the lush mountain rainforests of the Grand Etang Reserve, I saw that the tallest trees were stripped bare by the category three winds, sticking out like giant toothpicks from the brilliant green canopy. Down from the rainforests, on the eastern coast of the island, a portion of the old seaside transit road had been pulled underwater by the churning Atlantic surf; vine creepers, a sign of disturbed tropical soil, swarmed; houses everywhere were missing windows and roofs.

Roger insisted that this was all a major improvement from the year before. "Ninety percent of the buildings in Grenada were destroyed or damaged by Ivan," he told me. "A fifth of the people on the island were left homeless. And it wasn't like what happened with Katrina, where the rest of your country could help; here, the whole country was affected, so we were forced to help ourselves as best we could."

Of all the ways Grenadians were helping themselves recover from Hurricane Ivan, perhaps the most novel was the Ivan Bar, which the Grenada Chocolate Company sold via overseas distributors to raise money for hurricane relief.

Driving up from the eastern coast into the cool, plantation-fringed highlands of the north, we arrived at the village of Hermitage, where—just uphill from the police station—I could smell the Grenada Chocolate Company before I could see it. Thus, I was surprised to discover that the source of this rich aroma was a single, pastel-colored building, no bigger than a small suburban house. With seven employees and a 300-pound-a-week output, it was quite possibly the smallest chocolate factory in the world—and the only one operating on solar power.

Edmond Brown, the dread-locked forty-one-year-old Hermitage native who runs the chocolate factory with the help of two American partners, took Roger and me on a tour of his operation. "In the past, Caribbean farmers supplied cocoa beans to

Europe, and got chocolate in return," he said. "We started this factory to take out the middle-man and benefit local growers. Everything about our chocolate is 100 percent organic, from the cocoa beans, to the cocoa butter, to the cane sugar."

Moving from room to room, Edmond showed how freshly harvested cocoa is fermented, dried, roasted, winnowed, ground, mixed with sugar and cocoa butter, tempered, and molded into bars. By the time we returned to the front room for a tasting, I was salivating like an overheated St. Bernard. Edmond offered a choice between chocolate samples that were 60 percent and 71 percent cocoa, and—not wanting to come off as a wimp—I opted for the stronger morsel.

Having been weaned on the common milk chocolate found in the United States, I'll admit I wasn't ready for the bitter, slightly fruity taste that came with my first bite. As I chewed, however, a singularly rich chocolate flavor bloomed across my palate. Wielding my wallet, I bought five bars from Edmond.

"I can get more of this at the supermarket in St. George's, right?"

"Maybe," Edmond said. "But dark chocolate hasn't really caught on yet with Grenadians. Most of our product is exported; the supermarkets in Grenada still sell mostly milk chocolate, like Hershey's or Cadbury's, which comes from other countries."

Not wanting to leave things to chance, I plunked down my money and secured ten more chocolate bars for my stockpile. Gluttony accomplished.

For the ambitious sinner I was fast becoming, my original intended pursuit—sloth—posed a particular challenge. After all, by its very nature, this vice was difficult to combine with other, more rigorous sins, such as envy and greed—and sloth wouldn't be sloth at all if I indulged in the (lack of) activity merely to tick it off a list. Hence, in the spirit of proper iniquity, I was forced to spend three consecutive days in Grenada doing nothing in particular.

Fortunately, as Roger had assured me on our journey to the chocolate factory, doing nothing in particular was a classic Grenadian social activity. "It's called 'liming,'" he'd told me. "Hanging out. That's what tourists do when they come to Grenada: they lime."

For Grenadians and tourists alike, ground zero for liming was Grand Anse Beach, the two-mile curve of fine white sand, coconut palms, and clear turquoise water that sprawls along the island's southwestern coast, just below St. George's Harbor. A classic Caribbean beach by anyone's standard, Grand Anse also had the virtue of being uncrowded—especially along its southern end, where hotels and restaurants gave way to beachside pastures. For more social moods, the northern stretch of Grand Anse was dotted with restaurants, beach vendors, Grenadian families, honeymooning couples, and students from the nearby medical school.

My hotel, the posh Spice Island Resort, sat smack in the middle of Grand Anse beach, and was itself a marvelous venue for liming, particularly since (in a detail that risked the sin of covetousness) my suite featured its own private courtyard, complete with sauna and swimming pool. Typically, I started my daily lime at the resort's beachside dining veranda—a spotless gallery of arching ceilings and airy sea views that just one year before had been a pile of post-Ivan rubble. After breakfast, I would hit Grand Anse when it was still relatively quiet and the coconut palms gave shade at the proper angle, then retreat to my suite pool during the heat of the day. In the afternoons, I would either return to Grand Anse to play pickup beach soccer, or take a taxi out to La Sagesse—a gem of a beach on the southeastern edge of the island, which featured silver sands, shallow calm waters, proximity to an excellent nature preserve, and the isolated sense that I had just stumbled out of the jungle on a deserted island.

Indeed, liming is a splendid default activity in Grenada (many travelers to the island choose to do little else) and I might have indulged my sloth indefinitely had Roger, my driver, not earlier invited me to a Friday night fish barbecue in the coastal village of Gouyave.

Considering that I was only one deadly sin from collecting the full set—and with my time on the island running out—I cut my lime short, donned my nicest clothes, and joined Roger in a drive up the winding road that hugs Grenada's western coast.

On some of the more heavily touristed Caribbean resort islands—where nightlife can be loud, late and boozy—seeking out a provincial fish fry on a Friday night might have seemed like a lame social choice. On Grenada, however, where bars close at eleven and a devoutly Christian populace takes its brotherly love seriously, I found that weekend nightlife exuded an intimate, small-town charm. According to Roger, nightclubs on the island faced stiff competition from outdoor bingo tournaments (which, in true Caribbean style, featured music and dancing between rounds), and the runway of the old airport in St. Andrew's parish had been appropriated not by international developers, but by weekend drag racers.

Since no drag races or bingo tourneys were slated for the weekend, Gouyave's weekly "Fish Friday" was the place to be seen. Located half an hour north of St. George's on winding coastal roads, Gouyave has long been the hub of the island's fishing industry. When we arrived, the streets of the town were packed with cars from other parts of the island. A couple of streets near the old eighteenth-century French church had been blocked off, and local vendors grilled mahi-mahi, red snapper, and sea bass under dozens of white tents. Children ran in the streets, adults flirted in the shadows, and strings of Christmas lights glowed like multicolored fireflies amidst the grill smoke.

Spotting a booth selling succulent shrimp kebabs, I proffered my money, and was surprised to find that the vendor was a tall Swiss man who sported a graying mustache, a chef's smock, and a red beret. He introduced himself as Urs Pfister.

"How did you end up in Grenada?" I asked him.

"I married into Grenada," he said, nodding over at a bright-eyed black woman wearing a floppy white chef's hat and a red corsage. "That's Cheryl, my wife."

"You met Cheryl here in Gouyave?"

Urs shot me an ironic grin. "Not exactly. I met her in Pyongyang."

"North Korea?"

"That's right. We were both working for international aid agencies at the time. Later we lived in Afghanistan, operating a United Nations hostel, but we decided to leave when we were almost taken hostage."

"And now you sell fish in Grenada."

"Among other things. We've been doing this every Friday for seven months, and now we go through eighty pounds of shrimp in a night. Fish Friday has become so popular that people recognize me everywhere I go—even in St. George's. Of course, most people don't remember my name, so they just call me 'Fish Kebob.'"

As I ate my shrimp and listened to Fish Kebob describe the languorous pace of his weekly schedule, I felt the distinct twinge of one final sin: envy. After nearly a week on Grenada, I coveted Urs's happy-go-lucky island lifestyle.

Gazing around at the laid-back street festival in the smoky streets of Goyave, I wondered what kind of enterprising gimmick I could bring to Grenada that might allow me to be the American version of Fish Kebob. Saltwater-taffy Saturday? Bison-beef Wednesday? Vidalia-onion Monday?

It wasn't until later that night, when I returned to my hotel, that I had the epiphany that might well have turned me into a prospering expatriate entrepreneur: As I drifted off to sleep, I decided I would sell extra large flip-flops.

In the end, of course, my new business never got off the ground. The following morning I woke up early, strapped on my

Rastafarian jellies, and headed off for one last day of liming on the brilliant white sands of Grand Anse.

∾

ENDNOTES

1. Page 201: *Seven (Or So) Sins on the Isle of Spice*: Of all the stories in this book, "Seven Sins" is probably the least compelling at a pure narrative level. This is because it's a destination story, and destination stories don't typically address broader issues, explore larger ideas, or stand the test of time: By definition, all these stories do is creatively explore interesting tourist sights and/or activities at a given destination.

I decided to include my Grenada story for a couple reasons. First, destination articles are the bread and butter of travel writing, as they are in constant demand from newspapers and glossy magazines. Since they are consumer-oriented by nature, these stories have a fairly strict mandate to include typical vacation motifs. Thus, had I stumbled across a cricket stadium full of naked midgets calling for armed revolution while I was in Grenada (and sadly I did not), I still would have been obligated to work in mention of beaches and chocolate bars when I got around to writing the story.

Vacation motifs aside, my primary interest in sharing this tale is that (while not fictional in the technical sense) it is perhaps the most spectacular narrative deviation from lived reality in the history of my travel-writing career.

These endnotes explain how this came about.

2. Page 203, paragraph 9: *My sincere travel goal…was to find a nice, quiet beach and do absolutely nothing for a full week*: Admittedly, the impetus for my Grenada journey had very little to do with sitting on a beach and doing nothing. I went there because a certain glossy travel magazine wanted to do a story about the island, and an editor there asked me if I was interested in writing it. In theory, doing "absolutely

nothing for a full week" sounded nice, but it was no way to research my travel story.

Moreover, the magazine had utilized the local tourist board to under-write most of its travel costs, so I'd arrived in Grenada to discover that nearly every day of my visit had been scheduled with activities. At first I thought this might be an efficient way to familiarize myself with the island—but it didn't turn out to be that simple, since I was sharing the itinerary with a photographer I'll call "Donny Downer."

At a very basic level, travel writers and travel photographers have utter-ly unrelated travel goals: Writers are looking for interesting experiences; photographers are looking for interesting visuals. In this way, a photogra-pher will happily spend three hours using different lenses and angles to shoot an abandoned fort, while a writer will just scribble down a quick note about the place and be done with it. Similarly, a writer might be thrilled to meet an old lady who says she served breadfruit to American troops during the 1982 military intervention, while the photographer just wants her to get the hell out of the way so he can get a better shot of the marina. Keeping this discrepancy in mind, I generally try to tolerate the idiosyncrasies of the photographers who work with me on assignment.

Unfortunately, Donny turned out to be the most indecisive, scatter-brained, world-weary person I've met in any professional context. After, say, photographing a nutmeg plantation for two hours, Donny would sigh dejectedly and announce to nobody in particular that he hadn't got-ten any decent shots. Thirty minutes later, when the tourist-board van was about to stop at a village on another part of the island, Donny would announce his desire to go back and re-shoot the nutmeg plantation. We'd drive back; he'd re-shoot it, then sigh dejectedly and declare that he *still* hadn't gotten any decent shots.

This routine continued when we took a hydrofoil to the Grenadian island of Carriacou (which isn't mentioned in the story, for obvious rea-sons). Here, Donny decided he wanted some shots of snorkelers in L'Esterre Bay. Since snorkeling is an activity I theoretically might enjoy in Grenada, I consented to pose for the pictures—but by the time our water taxi had taken us out into the bay, Donny decided he wanted to shoot an anchored sailboat instead. When the owner of the sailboat came out on deck and asked him to stop taking pictures, Donny just kept shooting and demanded that the water-taxi driver move in closer. After what seemed like an eternity of rapid-fire shooting, the sailboat owner was hoarse from screaming at us and the water-taxi driver was on the verge of a nervous breakdown. Unperturbed, Donny just sighed and declared that he hadn't gotten any decent shots.

While I spent my days trapped in minivans and water-taxis as Donny dithered over what he wanted to re-shoot, I spent my evenings attending restaurant dinners that had been arranged in advance by the tourist board. These dinners were always quite tasty, but they invariably involved the restaurant manager coming out, making awkward small talk, and presenting me with CD-ROMs and glossy brochures full of information about the food and the facilities.

By the end of my third day on the island, I had a fat stack of restaurant brochures, a reporter's notebook laced with terse observations about my photographer, and no idea how I would write my story.

3. **Page 204, paragraph 3: *…I couldn't truly appreciate Caribbean sloth until I'd braved a few more deadly sins*:** Though the article implies that I was out looking for gluttony by my second day on the island, this was actually a retroactive realization. In truth, I didn't come up with the "seven sins" thesis until my fourth day in Grenada.

This theme was essentially born out of panic, since I knew I couldn't write an article about dining with restaurant managers and riding around in a tourist-board minivan with an indecisive photographer. Sitting in my hotel room that morning, I'd tried to itemize every interesting and authentic encounter I'd had since arriving on the island.

The best I could come up with was the three hours I'd spent shopping in St. George's after the airline had lost my luggage the first day. I remembered how, when I'd bought an ugly pair of plastic shoes to replace my missing flip-flops, the shopkeeper had told me how the only truly ugly thing in the world was sin. Recalling how I'd sampled the "aphrodisiac" drink at Marvelous Marva's earlier that day, I scanned my notebook for interesting details that might connect the two experiences. When I found Ronald's comment about lust, I realized I was on to something.

Thinking back to my journeys around the island in the tourist-board minivan, I tried to sort out the places I'd been able to enjoy when Donny wasn't sending us back to the hotel to find some misplaced telephoto lens. The Grenada Chocolate Company had been a highlight, and I realized I'd bought enough candy bars (which were actually gifts for my girlfriend at the time) to justify a gluttony reference. Further brainstorming helped me realize that tree-damage at the Grand Etang Reserve was evidence of Hurricane Ivan's wrath, and that the old colonial spice trade was a manifestation of greed. Considering that sloth was a no-brainer on a resort island like Grenada, all I had to do was find something that evoked envy.

In this way, I was able to go from no story at all to it being six-sevenths conceptualized in less than an hour.

4. **Page 205, paragraph 3: ...*Roger Augustine, an athletic thirty-one-year old with a passion for all things Grenadian*:** Roger drove the tourist-board minivan. He proved to be a terrific source of information about the island, and a model of patience and sanity as Donny stood at the side of the road trying to decide whether the light was good enough to photograph a coconut palm. Though I only mention Roger in the context of the chocolate factory and the fish fry, I saw him nearly every day on the island.

It's often said that to write an effective nonfiction story you need to accumulate far more research information than you'll end up using. These unused details are like the underwater mass that buoys an iceberg: they help float the story; they give it an inherent sense of stability and authority.

Thanks to Roger, I learned all kinds of curious facts that helped deepen my understanding of Grenada: the village decorating competitions that date back to the island's brief communist era; the "Shakespeare Mas" in Carriacou, where contestants recite speeches from *Julius Caesar* and reenact the bard's fight scenes with electric-cord whips; the calypso and extempo lyrics that serve as a de facto op-ed page for events on the island. It was from Roger that I learned how "soul case" is Grenadian slang for the human body, and that a *ligaroo* is a flying Grenadian werewolf that enters your house through the keyhole and tries to suck your blood (to slow him down, Roger told me, just leave sand on the doorstep and he'll get distracted counting the grains).

Through his sheer enthusiasm and depth of knowledge, Roger helped me accumulate the telling details that were to color my Grenada story once I'd formulated the "seven sins" framework.

5. **Page 208, paragraph 3:** *My hotel, the posh Spice Island Resort:* Though the middle portion of my Grenada sojourn was much saner for me than the initial days, I didn't exactly "lime" that whole time. Leaving the tourist-board minivan to Donny, I'd spent a good portion of those days wandering the island by myself. Among the many minor adventures that resulted (including getting kicked out of a St. George's KFC for wearing a tank-top), one of the more memorable encounters came in meeting the owner of the Spice Island Resort, Sir Royston O. Hopkin.

As far as I've been able to determine, Sir Royston is the only person in the British Commonwealth to have been knighted for his contributions to the hotel industry. I'd been hearing about him since I'd arrived at the Spice Island Resort. Apparently, his staff had been so well trained that when Hurricane Ivan destroyed half the hotel they'd coolly transformed the place into a safari camp, reassigning guests to undamaged rooms and cooking splendid steak-and-lobster meals over beach bonfires. Sir Royston had been away from the island at the time, but I figured he might be able to flesh out my "wrath" angle by sharing some perspective on Grenada's post-Ivan perseverance.

Sadly, our interview turned out to be a highly formal non-event, wherein I doodled notes about his appearance ("silver ring, silk shirt, resonant voice, graying hair, cocoa skin") while Sir Royston outlined his accomplishments in sequential, résumé-like fashion. Whenever I tried to get him to talk about his staff's response to Hurricane Ivan, Sir Royston would respond with a proud itemization of the hotel's post-hurricane amenities (Spanish floor-tiles, Bulgarian cutlery, Italian glassware). When I'd ask him how tourism had transformed Grenadian life since the 1980s, he'd give me a dry lecture on room occupancy rates and international markets.

No doubt Sir Royston's single-minded obsession with hotel-business minutiae is what made him successful—but in his compulsion to talk about stats and status instead of telling me stories, the regal old Grenadian knight had talked himself right out of my article.

6. **Page 209, paragraph 4:** *Since no drag races or bingo tourneys were slated for the weekend:* In the forty-eight hours before I went to Fish Friday, I embarked on a number of aborted missions to track down envy—my lone remaining sin. These forays took me to a rum distillery in St. David's parish, an evening worship service at the evangelical church in St. George's, and the Morne Fendue Plantation House near Mount Rich.

By the time I got to the plantation house I was getting nervous about rounding up my final sin. A kindly old physician named Jean Thompson owned the place, and I think I startled her by continually trying to steer our conversation to the topic of envy. When Dr. Jean told me how Princess Margaret had slept at the plantation house when she'd visited the island in the 1950s, I asked if the locals were envious of Margaret's royal lifestyle. When Dr. Jean commented on the happy simplicity of Grenadian rural life in the early twentieth century, I asked her if she envied the people that lived in that era. When she said no, I asked her if the people of that era might envy the relative prosperity of modern Grenadians. "What's all this about envy?" she'd finally blurted. "What kind of story are you writing, anyway?"

Fortunately, I found my envy that very evening at the fish fry in Goyave.

Five months later, my Grenada story debuted in the glossy travel magazine. All things considered, I think the narrative held together pretty well.

And, contrary to Donny's ongoing pessimism, the photos turned out great.

✌ 14 ✌

Virgin Trail

I. THE MORE LOOKERS, THE LESS THERE IS TO SEE?
Antigua, Guatemala

A few blocks from the ruined colonial churches and tourist sports bars of Antigua, Guatemala's tourist district, I stumble across a barbershop where it's not necessary to speak Spanish to get a haircut. Rather, without even uttering a word, I can peruse a wall-mounted poster and point to the Latin American hairstyle of my choosing. At first blush, this option comes as a relief, since my Lonely Planet Spanish-language phrasebook (which for some reason is flush with dubiously useful drug-Spanish, such as "I take cocaine occasionally!") is completely bereft of barbershop phrases.

Unfortunately, all the hairstyles from the point-and-choose poster seem to hearken from distant decades. The coiffure labeled "Serpentina" (which leaves one's ears largely obscured by lightly feathered tresses), for example, looks as if it would prepare me to shimmy under the disco balls of Raytown, Missouri, in, say, 1977. "La Musica" (a gently wavy hairdo that runs longish in the back), on the other hand, is Guatemalan vernacular for the 1980s barbershop staple now known as the mullet. Even the illustration for a "Normal" haircut seems to suggest that normal hair was invented by the Beatles sometime around 1964.

Because I've been living out of a Land Rover since I left San Francisco four weeks ago, I elect to skip the bewildering menu of hairstyles and keep things simple. "*Dos*," I say to the barber, pointing two fingers at his electric clippers. He grins and snaps a No. 2 setting onto the clippers. Three minutes later, I have a crew cut that is, mercifully, too basic and utilitarian to merit a space on any Latin American hairstyle posters.

For me, this haircut offers a welcome chance to slow down and enjoy the quirky ambience of Latin America. For the past month, I've been part of "Driving Around the World," a global Land Rover expedition that aims to raise money for charity. Our goal— to circumnavigate the globe on lines of longitude—may have a romantic ring to it, but the reality of endurance-driving expeditions is that they don't leave you with much time to see the countries through which you're traveling. Thanks to our ambitious schedule, our nine-person, four-vehicle expedition team blew through Mexico in just two weeks. As we raced to keep up with our itinerary, the countryside and culture outside our windshields sped by in a blur of tollbooths, gas stations, road signs, stray cattle, cacti, and one-night cheap hotels.

Now, however—thanks to a fortuitous change of the day our Land Rovers ship from Panama to Ecuador (thus bypassing the roadless Darien Gap)—we'll have a chance to slow down and enjoy our Central American surroundings. For the next week, as we travel relatively short stretches from Guatemala into El Salvador, Honduras, and Nicaragua, we'll have the novel opportunity to linger in places.

This change of pace is perfectly timed for me, since Antigua is the last major tourist destination on our route until we roll into Costa Rica a week from now. Places like El Salvador and Nicaragua have little tourist infrastructure and bad political reputations—and that's exactly why I think I'll enjoy traveling there. I don't say this merely because places known for wars and crises are off the beaten path; I enjoy such places because they reveal more about the traveler-host relationship than your average tourist "hotspot" can. Just as, in previous travels, Laos revealed a spontaneous vitality I found lacking in Thailand—just as Syria surprised me in ways Egypt never could—I suspect that El Salvador and Nicaragua will show me more about travel than I could find here in the gringo-saturated streets of Antigua.

Admittedly, preferring obscure destinations to popular ones is not a particularly original travel strategy. In the nineteenth century, an American visitor named William Brigham observed that travel veterans in Guatemala preferred far-flung places because they "know how soon the individuality of a country is lost once the tide of foreign travel is turned through its towns or its byways." At the time, Brigham was bemoaning the demise of mule paths in the face of Guatemalan railroads; I could just as easily grouse about the Guatemalan fast-food restaurants and Internet cafés that have colonized Antigua's colonial buildings.

Internet cafés notwithstanding, however, I'll admit that Antigua is a wonderful place to linger for a few days. Once the Spanish administrative capital of Central America, it is said to be the best-preserved colonial city in the Americas. Surrounded by volcanoes (including the active Volcan Fuego, which belched a faint puff of smoke into the southwestern sky this morning), Antigua's narrow cobblestone streets are crowded with flat-fronted pastel buildings that were originally built in the seventeenth and eighteenth centuries. Horse-drawn buggies clop through the main square, where Mayan women gracefully balance baskets full of fabric atop their heads. Bougainvillea vines climb the facades of ruined churches, and locals still gather to do their laundry in the pools of the public plaza. Antigua's laid-back, college-town vibe attracts students to its six-dozen (and counting) language schools, and it's not uncommon to walk into a café and hear Germans, Koreans, Israelis, and Iowans chatting away in rudimentary Spanish.

As I leave the barbershop with my expedition teammate Daisy Mae Scheisskopf, we stumble across a strange sight near the Parque Central: Outside of a solemn church sanctuary, a mortar-like tube sits in the middle of the street. Every few minutes—at certain points in the worship service—a middle-aged man jogs out of the sanctuary and drops fireworks into the mortar tube. A half-dozen powdery red and yellow bursts stain the sky above us, then the middle-aged man trots back inside and rejoins the worship service. Ten minutes later—after a bit of singing and kneeling and chanting—the man pops out with another armful of fireworks and repeats his routine.

Daisy knows a little Spanish, but her inquiries yield little specific information from locals (and, sadly, my Spanish phrasebook—full of useful lines such as "Do you have a methadone program in this country?"—doesn't cover inquiries about festivals). Before long, a crowd of gringo travelers assembles outside the church, and there is much discussion about what could possibly be going on with the explosive worship service. Could it by chance be an Advent ritual? Some synthesis of old Mayan traditions? Independence Day? The start of the Guatemalan World Series? Guidebooks are consulted, jokes are made, cameras flash, and—strangely—I begin to lose interest in the entire spectacle. Against my better intentions, I find myself longing for the same experience in different, more solitary circumstances.

The writer Walker Percy once pondered this weird contradiction of travel. "How does one see the thing better when others are absent?" he asked wryly. "Is looking like sucking: the more lookers, the less there is to see?"

The answer, of course, is that there is still plenty to see—but this doesn't stop me from wandering off to watch the proceedings from a different vantage point. By the time I go to bed, the divine purpose of the fireworks is still a mystery to me.

The following morning, our expedition team arises early, loads the Land Rovers, and heads into El Salvador.

II. Carlos Don't Surf
La Libertad, El Salvador

Just as biologists use bird populations to gauge the ecological health of natural areas, travelers can use populations of stray dogs and cats to determine the status of beach-hangout scenes. If the dogs and cats are skittish and skinny, for instance, the beach is probably well away from the tourist trail; if stray dogs and cats are nonexistent altogether, the beach-scene is likely catering to mass resort tourism. If the strays display nonchalant charm, however—if the random mutts and kitty cats flirt for their food from travelers—that beach scene has probably arrived at an enlightened middle point in its evolution.

On the volcanic beaches west of La Libertad, El Salvador, stray dogs saunter up to the open-front restaurants and sorrowfully flop their heads into the laps of diners; stray cats blink, purr, and mew under the tables. The patrons here, mostly young surfers and backpackers from the United States and Europe (as well as a few middle-class weekenders from San Salvador), are happy to oblige with morsels of food. Bob Marley tunes play endlessly on café sound systems, and bottles of locally brewed Pilsener beer come cold and cheap. It's a nice little vibe, and at times both the travelers and the strays look genuinely stunned by their good fortune.

With its warm waters, sandy beaches, cheap lobsters, and gorgeous sunsets, La Libertad could easily become a major beach resort—were it not for the fact that (despite the remarkable effectiveness of a 1992 peace accord) most people still associate El Salvador with war and suffering. Tell folks you're going to a beach in El Salvador, and the notion carries the vague suggestion of Robert Duvall blasting his way through the Mekong Delta in *Apocalypse Now* ("Carlos don't surf!"). Hence, outside of international surfing circles, the black-sand beaches near La Libertad (Playa El Zonte, Playa El Sunzal, Playa El Tunco) are virtually unknown.

Ironically, El Salvador's dangerous reputation is an integral part of the appeal for the people who travel here. I've been staying at Playa El Tunco since arriving from Guatemala yesterday, and I've found that traveler conversations invariably steer their way toward presumed dangers: gun-toting Salvadorans on the beach at night, street gangs near the cities, leftover land mines in the jungles. This talk is a standard traveler safety ritual, but it's also part of the vicarious thrill of being in a place with a bad reputation and no major guidebook coverage. Just as I've seen in the (largely peaceful) tourist environs of former war zones like Phnom Penh and Beirut, the suggestion of violence is an undeniable selling point for young travelers here—and an otherwise languorous afternoon of surfing and beer drinking can readily be passed off as an edgy adventure.

This morning I took the Land Rover into central La Libertad to rent a longboard that suited my novice surfing abilities. Rolling into the city, I noted the seeming contradictions of life alongside the road: the young woman wearing a midriff-baring Britney Spears shirt as she balanced a bundle of firewood on her head; the old *campesino* talking into a cell phone as his horse grazed in a traffic median. The tourist police wore shorts and darted their mountain bikes past oxcarts full of sugarcane; Internet cafés competed for storefront space with farm-implement shops and fundamentalist Christian chapels.

Perhaps to confirm my own prejudices (and to tap into that vicarious buzz of danger), I've been asking the Salvadorans about their war stories—but they mostly prefer to share their success stories. Oscar, the laid-back Salvadoran-American who runs our hotel on Playa El Tunco, may have dodged death squads as a teenager, but he's far more interested in sharing the tale of how he came to own a neon sign business in Los Angeles. Fifteen percent of El Salvador's population fled during the civil war in the '80s, and the influence of American-bred Salvadorans can be seen in everything from strip malls to gang graffiti (not to mention the economy: Salvadoran-Americans send over $1.5 billion back to El Salvador each year). Of the half-dozen or so locals I've chatted with today, two have lived in Southern California; one has spent time in Tempe, Arizona; and a fourth offered me casual advice on nightlife in Conyers, Georgia.

Aside from those passing conversations, however, I'll confess that I haven't spent all that much time with the locals. As with the other gringos here, I've mainly been indulging in standard beach-scene pleasures. This morning, I paddled against the current off Playa El Sunzal and jockeyed for waves along the long, rocky right-break. This afternoon I drank three beers and fell asleep in a hammock. This evening I will walk to one of the restaurants that line the beachfront, where I will have the option of ordering french fries and a medium-rare bacon burger. If by chance that restaurant is playing a cheesy Hollywood action-adventure movie on DVD (and most of them here do), I'll probably end up watching it. If that restaurant also has an Internet connection, I'll likely check my e-mail.

I realize the insipidity in traveling to a far-flung clime merely to discover the same small pleasures that can be found at home, but that's how these insouciant little beach scenes work. The formula has already been set: Attract enough travelers to a place, and before long that place will figure out how to cater to the fashions and tastes that travelers bring with them. If, as a visitor, you bemoan the presence of these comforts, you may as well bemoan the presence of yourself.

And that may well be the ironic allure of traveling to lesser-known destinations like La Libertad: Here, you can indulge yourself in a few comforts of home and still feel like you're some-place wonderfully exotic.

As I walk my way toward dinner, a stray mutt trots in the sand behind me, looking optimistic.

III. BUREAUCRACY, REST, AND MOTION
The El Salvador-Honduras Border at El Amatillo

After the beaches of La Libertad, our expedition team heads east along the Pacific coast, faced with the task of traveling through two borders (El Salvador-Honduras and Honduras-Nicaragua) in thirty-six hours. As I steer the Land Rover toward the Honduran frontier, I watch the sights of El Salvador race by outside: farmers drying grain on the shoulder of the road; clusters of spandex-clad bicyclists training on the highway; coffee fields curving up vol-cano slopes and disappearing into the clouds; a lone boy clutch-ing a dead armadillo at a crossroads; morning commuters packed into refurbished American school buses ("Dodge County Schools" reads one; "The Love Machine" another). We stop for lunch in the thriving eastern city of San Miguel, then roll on to the Honduras border check-post at El Amatillo.

For air commuters, customs proceedings are a passing has-sle—but on a multinational vehicle expedition, border zones become a major part of the experience. And, while border towns have a reputation for being artificial anti-places, devoid of cul-ture and character, I find them fascinating. A quarter of a centu-ry ago, social critic Paul Fussell observed that politically imposed frontiers have little regard for time or tradition and "imply an awareness of reality as disjointed, dissociated, fractured." In the time since he wrote that, however, the same words have been used (in the context of "globalization") to describe the world in general. Indeed, in an amplified and chaotic way, border towns remind us of how we're already living: They reveal the very uncertainties, inequities, and absurdities we've come to ignore in our domestic routines.

A tidy narrative explaining the intricacies of the El Amatillo border crossing simply can't do the experience justice. Granted, there is a very clear beginning to the process (when a crowd of teenage boys mobs our convoy at the edge of town, hoping to earn tips by guiding us through the bureaucratic process)—as well as a definite ending (when a soldier on the Honduran side makes a half-hearted pitch for a bribe before waving us on)—but I've found that there's no coherent progression to what happens in between.

On this day, the El Salvador checkpoint is being bombarded by tuneless hymns and rhythmic clapping from a charismatic gospel church housed in a small cinderblock hovel just across from the customs station. When I wander over and peek inside the church, I discover that all the noise is being generated by one man, one woman, two microphones, and a rather sophisticated electronic sound system. The audience consists of an enraptured old woman and two bored-looking little girls. The amplifiers—which sit in the doorway, aimed at the heathen outside—look like they weigh more than the entire congregation combined. Nobody in the street pays much mind.

Opting out of church, my next order of business involves buying explosives. Actually, I have little personal interest in this activity—but our documentary video crew seems to think my interactions with a Salvadoran fireworks vendor might result in a humorous border moment for their outtakes. Trailed by cameras and microphones, I obligingly walk over to the local fireworks stand, where (apart from a few imported Russian and Chinese bottle rockets) most of the merchandise appears to have been assembled locally from newsprint, gunpowder, and red wax paper. After a bit of discussion, the vendor brings out some dynamite-sized specimens that look like they were designed while watching Wile E. Coyote cartoons. "*Demasiado peligroso,*" I tell her, "—too dangerous." The firecracker vendor shoots me a pity-ing look, no doubt reserved for retards and sissies. "*Por los niños,*" she snorts. "These are for children." I can't imagine how anyone would let children handle fireworks that look big enough to kill cattle—but, since the video crew has their outtake moment, I drop the issue and wander back to the Land Rovers.

Once our stamped passports come back from the El Salvador customs office, our expedition team drives the Land Rovers to the Honduran side of the Goascoran River. As we cross the bridge, I look down and see a baggage-laden Salvadoran family fording the river on horseback. This goes on in plain sight of the immigration authorities, and I can think of no more vivid reminder of the fact that most international borders are purely political-bureaucratic abstractions.

The first official we meet on the Honduran side is a fat, mus-tached police officer who collects our drivers licenses, then informs us that we can have them back when we produce our vehicle fire extinguishers. When we show him the red canisters in the back of our Land Rovers, the policeman nods officiously and mentions that what he is *really* concerned about is whether or not we have our orange safety-hazard triangles. When we produce one, he tells us we need four. When we produce four, he tells us we need eight. When we tell him we don't have eight safety-haz-ard triangles, the policeman clicks his tongue and discreetly offers to overlook this horrible safety breach for the modest sum of $100 per vehicle.

As we have learned over past few weeks, $100 is the opening bid on all vehicle infractions south of the U.S.-Mexico border. In Mexico City, for example, a trio of police officers tried to fine us $100 when we failed to signal a lane-change; two days later, another team of Mexico's finest demanded $100 from us for hav-ing the wrong numbers on our license plates. As happened in those cases, Nately Sanchez (our best Spanish speaker) launches into negotiation mode—telling the Honduran officer how we are all volunteers, how the Land Rovers are actually on loan to the project, and how our drive-a-thon is raising money for charity. Before long, the going rate for our missing safety triangles is down to $5 per vehicle, and our licenses are returned to us intact. Nately takes a huge stack of paperwork from his vehicle and, joined by expedition leader Kenny Cathcart, heads over to the Honduran customs office.

Since the paperwork indicates that Dirk Wintergreen (my driving partner) is the primary operator of my Land Rover, I am usually spared the tedium of border formalities. In the interest of reportage, however, I jog off to join Nately and Kenny in the customs office. Inside, I see them sitting in front of a wooden desk, clutching their paperwork in bewilderment as an *Alvin and the Chipmunks* version of "Silent Night" shrieks out from a vacant desktop computer.

Figuring this is as entertaining as the paperwork process is going to get, I wheel around and walk back outside. It is four hours before I see Nately or Kenny again.

While the bureaucracy plods on, I hang out near the Land Rovers with the rest of the expedition team and a rowdy knot of Honduran snack vendors, moneychangers, drunks, rubber-neckers, and schoolchildren. As happens everywhere we go in our expensively kitted vehicles, the financial gulf between host and traveler creates an instant cultural-economic free trade zone. At times, the barrage of yes/no inquiries from curious onlookers and potential middlemen makes me feel like a harried celebrity.

"Yes, *señora*," I say, "I do have Honduran money. No, I don't want another Coke. Yes, *señor*, I am from the United States. No, I don't live in Beverly Hills. Yes, amigo, you can watch movies on this laptop. No, I don't think I will give it to you. Yes, sister, I've heard that Jesus died on a cross for my sins. No, I would not like to buy a Virgin Mary air freshener. Merry Christmas to you too, ma'am. Yes, sir, you do indeed have a lovely looking family. No, I will not lend you the money to buy a chain lamp for your living room. Yes, *muchacho*, I am the driver of this car. No, I don't need you to guard it for me. Sure, I'll say hello to your cousin in Bakersfield. No, I don't need cashews. Sure, if you find a soccer ball, I'd be happy to play a game. The cars? I'm not sure how much they're worth. The computer? I'm not sure how much it's worth, either. No, that's a satellite phone. I don't know how much it's worth. I don't know how much the mountain bikes are worth. I don't know how much my shoes are worth. Yes, probably more than your shoes. No, I don't have a wife. No, I don't need to find a wife just this moment. Yes, we have Santa Claus in America too. No, I've never met Arnold Schwarzenegger. Yes, I know he's the governor of California. Thank you for the offer, but we're not going to Tegucigalpa. No, I can't give you a ride to the hardware store. No, I still don't want a Coke. Yes, you too, and a happy New Year to you as well."

At sunset, a small parade of vehicles rolls up to the border from the Honduran side. A brass band in the front truck belts out a spirited Latino oom-pah tune, and a pretty teenage girl in a prom dress stands in the back of a second truck, looking happy and nervous under a makeshift wooden canopy. Balloons flutter from the windows of the other cars, and an old man begins to throw candy from the window of a Ford Escort. As the school-children near me bolt off for the sweets, I inquire with the adults about the meaning of the parade.

I don't, unfortunately, get a clear answer. A few folks inform me that the girl in the truck is a virgin. Others tell me there will be a party tonight in El Amatillo. Nobody can tell me exactly what's going on, except to vaguely suggest that it has something to do with Christmas. As with the church fireworks in Antigua, I feel as if I've stumbled across an odd little party that everyone knows about but nobody can tell me about. I have a suspicion, however, that it's all the same party, even as we change countries.

Nately and Kenny come out of the customs office after nightfall, paperwork in hand, and we head off in darkness for the small Honduran commercial center of Choluteca. When we arrive, the only restaurant still open is a place run by Chinese immigrants. Exhausted, we watch Mandarin-dubbed karaoke videos as we gobble down our spicy chicken curry.

The following day we rise at six in the morning, drive to the Nicaraguan border at Guasaule, and (with a few slight variations) repeat this entire routine again.

IV. THEY EAT MERMAIDS, DON'T THEY?
Mombacho Volcano, Nicaragua

After two hours of hiking through the cloud forests of Nicaragua's Mombacho Volcano, my companions and I have seen no sign of the pumas and howler monkeys that are said to lurk here. Admittedly, it's difficult to spot wildlife when you're tromping through the jungle with eight other people—and I suspect our collective expectations of ecotourism are rooted more in the Discovery Channel than in any meaningful knowledge of nature itself. At times, our adventure here carries a postmodern kind of pathos: Because we haven't spotted any of the animals we'd hoped to see here, the jungle seems slightly *wrong* somehow.

We certainly aren't the first outsiders to come to this part of the world and get stymied by our expectations. When Christopher Columbus first sailed to the Caribbean coast of Nicaragua, he claimed he saw three mermaids cavorting in the shallow waters. The creatures, he wrote, "raised their bodies above the surface of the water, and, although they were not as beautiful as they appear in pictures, their round faces were definitely human." One wonders if the legendary explorer would have been disappointed if he'd known he was looking at manatees.

Though Columbus died none the wiser, the reality check for our group comes from an American biologist named Eric Vandenberghe, whom we find skulking on the northern ridge of the volcano, butterfly net in hand. Eric has been studying wildlife in Nicaragua for seven years, and—like many other naturalists I've met—he is soft-spoken and passionate about his work, with a tendency to giggle absently whenever I ask him a stupid question.

The first giggle comes when I inquire about where we might be able to spot some wildlife. "It depends on what you mean by wildlife," he says. "Bring a UV light here tonight, and you'll be able to catch forty varieties of hawk moths before the sun comes up. I've identified seventy-five different species of butterflies since I arrived yesterday. This volcano is an island of biodiversity: Keep your eyes open, and you could spend an entire day going 100 feet any direction into the jungle."

"Unfortunately," I say, "we don't have a whole day to spend here—and we were hoping to at least see some monkeys."

This is obviously a telling statement, as it elicits another involuntary giggle from the biologist. "Try the Embarcado Oriental— the big market in Managua," he says. "You can see nearly any monkey species in the country there. For $15, you can buy one. You can also buy just about any species of parrot. Green turtle meat will cost you fifty cents a pound."

"But aren't green turtles endangered?"

"Sure they're endangered. They're also the cheapest meat you can find in Nicaragua. Cheaper than chicken. And green turtle eggs are cheaper than chicken eggs. In the market, nothing is sacred. People eat manatees in Nicaragua; it's a very prized meat in some parts of the country."

I ponder the grim prospect of shopping for one of Columbus's mermaids in central Managua. "But can't you find these animals in nature anymore?"

"Of course you can find those animals in nature," Eric says with a wry grin, "but you just told me you don't have a day to spend looking for them."

In the course of a three-minute conversation, it appears that Eric and I have struck upon a basic contradiction of ecotourism: To truly immerse yourself in nature, you need time and patience, yet short-term tourists rarely have much time to spare. The "product" of ecotourism, after all, is *experience*—yet a meaningful experience of nature is not something that can be delivered in quick, standardized packages.

If any country in the world has come close to making ecotourism work, it is Costa Rica, Nicaragua's neighbor to the south. And, despite the fact that Mombacho Volcano hasn't produced any marquee fauna for us today, this Nicaraguan nature reserve is very much an extension of the Costa Rican success story. The trails here are well maintained, the interpretive information is scientifically accurate (albeit only in Spanish), and an eco-marketed "canopy tour" has opened up on the lower slopes. Nature Air, a San Jose-based airline, makes regular flights to nearby Granada, and nature lovers weary of overcrowding at Costa Rican hotspots like Monteverde are increasingly looking to Nicaragua's abundant volcanoes and lakes as quieter (and less expensive) eco-alternatives.

That said, Nicaragua doesn't look set to steal Costa Rica's nature-travel crown any time soon. For starters, many would-be tourists still regard Nicaragua as a humid cesspool of chaos and revolution—despite the fact that the Sandinistas were voted out of power here in 1990. And, political reputation aside, this country is sorely lacking in tourist infrastructure: Of the seventy-three nature reserves in the country, less than ten maintain a permanent staff, and many of the parks aren't even marked with signs. Merely finding most of the reserves requires good Spanish skills, accurate maps, independent transportation, and patience. Moreover, according to Eric, the actual extent of Nicaragua's biodiversity is largely unknown. "The number of scientists in this country who even know taxonomy can be counted on one hand," he says. "Since Darwin's day, there's been almost no systematic scientific work here."

In a way, one could find comfort in the idea that Nicaragua's nature reserves are unknown and inaccessible. Perhaps, in their isolation, these habitats could thrive.

Another giggle. "It's just not that simple," Eric says. "Those areas might be isolated from tourists, but not from Nicaraguans."

I think back to the mermaids and turtle meat in Managua's market. "Is hunting the problem?"

"Hunting is a problem, but it's a limited one. I've studied animal bones that archaeologists have turned up at dig sites across the country, and I found that the pre-Columbian people here had pretty much the same tastes as Nicaraguans do now. They craved deer and armadillo meat, but didn't care much for sloth or howler monkeys. Animal populations have always adapted to hunting. The biggest environmental threat here is habitat destruction. It doesn't help that the birthrate in Central America is one of the highest in the world."

When I ply the biologist for the solution to this problem, our discussion gets complicated. On one level, he says, what my companions and I have been doing all morning—wandering in the cool air near the volcano summit, scanning the treetops for monkeys—could be a small part of the solution. As Costa Rica has proved, ecotourism creates alternative forms of income, promotes local efforts at wildlife protection, and instills national pride for unique habitats. The challenge, however (as Costa Rica is discovering), is balance: A tourist economy requires a steady influx of visitors, yet wildlife areas will suffer if you build too many roads and bus in too many animal lovers.

All this in addition to that fact that—as we have discovered this morning—pumas and howler monkeys don't always appear on cue.

From the breezy summit of the Mombacho Volcano, I see the tree-lined streets of Granada spidering back from the shores of

Lake Nicaragua below. Amid the terra cotta rooftops, I note a sudden pinprick of light over the white bulk of the Granada Cathedral. After five full beats, the faint noise of fireworks echoes up the volcano.

By sundown, I will be face-to-face with the mystery that has been following me since Antigua.

V. Virgin Territory
Granada, Nicaragua

It is three hours after sunset, and pandemonium has broken out in Granada's central square. Old women duck for shelter in the cathedral as staccato blasts shake the humid air and flaming debris rains down from the sky. Teenage boys dash through swirling clouds of blue smoke as errant rockets skitter across the cobblestones. Women scream and children scatter as Los Toros—men dressed in crude, wooden, firecracker-rigged bull costumes—sprint through the plaza like human fireballs, trailing embers. A glittery parade float, which minutes ago was the center of attention, now sits abandoned in the chaos—its cardboard angels still leaking dry-ice fog. As I dodge the explosions in the plaza, I run into our expedition videographer, who cheerfully reports that his wallet has been stolen and that he has temporarily lost hearing in one ear. To hear him talk, you'd think he'd just won the lottery—and, in travel terms, we have.

Indeed, there are moments on the road when you stumble across an unexpected spectacle that makes all the hassles and uncertainties of the journey worthwhile. Without a doubt, Nicaragua's Festival of the Virgin (referred to locally as La Purísima) is one of those moments. A weird Latin American synthesis of Advent, Halloween, and Christmas (with an explosive Fourth of July touch thrown in), La Purísima is a nine-day festival commemorating the Immaculate Conception. All over the country, Nicaraguans build altars to Mary in their homes, using palm leaves, flowers, and candles. Children go door-to-door singing hymns to the virgin, and are rewarded with candy and toys. Neighborhood committees design and build elaborate floats, which are paraded through city streets carrying an honorary "virgin" (usually a sixteen-year-old schoolgirl) and a statue of the Virgin Mary. Prayers are chanted, brass bands belt out Christmas tunes, and fireworks rock the streets well into the night.

In this particular corner of Nicaragua, the Purísima celebration revolves around a Virgin icon known as "La Conchita"— which traces its history back to the day when Granada was one of the most important cities in Latin America. Indeed, long before a canal was cut across the isthmus, freight from the Caribbean Sea was carried up the San Juan River to Lake Nicaragua, where it was offloaded in Granada before continuing overland to the Pacific Ocean. Thus, perched on a trade crossroads (overland commerce between Guatemala and Colombia also passed through the city), Granada grew rich—and all the new wealth attracted pirates. As local legend has it, freebooters plagued Granada until one December morning in 1721, when local women found a Franciscan statue of the Virgin Mary floating in the waters of Lake Nicaragua. Dubbed "La Conchita," the icon reputedly protected the city from marauders (as well as plagues and volcanic eruptions) for over a century.

Unfortunately for Granada, La Conchita had little effect on a runty, thirty-one-year-old Tennessean named William Walker, who sacked the city with a small band of American mercenaries in 1855. The following year, with the tacit endorsement of the United States, Walker declared himself president of all Nicaragua—and his first act in office was to legalize slavery and institute English as the national language. Eventually, when Walker made it clear that he intended to conquer the rest of Central America and annex it to the American South, Salvadoran and Guatemalan generals united with Nicaraguan insurgents to oust the megalomaniacal American from power. Walker's last act as he retreated from Nicaragua was to burn Granada to the ground. Housed in the city's cathedral, La Conchita is said to have miraculously escaped the flames, but—in spite of her patronage—Granada never recovered as a hub for transoceanic trade. By the early twentieth century, the Panama Canal had redrawn the strategic map of Central America, and Granada had reverted to a sleepy little colonial town on Lake Nicaragua.

Earlier this evening, the La Conchita Virgin was ceremoniously paraded through the streets before being removed from the float and carried into the towering halls of Granada Cathedral. The city's devout have now lined up inside the sanctuary to offer prayers and kiss the feet of the virgin. Outside the sanctuary, Granada's less-than-devout are turning the central square into something resembling a war zone. And, despite the ever-present danger of getting taken out by a stray bottle-rocket, I'm thrilled to be witness to it all.

The irony here is that I've been traveling amid La Purísima festivities since I arrived in Central America several days ago. In retrospect, I realize that the peculiar church fireworks in Antigua (as well as the virgin parade on the El Salvador-Honduras border) were a part of this same celebration. Had I not been obsessed by the presence of the other gringos in Antigua, I might have figured this out from the beginning. Instead, three countries later—surrounded by Granada locals (and a token handful of backpackers and expatriates)—I am seeing the festival for the first time. It occurs to me how profoundly my perception of foreign places is tied into the slippery notion of what I think the exotic is supposed to look like.

As I wander through the crowds of the square, I note the similarities between Granada and Antigua: colonial churches, pastel facades, courtyard gardens, cigar vendors, horse-drawn taxis, volcano-etched horizons, coffee-scented humidity. In the windows that face the plaza, I notice ads for pizza parlors, kayak tours, sports bars, yoga classes, and Internet cafés. I see an English-language flyer taped in the door of a real estate office, and it reads, "Having seen the miracle migrations in neighboring countries, we knew it was only a matter of time before Nicaragua was discovered as the last frontier."

I suppose I could draw connections and conclusions here, but La Purísima beckons.

Hearing another barrage of fireworks I look skyward, hoping to spot the bursts of color before they fade into smoke ribbons and drift their way back down.

∾

ENDNOTES

1. **Page 218, paragraph 3: ...*a global Land Rover expedition that aims to raise money for charity*:** Off the written page, I probably tell more stories about this Land Rover expedition than any other journey in my years as a travel writer. These stories have very little to do with the places I visited; they revolve around the eccentric and dysfunctional dynamic of my Land Rover expedition team. Imagine a hybrid of *The Office* and *Arrested Development* (combined with the physical setting of a 1970s National Geographic TV special) and you get a vague sense for what I experienced on the expedition.

I wrote "Virgin Trail" for *Slate*, and I later penned a few South America stories about the expedition for the *San Francisco Chronicle Magazine*. In each case I was tempted to write about the curious antics of my fellow adventurers (and nothing in my expedition-journalist arrangement would have prevented me from doing so), but ultimately I decided to focus these articles on the places and cultures we were visiting. I did this for standard journalistic reasons, but also because it was too difficult to weave the idiosyncrasies of my expedition teammates into a concise and coherent story.

This postscript is an attempt to make up for that omission.

I'll note upfront that these endnotes are neither even-handed nor comprehensive. They don't expand much on the story in question, nor do they instruct the reader in the ways of travel writing.

All they do is offer a brief glimpse into the bizarre little universe that can exist behind a seemingly straightforward travel story.

2. **Page 218, paragraph 3: ...*a blur of tollbooths, gas stations, road signs, stray cattle, cacti, and one-night cheap hotels*:** I became involved with the Land Rover expedition quite by chance: My cousin was acquainted with the trip leaders, and while I was visiting San Francisco on a book tour in early 2003 they asked if I was interested in joining their expedition as the team journalist. I only had a few weeks free that coming winter, but the journey sounded interesting, so I flew in from Asia in the fall for team training in the Bay Area. Since I'd spent much of the previous five years traveling alone and on the cheap, it was quite the shock to join a nine-person expedition team wherein everyone drove expensive vehicles and wore matching uniforms. On a certain level it was a classic opportunity to journey overland from California to Patagonia—but in practice it was far less glamorous than it sounded.

During team training I discovered that most of my companions had joined the team because of an interest in Land Rovers, and few of them had much independent travel experience. To all appearances, the expedition was less about travel than the vehicles in which we were traveling—and I soon learned that this was not at all unusual. When veterans of previous Land Rover expeditions were brought in to train us in off-road driving, for instance, I was surprised at how little they knew of the countries they'd visited. The only story these advisors shared about interacting with local people overseas involved giving an I.V. drip to a man they'd met *after they hit him with their vehicle* in Borneo.

Once the expedition began and we headed south through the Americas, I realized just how profoundly the lack of travel experience affected our team worldview. Although I'm sure everyone on the expedition team meant well, they took only a passing interest in the places we visited: Our standard routine was to drive all day, surf the Internet or watch DVDs at night, and occasionally get rip-roaring drunk. Kitted out in expensive vehicles that got twelve miles to the gallon, the expedition motored through the most fascinating corners of the developing world in perky, self-satisfied oblivion.

Despite my frequent embarrassment at the way the expedition operated, I developed a genuine affection for my travel companions. If at times I skewer them in these endnotes, it is purely out of love.

3. **Page 220, paragraph 2:** *...my expedition teammate Daisy Mae Scheisskopf:* In the interest of discretion, "Daisy Mae Scheisskopf" is a *Catch-22*-inspired pseudonym—as are all of the names in this story. To keep things lighthearted, I have also tweaked and embellished some of the descriptive details below, to the point that the following endnotes occasionally stray into fiction. Still, I'll assert that these are exaggerations of detail—not of individual personality-quirk—and that my companions were every bit as flamboyant as the altered details imply.

Daisy Mae was a charismatic Marine Corps reservist from Texas who was obsessed with physical fitness and junk food. About once a week during the expedition, she would walk up and loudly announce that she was headed off for, say, a seventy-mile run into the local mountains (or jungle, or desert, if applicable). When you asked her what she would do for food, she'd tell you she'd kill grizzly bears with her bare hands and eat their babies. When you asked her how she would communicate with the team if she got lost, she'd tell you she'd tear boulders from the mountainside and hurl them into the sky to spell out messages in Morse code. She would go on like this for much of the morning, until each team member (except Simon Flume; see below) had personally begged her not to go on a seventy-mile run in the mountains. Declaring us all a "bunch of pussies," Daisy Mae would then chug a six-pack of Red Bull, go for a three-mile run, do 200 jumping jacks, shotgun a beer, eat two bags of potato chips, watch an entire season of *The Simpsons* on her computer, and drive to the nearest town to buy souvenir refrigerator magnets.

Though Daisy Mae loved driving the Land Rovers, I suspect her truest motivation for joining the expedition was the free swag we got from our various corporate supporters. While the rest of us spent the pre-trip planning period finding sponsors that could provide tires, camping gear, clothing, computer accessories, and travel guidebooks,

Daisy hit the phones to solicit things like snowmobiles and bow-hunting equipment. If you had the temerity to ask her how the expedition stood to benefit from a donation of, say, one 40-horsepower bass-boat engine, Daisy Mae would yell, "Bite me!" and drop to the floor to crank out bare-knuckle pushups until you went away.

Kenny Cathcart, our expedition leader (see below), was in awe of Daisy Mae, and he gave her all kinds of official job titles, from "security consultant" to "team recon leader." Though she seemed to enjoy collecting job titles, the only job she actually did was write press releases (which, as it turned out, is exactly what she'd done in the Marine Corps). Daisy churned out dozens of press releases each week, announcing everything from border crossings to holiday greetings to flat tires. Nobody was sure where she sent the press releases, and whenever Kenny asked her if she'd followed up on them, she'd just walk away without answering. If by chance Kenny walked after her, Daisy would walk faster. If Kenny managed to keep up, Daisy would start singing, and if Kenny tried to talk over the singing, Daisy would sing louder. In this way, Kenny learned to stop asking about Daisy Mae's press releases.

4. **Page 225, paragraph 4: ...*I have little personal interest in this activity—but our documentary video crew*:** The documentary video crew was headed up by a guy named Simon Flume, who grew up in a wealthy suburb of San Francisco and had recently graduated from film school. Simon's defining trait was his apparent loathing for the expedition, and his simmering hatred for most everyone involved with it. One of his conditions for joining the journey was that he bring along his best friend, a happy-go-lucky surfer named Nately Sanchez—and he spent most of his time either filming Nately or sulking in his Land Rover.

Simon never made any suggestions for the expedition itinerary, nor did he offer much direction when he was filming us—though in the rare moments when he did speak with non-Nately team members, he would invariably mention that we never drove anyplace interesting, and that we were all dreadfully incompetent in front of the camera. To an extent I think Simon was frustrated by people's eccentricities as the expedition wore on—though I can't recall a time when he regarded his teammates with anything but contempt. Before the expedition started, for example, when I was passing out travel guidebooks, Simon just stared up at me like I was offering him a pile of horseshit. When I tried to explain how the guidebook might be useful in researching places and events for his documentary, he waved me off, muttering something about how sick he was of everyone telling him how to do his job.

I eventually learned to steer clear of him, though that proved hard to do on a vehicle expedition. I recall stumbling across Simon while gathering firewood one night in Chilean Patagonia. It had been days since I'd interacted with him, so I tried to make small talk by mentioning how bright the Southern Cross was that night. Simon didn't even look over at me. "I'm so fucking tired of people talking about the Southern Cross," he said.

Interestingly, Simon's documentary turned out quite well. Its main weakness was similar to that of my *Slate* story: Just as I'd focused on Central America at the expense of quirkier team details, Simon's focus on Nately meant the show never quite captured how profoundly weird everyone else was (Simon included).

5. **Page 227, paragraph 1:** *...joined by expedition leader Kenny Cathcart*: Kenny was an attention-deficit Silicon Valley engineer who'd made a gazillion dollars in the tech boom of the late 1990s and retired in his mid-thirties. Though he had an obsessive love of Land Rovers and a genuine interest in charity, it often felt as if his main motivation in organizing an international vehicle expedition was the hope he might get to appear on national television.

Kenny was ceaselessly optimistic in this regard, and during the planning stages of the journey, he would occasionally stride into the expedition office and announce something along the lines of, "We've been invited to appear on the *Oprah Winfrey Show!*" After an initial buzz of excitement, someone would ask him how we got invited on *Oprah*, and Kenny would reply that his mechanic's cousin had done time in Sing-Sing with Oprah's gardener's brother-in-law, and that he'd scored us studio tickets for just $50 each. After a long pause, someone would point out that (a) attending an *Oprah* taping is not the same as being on *Oprah*, and (b) studio audience tickets are supposed to be free. Undaunted, Kenny would insist that Oprah might well invite us onstage if we wear our matching expedition uniforms—and that we should pack immediately, since the taping would begin at eight o'clock the following morning. After another pause, Dirk Wintergreen (see below) would point out that Chicago was two thousand miles from San Francisco, and that we would have to drive at 125 miles per hour for the next sixteen hours if we wanted to get there on time. Kenny would then insist that our Land Rovers could hit 125 miles per hour if we removed the roof racks, and the rest of us would have to argue for another couple hours before we could convince him that an *Oprah* appearance was simply not going to happen.

Once we were on the road in Latin America, Kenny showed a keen aptitude for border paperwork, and a spotty track record on most everything else. At least once a week, for example, he would forget to show up for a team meeting he'd organized himself—and he rarely woke up in time to meet his own departure schedule. On the day we drove to Mexico City, Kenny kept radioing the lead vehicle to insist we were traveling in the wrong direction—and he went on like this for nearly an hour before he realized he'd mounted his GPS upside-down.

On the bright side, Kenny was an exceptionally laid-back expedition leader, and we quickly discovered you could get away with most any behavior on his watch so long as you didn't damage the Land Rovers or criticize the expedition. When Daisy Mae spent an hour shopping for potato chips during a fuel stop that should have lasted four minutes, Kenny cheerfully sat in his Land Rover and waited for her; when the film crew drank tequila until dawn and slept till noon on a day when we were scheduled to drive 500 miles, Kenny clapped them on the back and told them they were hilarious.

Unfortunately, Kenny considered it deeply insubordinate to suggest ways of improving the expedition—and this meant I was most always on his shit list. Before the expedition, for example, when I suggested he didn't need to pack a one-gallon bottle of Costco mouthwash, he angrily insisted it was vital to the success of the expedition. When in Mexico I pointed out that we'd missed the Oaxaca crafts market because he'd spent two hours that morning taking pictures of a donkey, Kenny earnestly argued that donkeys are far more interesting than cities. At first I thought Kenny was clinically insane, but over time I came to realize he took all corrective suggestions as an affront to his leadership. Apart from the El Salvador fireworks encounter, my only significant appearance in Simon's documentary video is a surreal scene wherein I argue with Kenny about how he should stick to his own departure schedule while Kenny keeps insisting that his departure schedule is of no importance whatsoever.

Eventually, when I stopped offering suggestions and started drinking tequila till dawn, Kenny thought I was the greatest.

6. **Page 227, paragraph 2:** *...paperwork indicates that Dirk Wintergreen*: Unlike most everyone else I was traveling with, Dirk could plan ahead, wake up on time, read maps, utilize an instruction manual, organize team supplies, program the GPS, perform advanced first aid, balance budgets, troubleshoot automotive problems, write compelling blog entries, do complicated math equations in his head, pick up local languages, and cook for large groups of people.

Dirk's Achillean weakness was that every shred of poise and competence would evaporate whenever the video crew was around. In day-to-day life Dirk was a genuinely funny guy, but with the cameras rolling he would mug like a goofball and spout lame jokes. He faithfully studied local history and culture as we traveled from country to country, but whenever the camera-lens panned in his direction he would instantly confuse event-dates and mispronounce place-names. Once, when we happened onto a crashed car on a Mexican back-road, Dirk quickly (and accurately) determined that there were no victims—but when the camera crew ambled over he sprinted off for the first-aid kit and commenced tugging at the wreck's crumpled doors, as if the Virgin of Guadalupe was trapped inside and screaming for help.

Dirk's secondary weakness was he'd spent the early years of his adulthood living in a fraternity house, and thus he assumed it was perfectly normal to, say, wrestle newfound acquaintances to the ground and fart on them. He also had a habit of calling all Spanish-speaking locals "Mexicans" well into Central and South America.

7. **Page 236, paragraph 3:** *...fade into smoke ribbons and drift their way back down*: Though my Central America dispatches for *Slate* went

on to win a Lowell Thomas Award (an annual competition for American travel writers), the response from my expedition teammates was not nearly so positive. When the series debuted online six weeks into the expedition, they all seemed irritated that the story was about Central America and not about them.

Well guys, here's hoping this postscript has made up for that.

PART FOUR

People You Don't Forget

ᴄ 15 ᴄ

My Beirut Hostage Crisis

FIRST met Mr. Ibrahim in the Hamra district of West Beirut. At the time, I'd been searching for a pub that had been recommended to me second-hand, and I wasn't having much luck. I was studying my street map on the corner of Hamra and Rue Jeanne d'Arc when Mr. Ibrahim approached me, looking innocuous in his blue jeans, plaid shirt, and neatly trimmed goatee.

"Are you lost?" he'd asked me.

"Not really," I said. "I know where I am; I just can't find the place I want to go."

"I am Mr. Ibrahim," he said, gesturing grandly at the buildings of Beirut, "and this is my city." He looked to be in his early thirties, but he spoke like he thought of himself as a wizened old patriarch. "Where do you wish to go?"

"Well, it's a pub that a friend of a friend told me about, but I'm not sure if you would know where—"

"THIS IS MY CITY!" Mr. Ibrahim bellowed happily.

"Oh, right. Well, I'm looking for a—"

"Where are you from?"

"I'm from America."

"AMERICA!" Mr. Ibrahim yelled, his voice echoing through

the street. He pulled out his wallet and produced a dollar bill. "What is this?" he asked me.

"Um, it's a dollar."

"And what does it say?"

"It says, 'one dollar.'"

"NO!" Ibrahim boomed. He held the dollar up in front of my face. "It says '...IN...GOD...WE...TRUST'!"

"In God we trust," I repeated, not sure what the point was.

"That's why your country is great: Because you trust in God." Mr. Ibrahim magnanimously handed me the dollar bill. "You keep this," he said.

"Well, that's nice," I said holding the dollar back out to him, "but I don't need a dollar as much as I need to find—"

"YOU KEEP THIS!" Mr. Ibrahim hollered cheerfully, snatching the dollar from my hand and stuffing it into my shirt-pocket. "Every day you must pray to God for sex, and he will give you more dollars than you ever dreamed of."

"Pray for sex?"

"Yes, pray for sexus!" He beamed proudly, as if he'd just changed my life.

"Oh," I said, catching his accent. "Pray for success."

"SEX-CESS!" Mr. Ibrahim yelled, suddenly looking impatient. "Where do you want to go? This is my city, and I can show you anywhere."

"Well, a friend's friend told me about a pub called the Hole in the Wall..." I began. As I spoke, Mr. Ibrahim pulled out his cellphone and began to furiously punch in numbers. "...I'm just not sure if I'm even in the right—"

I paused as Mr. Ibrahim began to shout Arabic into his cellphone. He stopped for a moment and looked over at me. "Where do we go?"

"The Hole in the Wall."

"THE HOLY DIWAH!" he yelled at his phone. He punched another button and put the phone back into his pocket.

"Who was that you were talking to?" I asked.

"It's O.K., we will take you there. It is my pleasure."

"Yes, but who's we? Who was on the phone?"

"That was Abdul."

"Is he a friend of yours?"

"OF COURSE NOT!" Mr. Ibrahim boomed, laughing. "Abdul is my bodyguard!"

Five minutes later, a massive young man drove up in a gold Mercedes E300. The door locks, I noticed, were tipped with rhinestones. At Mr. Ibrahim's grand insistence, I took the shotgun seat, and—for all practical purposes—I was his hostage for the next three days.

The hours before my first encounter with Mr. Ibrahim stand out in vivid contrast with what was to follow, if nothing else for their relative peace and coherence.

I'd arrived in Beirut the previous afternoon, but I hadn't set off to explore the city itself until that morning. Striking out from my hotel, I strolled past the impressively redeveloped central business district, the Roman ruins of Cardo Maximus, and the idyllic campus of the American University.

The most intriguing thing I discovered that morning, however, was the stark evidence of the civil war that had once raged through the city. An abundance of bullet-scarred buildings stood in bleak contrast to the ongoing renovations, particularly along the Green Line that once separated Muslim West Beirut from the Christian East.

I'm not sure why these war remnants proved so fascinating for me. In a way, I don't even like war tourism, as it reduces certain places—Sarajevo, Belfast, Phnom Penh—into dull, de facto thrill-destinations, relevant only for the visceral buzz of recent history. Here, travelers photograph soldiers and barbed wire with the same blind compulsion that inspires them to photograph the Eiffel Tower in Paris.

In Beirut, which has only been open to American travelers since 1997, I found it difficult not to be a war tourist. The battered buildings of the old buffer zone proved a grim reminder of not just the Muslim-Christian discord that symbolized the war, but the international factors that started and prolonged it: French favoritism, American geopolitics, Syrian opportunism, Israeli brutality, Iranian radicalism, Palestinian rage. In some places, bullet holes in buildings were so common that they seemed a part of the architecture—a congenital concrete defect that just happened to afflict that neighborhood.

By its very definition, war tourism is a fickle activity. Stunned as I was by the evidence of war—sobered as I was by its devastation—I left the Green Line that evening looking for a place to party.

Using directions copied from a month-old e-mail, I began to walk in search of the Hole in the Wall pub. Less than an hour later, I found myself in the ruthlessly gung-ho custody of a man who called himself Mr. Ibrahim.

When I first got into Mr. Ibrahim's Mercedes, I thought maybe he was one of those rich guys who runs with showgirls and compulsively hands out bottles of Hennessey and boxes of Cuban cigars. As it turned out, he was a celibate teetotaler who vetoed our trip to the Hole in the Wall the moment I mentioned that the place served alcohol.

We ended up driving to the Weekland, an upscale buffet restaurant that had been booked up that night for a Sunni Muslim wedding. Unfazed by our lack of a reservation, Mr. Ibrahim bullied his way into getting us a table overlooking the courtyard fountain. As Mr. Ibrahim instructed Abdul the Bodyguard to fill my plate with lamb, kibbeh, and hummus from the buffet, I took in my surroundings. Down in the courtyard, an immaculately dressed bride and groom cut their cake and posed for a photographer. Across the restaurant, groups of relatives watched this unfold live on a big-screen TV. At the tables around us, tuxedo-clad Sunni men smoked cigarettes and squinted at their cell-phones. The Sunni women chatted amongst themselves, looking refined and downright sexy in their designer dresses and silken headscarves.

The Lebanese food was fantastic, and Mr. Ibrahim was thrilled that I ate it with such enthusiasm.

"Do you like my food?" he asked me, grinning like a madman.

"It's great," I said between mouthfuls.

"How about my city? Did you see my city today?"

"Yes, I walked around some this afternoon."

"What did you see? Did you see the Hard Rock Cafe?"

"No, but I visited the American Univ—"

"That was a trick question: Beirut has TWO Hard Rock Cafes!"

"Wow. Well, I haven't seen either one of them yet, but—"

"TWO HARD ROCK CAFES!" Mr. Ibrahim hollered happily.

"Right, but today I went walking along the old Green Line and—"

"I'm sorry, where did you say?"

"The Green Line. I went walking—"

"THE GREEN LINE IS NOT FOR TOURISTS!" Mr. Ibrahim yelled, shaking his finger at me. For the first time since I'd met him, Mr. Ibrahim was not grinning, and this gave me a chill.

"What?" I stammered.

"The Green Line has only bullets and old buildings. Why do you want to see that?"

"Well, I thought it would be interesting to—"

"DO THESE PEOPLE LOOK LIKE TERRORISTS?" Mr. Ibrahim gestured angrily at the wedding guests, his voice echoing off the walls.

"Of course they don't look like terrorists."

"OF COURSE NOT! Look at them! This is like Europe. Does this not look like Europe?"

"Yes, it's very nice."

"Then why do you go to look at buildings with bullets?"

"I don't know. I guess it just seemed—"

"THERE WERE 180 LEBANESE ON THE *TITANIC*!"

I stared at Mr. Ibrahim, momentarily speechless. Since it looked like his grin might return, I decided to play along. "Really?" I said, completely oblivious to how this factoid could have any relevance. "One-hundred-eighty Lebanese were on the *Titanic*?"

"Of course! They were all rich men. Businessmen. Like Europeans. Do you think they would let terrorists onto the *Titanic*?"

"I'd imagine they wouldn't."

"Of course not! The Lebanese have always been rich people. Important people. Do you know how many Lebanese there are in Bill Clinton's cabinet?"

"I don't know."

"FOUR! There are four Lebanese in Bill Clinton's cabinet. I know this, and I am not even American! And the president of Ecuador. Do you know where he is from?"

"Well I'd imagine he's from Ecuador."

"HE IS FROM LEBANON!" Mr. Ibrahim roared, obviously having a good time again. "And when Boris Yeltsin needed surgery for his heart, where do you think his surgeon was from?"

"Lebanon?"

Mr. Ibrahim beamed at me. "I think you are a genius. The surgeon was from Lebanon. He could have had any surgeon in the world, but he wanted the best, and the best was from Lebanon."

Mr. Ibrahim went on like this nonstop for twenty minutes. Once he had exhausted the topic of Lebanese pride, he went on to rant about the evils of tobacco and alcohol, the virtues of America, the scourge of foreign laborers in Lebanon, and how Syrians smell like pigs and dogs. The whole time this was going on, Abdul the Bodyguard blissfully ignored his boss, shoveling down plate after plate of the buffet food. Whenever, Mr. Ibrahim would leave the table to get more food or bully the wait staff,

Abdul would smile mischievously and point out cute girls in the wedding party.

Later, when Abdul was driving us back to my hotel, Mr. Ibrahim laid out our plans for the next day. "Tomorrow, we will go to Byblos," he said. "I will show you Lebanon, and you can teach me English. How is my English? Is it bad?" Mr. Ibrahim grinned at me from the back seat, obviously fishing for a compliment.

I decided to shoot him straight. "Well, your vocabulary is good, but your—"

"I took many lessons from an institute near the American University."

"Yes, well your pronunciation could—"

"I SPEAK ENGLISH LIKE AN AMERICAN, YES?" Mr. Ibrahim shouted. He grinned, ebullient, in the back seat.

"Well, kind of. But your pronunciation could use some work."

Mr. Ibrahim looked concerned for just a fraction of a second. "You must teach me to make it better. We will be business partners: I will show you Lebanon, and you will teach me English."

"O.K., well the best way to improve your pronunciation is to—"

"I think you are the best teacher, so I will be the best tour guide!"

"…is to listen and practice. Listen and practice, and your pronunciation will get better."

"LISTEN AND PRACTICE!" Ibrahim yelled happily.

But of course he wasn't really listening.

Sightseeing with Mr. Ibrahim the next day turned out to be like some kind of bizarre religious penance or fraternity initiation. As we walked through the old Crusader castle and Roman ruins at Byblos, Mr. Ibrahim demanded that I peek into every single tomb, climb every single rampart, and photograph every single colonnade. "WHEN WILL YOU COME TO LEBANON AGAIN?" Mr. Ibrahim would shout every time I tried to complain about this. "THIS IS THE HISTORY OF MY COUNTRY!" As we walked from ruin to ruin, Mr. Ibrahim wanted to know my opinion about each detail of the experience, and he got grumpy whenever he thought I wasn't being enthusiastic enough.

Amidst this tireless touristic browbeating, I slowly learned things about my hell-bent host. Mr. Ibrahim, I discovered, was thirty-two years old, and the son of a Sunni Muslim father and a Maronite Christian mother. As a child, he and his family lived on the Green Line, and the young Ibrahim came to admire the American soldiers who patrolled his neighborhood. Sometimes, the soldiers would give him vacuum-wrapped MREs (Meals Ready to Eat)—dehydrated army food that tasted like chicken or beef or coffee. Ibrahim idolized the foreign soldiers, and—much to the consternation of his family—he hung a small American flag in his bedroom. Eventually, the Americans withdrew from Beirut, and Ibrahim's home was destroyed in the ongoing fighting. Salvaging what they could, he and his family moved in with relatives at the outskirts of town.

After the fighting subsided in 1990, Ibrahim went into business, first selling simple household items within Lebanon and later importing goods from overseas. He first became rich by introducing certain European detergents and soaps to the Lebanese market, and that's still his main line of business—even though he speaks of branching out into jewelry and women's shoes.

If there was one thing in which Mr. Ibrahim took the most pride, however, it was the fact that he had not so much as touched a girl in all of his thirty-two years. When we traveled back down the coast toward Jounieh, I quizzed him about this—and by the time we'd taken the cable car up to the Christian shrine at Harissa, Mr. Ibrahim was happily ranting about his utter lack of a sex life. As we climbed the winding staircase up to the huge Virgin Mary statue, Mr. Ibrahim told heroic stories of celibacy with the same lusty enthusiasm most men reserve for tales of sexual conquest.

"I've had thirty different women who wanted to do sex with me, AND I TOLD THEM ALL 'NO'!" Mr. Ibrahim bellowed, startling a group of Sri Lankan pilgrims as we spiraled our way up to the bronze Virgin. "Some of them rented hotel rooms for me! ONE OF THEM SHOWED ME HER PANTIES! But do you know what I told her?"

"What did you tell her?" I asked wearily.

"I TOLD HER 'NO'!"

Oddly enough, Mr. Ibrahim was equally preoccupied with people who were highly promiscuous. Abdul the Bodyguard, he repeatedly reminded me, had fathered two children out of wedlock. During his days as a competitive bodybuilder, Abdul had once had sex with five different women over the span of three days. Another associate of Mr. Ibrahim's, a sixty-year-old Saudi man, had supposedly been married to eighty different women, and had fathered forty-two kids. This man's latest wife was a seventeen-year-old Syrian girl, and on their wedding night he'd taken Viagra and had sex with her eighteen times. After that night, Mr. Ibrahim noted happily, the Saudi man was paralyzed for three days.

After Jounieh and Harissa, Mr. Ibrahim had Abdul drive us back to Beirut. At first I thought this meant I would finally get to go home, but instead we ended up cruising the city for two hours. Meticulously avoiding war-damaged areas, Mr. Ibrahim pointed out signs of the prosperous new Lebanon: shopping malls, cinemas, resort hotels, luxury high-rises. "LOOK!" he would holler obsessively. "THIS IS JUST LIKE EUROPE!"

Amidst all the shouting, Mr. Ibrahim seemed to be a man who very earnestly wanted to erase all the reputation and memories from a war that had ravaged his home. Somehow, through sheer force of personality, he hoped to turn Lebanon back into a booming, Westernized country. And I think he saw me as a kind of captive emissary who could bring the good news back to America.

Consequently, I shouldn't have been surprised when he arrived unannounced at my hotel the following morning, ranting about all the thousands of dollars in business he was passing up just so he could take me to the Chouf Mountains. Out of obligation, interpersonal cowardice, and lack of a ready excuse, I consented.

About five minutes out of Beirut, however, the presence of a Syrian military checkpoint got Mr. Ibrahim off onto an anti-Syria diatribe that hadn't let up by the time we'd entered the mountains. The solution to the Syrian military and political presence in Lebanon, he'd reasoned, was to have the United States bomb the bejesus out of Damascus.

After he'd demanded for the twenty-third time that I write a letter to President Clinton in support of this diplomatic strategy, I pointed out that—technically—he could go to the White House website and write that letter himself. Less than one hour later, our plans to visit Beit Ed-Dine Palace had summarily been scrapped, and I found myself taking dictation from Mr. Ibrahim in a West Beirut internet café.

"Do you have an e-mail reply address?" I'd asked him. "It's required if you're going to send a message to the White House."

"OF COURSE!" he boomed. "I use e-mail for business all the time."

"O.K., then what is it?"

"What is what?"

"Your e-mail address."

Mr. Ibrahim grinned and fluttered his eyelids. "I have many e-mail addresses. Ten, maybe twenty e-mail addresses."

"Just give me one."

Mr. Ibrahim's grin wavered a bit. "I don't remember."

"O.K.," I said diplomatically, "We'll use mine."

By the time we were ready to type the body of the message, Mr. Ibrahim was visibly nervous. "What do I say?" he demanded testily.

"It's your message," I replied. "Tell him what's on your mind."

"Dear President Clinton," he dictated. "It is my great pleasure and honor to write to you today, and if you ever come to Lebanon, I will be your tour guide and I will show you that we are a rich and beautiful country, and that we are not terrorists like you think we are." Mr. Ibrahim paused for a moment. "Is that good?"

"Sure," I said, keying in his greeting. "It's your message, so say what you want."

Mr. Ibrahim grinned thoughtfully and stroked his goatee. "Why do you support Israel when you ignore Lebanon?" he said. "Are we not as good at business as them? Are we not more fashionable? Do we not love America also? SO WHY DO YOU GIVE THEM A BILLION DOLLARS WHILE WE ARE BEING INVADED BY SYRIANS, WHO HATE AMERICA AND SMELL LIKE DOGS?"

"Whoa, slow down," I said, but Mr. Ibrahim had already gone manic.

"WHEN SADDAM HUSSEIN INVADED KUWAIT, YOU BOMBED BAGHDAD!" he yelled. "SO WHY NOT BOMB DAMASCUS NOW?"

I typed as fast as I could, wincing at Mr. Ibrahim's reckless bravado. In a way, there was a certain sadness to what he was saying. Though created under circumstances similar to Israel, the nation of Lebanon has always been too small, disorganized and divided to avoid getting bullied by its neighbors.

"LOOK AT US!" Mr. Ibrahim hollered. "LOOK AT THE PEOPLE IN THIS ROOM! WE ARE LIKE AMERICANS! WE ARE LIKE EUROPEANS! WE NEED BUSINESS AND TOURISTS IN LEBANON! WE NEED THE POPE AND MICHAEL JACKSON TO COME AND SEE OUR FACES—"

"I think that's enough for now," I interjected.

"I AM NOT FINISHED!" he yelled indignantly.

"The president is a busy man," I said sagely. "It's best to keep it short."

"Yes, you are right," Mr. Ibrahim said, looking a bit dazed. "Do you think he will write back?"

The following day, Mr. Ibrahim had to work, so I visited the village of Qana, near the Israeli-occupied zone in south Lebanon.

Of course, it wasn't that simple. The night before, Mr. Ibrahim had asked me what I was going to do in his absence, and when I told him Qana, he'd nearly lost it.

"YOU SHOULD NOT GO TO QANA!" he'd yelled. "THERE IS NOTHING TO SEE THERE!"

By "nothing to see," Mr. Ibrahim meant that the place was a reminder of war. In Qana, the main tourist attraction is a Syrian-built memorial to the 200 civilians who died when Israel shelled the town in 1996. However, since Qana is also one of the possible locations of Cana—where Jesus was said to have turned water into wine at a wedding festival—I was able to use this seemingly pious pretext to convince Mr. Ibrahim of my good intentions.

Insisting that I should also visit Sidon during my southbound trek, Mr. Ibrahim gave me $20 to cover transportation and admission fees. Each time I tried to refuse the $20, Mr. Ibrahim accused me of not really wanting to go to Sidon. This accusation, of course, was completely valid. I finally convinced Mr. Ibrahim to keep the money, but he made me promise to call him with a full report as soon as I got home that evening.

By the time I'd taken two buses and a share-taxi down to Qana, the comparative serenity of traveling without Mr. Ibrahim had already made the trip worthwhile. Once in the town, I was more impressed by the sight of daily life in southern Lebanon than I was with the clumsy Syrian memorial to Israeli aggression. South Lebanon is a predominately Shi'ite Muslim area, and huge pictures of the Ayatollah Khomeini hung on buildings and along roadsides. Some neighborhoods flew the yellow flag of Hezbollah, while others displayed the green Amal flag. Despite the violent fanaticism associated with such symbols, however, the town itself went about its business at a casual, friendly pace.

Resolving to overcome my instinctive fear of all the Hezbollah iconography in the area, I hiked out into the countryside beyond the town. After about fifteen minutes of walking along a dusty road, I came to a U.N. roadblock manned by a couple of Fijian peacekeepers who introduced themselves as Vasco and Reef. The Fijians were stationed there as part of the U.N. Interim Force in Lebanon (UNIFIL), a mission which—despite its temporary-sounding name—had been in operation since the first Israeli invasion twenty-two years before.

After I chatted with the blue-bereted soldiers for a couple minutes, a loud explosion rang out, and a plume of smoke rose up from a hill on the horizon.

"Israelis?" I asked the Fijians nervously.

"No," Vasco laughed. "A rock quarry."

"How can you tell the difference?"

"Well, the Israelis usually call on the radio before they start shelling us."

Vasco encouraged me to hang out at the checkpoint for a while, and Reef went up to the watchtower to prepare some tea. Both Fijians seemed desperate to talk to someone who was fluent in English, and I was certainly thrilled to speak with someone who let me finish my sentences. When Reef returned with cups of milky tea and toast, the three of us chatted about politics, rugby and whether or not Jesus actually came to Qana. Reef was convinced that Jesus had turned the water into wine here in Lebanon; Vasco insisted that the miracle had happened at Kafr Kanna in Israel.

After a while, a couple of local teenagers walked up to greet the Fijians, and Vasco encouraged them to give me a tour of the area. Mahmoud, the older one, jogged off down the road and came back ten minutes later in his father's car.

"Mahmoud," I said as I got into the car. "Is that a Muslim name?"

"Yes, I am Sunni. But many of my friends are Christians. Maybe you've heard bad things about Lebanon, but we all get along in my town."

"What about Shi'ites, do you get along with them?"

"Yes, the Shi'ites are good people. But they don't like sin, so sometimes they stay to themselves."

"So does that mean you're a sinner?"

"Yes," Mahmoud said seriously. "I like to sin very much."

After showing me some Roman-era Christian caves on the far side of Qana, Mahmoud took me to an archaeological dig that contained a couple of ancient stone wine vats. A third stone urn sat, broken, at the edge of the pit.

"Were these used to turn water into wine?" I asked Mahmoud.

"I don't know," he said, "but I know they are very old. I feel bad for breaking that one." He pointed to the fractured urn at the edge of the pit.

"That urn is enormous," I laughed. "How could you have possibly broken it?"

"Well, my father owns a construction company, and I broke it with his bulldozer when we were building a street a couple weeks ago. I thought it was a rock until we took it out of the ground."

I looked again at the broken urn. Archaeologists go for years without finding anything that big or old, and here Mahmoud had discovered it during his after-school job.

That evening, I returned to Beirut in good spirits. Buoyed by my successful foray into the south of Lebanon, I went out for an evening stroll through East Beirut and ended up stumbling upon (though not entirely by accident) none other than the Hole in the Wall pub. There, I drank a couple of beers and listened to music until just short of ten o'clock.

When I arrived back at my hotel, Mr. Ibrahim and Abdul the Bodyguard were in the lobby waiting for me. I noticed that Mr. Ibrahim was cradling an enormous plastic tub full of pudding.

"I TOLD YOU TO CALL ME!" he bellowed as soon as he caught sight of me.

"Yes, well I was just going to call—"

"WHERE HAVE YOU BEEN?"

"Well, I started out by going to Qana—"

"Qana? WHAT ABOUT SIDON?"

At this point, I was too flustered to do anything but lie out-right. "Sidon," I said. "Well, wow! It was great."

"What did you see there?"

"The ruins. I visited the ruins." This was a stab in the dark; for all I knew, the big attraction in Sidon was a Tijuana-style donkey show.

"THE RUINS!" Mr. Ibrahim yelled. I wasn't sure what this meant until he grinned and held up the tub of pudding. "My sister made you some sweets!" he said. "We can eat it together."

Relieved at being off the hook, I plopped down next to Mr. Ibrahim and started to spoon up the chocolate dessert. After a couple of bites, Mr. Ibrahim tugged the bowl away from me.

"You smell like Al Cole," he said. One couch over, Abdul diplomatically picked up a magazine and pretended to read it.

"Al Cole?"

"Did you drink al-coal tonight?"

It dawned on me what he meant. "Just a couple of beers," I said.

"IN SIDON?" Mr. Ibrahim yelled.

"Um, no," I mumbled. "I had them here in Beirut."

"You didn't call me because...YOU...WERE...DRINKING...AL-COAL?" Mr. Ibrahim glowered at me. Obviously, this was a major betrayal in his moral world.

"Like I said, I was going to—"

"I HAVE BEEN WAITING HERE FOR TWO HOURS!"

"Well you didn't need to come all the way—"

Mr. Ibrahim shoved the tub of pudding over at me. "You eat this," he said quietly. "I'm not hungry anymore."

"I'm sorry, it's just—"

"EAT IT!"

"Doesn't Abdul want—"

"ABDUL IS NOT HUNGRY EITHER!"

I stared down at the pudding. The plastic tub was so big that I could have used it to smuggle a bowling ball through customs at the airport. There was no way I could eat all of it by myself, and I secretly suspected that he'd had his sister prepare it with the sole intention of punishing me for not calling him within the proper time-frame.

Gripping my spoon, I made my best effort. As I choked down the chocolate dessert, it occurred to me that my weird friendship with Mr. Ibrahim betrayed my own credulous, middle-class sense of judgment. Had someone as ruthless and narrow as Mr. Ibrahim been a penniless street-sweeper with a donkey-cart and a chicken instead of a Mercedes and a bodyguard, I doubt I'd have accepted his efforts to help me in the first place—and I certainly wouldn't have let him know where I was staying. Seeing Lebanon by Mercedes and eating gourmet meals had made me rationalize Mr. Ibrahim's idiosyncrasies. Somehow, I suspect that both his social life and his moral self-concept depended on people like me.

In the end, Mr. Ibrahim never did force me to eat all of the pudding. After verifying to his satisfaction that I was truly suffering from the effort, he melodramatically forgave me for not calling him, then went home for the night.

If he had any intention of surprising me with a sightseeing trek the next day, I didn't wait around to find out. Immediately after the pudding incident, I wrote Mr. Ibrahim a note. It read: "I'm sorry to have to tell you this way, but I had to go to Syria on short notice. Thank you for your kindness and hospitality. I will remember Lebanon well."

The following morning, I left the note with the manager of my hotel and took the first bus up the coast to Tripoli. For the first hour of the bus ride, I had trouble relaxing: I kept expecting the old lady in the seat next to me to pull off a polyurethane face-mask and reveal herself, grinning madly, as Mr. Ibrahim.

As for the note I left with the hotel manager, it wasn't completely dishonest: I will remember indeed Lebanon well.

It's just that too much of any good thing has a way of wearing a man down.

∾

ENDNOTES

1. **Page 255, paragraph 1:** ONE OF THEM SHOWED ME HER PANTIES!: Since Mr. Ibrahim had such a hyperbolic personality, this story pretty much wrote itself. The most difficult part in putting it down on paper was showing the quirkier details of Mr. Ibrahim's personality without making it sound like I'd invented those details just to be funny.

This is one of the more curious aspects of writing nonfiction: At times you have encounters that are so over-the-top you have to tone them down a bit to make them seem more believable. On one hand eliminating tangential facts is often necessary to keep a story focused (and for this reason I didn't mention the American girl from my hotel who'd joined us on the day-trip to Byblos)—but sometimes facts must be left out for simple reasons of credibility. This is always a judgment call during the writing process, and it can be interesting to retrospectively revisit the details that might have made it into the story.

For example, one of Mr. Ibrahim's favorite pop songs at the time was "Sex Bomb" by Tom Jones. Ibrahim wanted to sing along to the song when he was riding in his car, so he asked me to transcribe the lyrics for him. As it turned out, Mr. Ibrahim thought the song was called "Six Bombs"—and when he realized the lyrics were about sex he refused to let Abdul play it anymore.

Ibrahim's mix-up was hilarious, but it was also mystifying. Since he hated war as fervently as he protected his virginity, why was "Six Bombs" more palatable to him than "Sex Bomb"? I had no idea, so—not wanting to make Mr. Ibrahim seem too cartoon-like—I left the "Six Bombs" detail in my notebook.

From that notebook, here are five other completely factual details that were too befuddling to try to mention in the story:

Not long after Mr. Ibrahim had established that I was American, he mentioned that the Lebanese people had idolized John Candy, and the entire nation had been heartbroken when he died. I pointed out that, as far as I knew, John Candy was Canadian. This revelation came as a shock to Ibrahim, and we must have gone back and forth for five minutes before I noted his accent and realized he was talking about John Kennedy.

When it came to television, Mr. Ibrahim told me he enjoyed watching *Xena: Warrior Princess*, *Hercules: The Legendary Journeys*, and any show "where the Indians are better than the cowboys." When I mentioned I knew some Native Americans in my hometown, Ibrahim said that he wanted to come to Kansas and ride horses with them. When I pointed out that the Indians I knew didn't ride horses, Ibrahim insisted that they must not have been real Indians, because real Indians ride horses.

The name of Mr. Ibrahim's company was "Stuckhome Trading." At first I thought "Stuckhome" was a clunky transliteration of some Arabic word, but as it turned out his company was named after the capital of Sweden. When I asked him why he'd spelled "Stockholm" in such a peculiar manner, he admitted that he hadn't checked the spelling before he registered his company, and he didn't want to pay the $1,000 to re-register the name.

While I mention in the story that Mr. Ibrahim objected to "the scourge of foreign laborers in Lebanon," he later let it slip to me that most of his employees were Nigerians, Ghanaians, or Syrians.

During our visit to the Christian shrine at Harissa, Mr. Ibrahim declared that the first Christians had lived in Lebanon two thousand six hundred years ago. When I tried to explain how this put them a good six hundred years before Christ, Ibrahim heartily agreed with me. I never did divine his line of reasoning, but I suspect he liked to believe that Lebanese Christians had been way ahead of the curve; that Jesus had simply been a Jewish straggler at what was essentially a Lebanese party.

༈ 16 ༈

Up Cambodia without a Phrasebook

I AM fifteen minutes into my hike down the muddy little stream when a tree carving captures my attention. Sticky with sap and arcing brown across the bark, it seems to have been made recently.

I drop to my haunches and run my fingers over the design. After three days of living in the Indochinese outback without electricity or running water, I feel like my senses have been sharpened to the details of the landscape. I take a step back for perspective, and my mind suddenly goes blank.

The carving is a crude depiction of a skull and crossbones.

Were I any place else in the world, I might be able to write off the skull and crossbones as a morbid adolescent prank. Unfortunately, since I am in northwestern Cambodia, the ghoulish symbol can mean only one thing: land mines. Suddenly convinced that everything in my immediate vicinity is about to erupt into a fury of fire and shrapnel, I freeze.

My brain slowly starts to track again, but I can't pinpoint a plan of action. If this were a tornado, I'd lie face down in a low-lying area. Were this an earthquake, I'd run to an open space away from trees and buildings. Were this a hurricane, I'd pack up my worldly possessions and drive to South Dakota. But since I am in a manmade disaster zone, all I can think to do is nothing.

My thoughts drift to a random quote from a United Nations official a few years back, who was expressing his frustration in trying to clear the Cambodian countryside of hundreds of thousands of unmarked and unmapped mines. "Cambodia's mines will be cleared," he'd quipped fatalistically, "by people walking on them."

As gingerly as possible, I lower myself to the ground, resolved to sit here until I can formulate a course of action that won't result in blowing myself up.

For the past decade, northwestern Cambodia has been home primarily to subsistence farmers, U.N. de-mining experts and holdout factions of the genocidal Khmer Rouge army. Except for travelers headed overland from the Thai border to the monuments of Angkor Wat, nobody ever visits this part of the country.

If someone were to walk up right now and ask me why I'm here, who I'm staying with, and how I got to this corner of the Cambodian boondocks, I could tell them truthfully that I do not exactly know.

Technically, I was invited to come here by Boon, a friendly young Cambodian who shared a train seat with me from Bangkok to the border three days ago. Our third seatmate, a Thai guy who called himself Jay, knew enough English for the three of us to exchange a few pleasantries along the way. Our conversation never amounted to much, but as we got off the train at the Thai border town of Aranyaprathet, Boon asked through Jay if I was interested in staying with him and his family once we got to Cambodia. Eager to explore a part of Cambodia that had been a notorious Khmer Rouge stronghold only six months ago, I accepted.

Jay parted ways with us at the train station, and that was the last time I had any real clue as to what was going on.

Perhaps if I hadn't forgotten my Southeast Asian phrasebook in Bangkok, I would have a better idea of what was happening. Unfortunately, due to a moment of hurried absent-mindedness shortly before my departure to Aranyaprathet, I left my phrasebook languishing on top of a toilet-paper dispenser in the Bangkok train station. Thus, my communication with Boon has been limited to a few words of Lao (which has many phrases in common with Thai, Boon's second language) that I still remember from a recent journey down the Laotian Mekong.

My *Lonely Planet: Southeast Asia* guide also provides a handful of Khmer words; unfortunately, phrases such as "I want a room with a bathtub" and "I'm allergic to penicillin" only go so far when your hosts live in a one-room house without running water.

As a result, trying to understand the events of the last three days has been like trying to appreciate a Bengali sitcom: I can figure out the basics of what's going on, but most everything else is lost in a haze of unfamiliar context and language. In a way, this is kind of nice, since I have no social expectations here. Whereas in an American home I would feel obliged to maintain a certain level of conversation and decorum, here I can wander off and flop into a hammock at any given moment, and my hosts will just laugh and go back to whatever it was they were doing. At times I feel more like a shipwrecked sailor than a personal guest.

The majority of my stay here in Cambodia has been at Boon's mother's house, in a country village called Opasat. Boon's wife and baby daughter also live here, as well as a half-dozen other people of varying age, whose relation to Boon I have not yet figured out.

My first morning in Opasat, Boon took me around and introduced me to almost everyone in his neighborhood. I don't remember a single name or nuance from the experience—but everyone remembers me because I kept banging my head on the bottom of people's houses, which stand on stilts about six feet off the ground. Now I can't walk from Boon's house to the town center without someone seizing me by the arm and dragging me over to show some new relative how I'm tall enough to brain myself on their bungalow.

After five minutes of paranoid inaction in front of the skull and crossbones tree, I hear the sounds of children's voices coming my way. I look up to see a half-dozen little sun-browned village kids strung out along the stream bank. Suddenly concerned for their safety, I leap to my feet and try to wave them off.

Unfortunately, my gesticulations only make the kids break into a dead sprint in my direction. I realize that the kids think I am playing a game I invented yesterday, called "Karate Man."

The rules behind Karate Man are simple: I stand in one spot looking scary, and as many kids as possible run up and try to tackle me. If the kids can't budge me after a few seconds, I begin to peel them off my legs and toss them aside, bellowing (in my best cartoon villain voice) "I am Karate Man! Nobody can stop Karate Man!" Caught up in the exaggerated silliness of the game, the kids tumble and backpedal their way twenty or so feet across the dirt when I throw them off. Then they come back for more. It's a fun way to pass the time, and it's much less awkward than trying to talk to the adults.

At this moment, however, I'm in no mood to be surrounded by a field of exploding Cambodian children. "No!" I yell desperately. "No Karate Man!"

"Kanati-maan!" the kids shriek back, never breaking stride.

As the kids charge me, I clutch them to me one by one, and we sink to the ground in a heap. Convinced that they have just vanquished Karate Man, the children break into a cheer.

I stand them up, dust them off, then make them march me back the way they came. Thinking this is part of the game, the kids take the task very seriously. We walk in single file, the kids doing their best to mimic my sober demeanor. Nobody blows up. By the time the buildings of the village are in view, I begin to relax again.

Once I arrive back at Boon's house, one of the kids is immediately dispatched for a sarong. This, I have learned, is the signal that it's time for me to take a bath. I've already bathed once today, but my hosts seem to think it's time for me to bathe again. This could have something to do with the fact that I'm sweaty and dusty from the hike, but I suspect that my hosts just want an excuse to watch me take my clothes off.

Since there is no running water at Boon's house, all the bathing and washing is done next to a small pond out back. The first time I was hustled out to take a bath, I didn't realize that it would be such a social undertaking. By the time I'd stripped down to my shorts, a crowd of about ten people had gathered to watch me. Since I'd never paid much attention to how country folks bathe in this part of the world, I wasn't quite sure what to do next. I figured it would be a bad idea to strip completely naked, so I waded into the pond in my shorts. A gleeful roar went up from the peanut gallery, and a couple of kids ran down to pull me out of the murky water.

In the time since then, I have learned that I am supposed to wrap a sarong around my waist for modesty, and bring buckets of water up from the pond to bathe. Since I have very white skin, my Cambodian friends watch this ritual with great curiosity. My most enthusiastic fan is a wrinkled old neighbor woman who is given to poking and prodding me with a sense of primatological fascination that would rival Jane Goodall. When Boon took me over to visit her house two mornings ago, she sat me down on her porch, yanked off my sandals, and pulled on my toes and stroked my legs for about five minutes. At first I thought she was some sort of massage therapist, until she showed up at my bath this morning and started pulling at the hair on my nipples.

This afternoon, Old Lady Goodall manages to outdo herself. As I am toweling off under a tree, she strides up and starts to run her fingers over my chest and shoulders, like I'm some sort of sacred statue from Angkor Wat. If this woman were forty years younger and had a few more teeth, it might be a rather erotic experience; instead, it's just kind of strange. Then, without warning, Madame Goodall leans in and licks the soft white flesh above my hipbone. Comically, furrowing her brow, she turns and makes a wisecrack to Boon's mother, who erupts into laughter.

I can only assume this means I'm not quite as tasty as she'd expected.

By nightfall, I know something is amiss. Usually, my hosts have prepared and served dinner by early evening, and we have cleaned up and are playing with the baby (the primary form of nighttime entertainment, since there are no electric lights) by dark. But this evening there is no mention of dinner, and a group of a dozen young men from the neighborhood have gathered at Boon's place. They gesture at me and laugh, talking in loud voices. I laugh along with them, but as usual I have no idea what's going on. For all I know they're discussing different ways to marinate my liver.

About an hour after sundown, Boon indicates that it's time to go. I get up to leave, but I can't find my sandals. After a bit of sign language, a search party is formed. Since my size-13 sandals are about twice as big as any other footwear in the village, it doesn't take long to track them down. One of the neighbors, a white-haired old man who Boon introduces as Mr. Cham, has been flopping around in my Tevas. Mr. Cham looks to be about sixty, and he's wearing a black Bon Jovi t-shirt. When Boon tells him that he has to give me my sandals back, Mr. Cham looks as if he might burst into tears.

Finally ready, I hike to the village *wat* with Boon and the other young men. The *wat* is filled with revelers, and has all the trappings of an American country fair. Dunk tanks and dart-tosses are set up all along the perimeter, and concession tables selling cola, beer, noodle soup and fresh fruit dot the courtyard. A fenced-in dancing ring has been constructed around the tallest tree in the *wat*, and a sound system blasts traditional and disco dance tunes.

Boon nods at me and sweeps his hand at the courtyard. "Chaul Chnam," he says. "Khmer Songkhran."

Songkhran is the Thai New Year celebration, so I gather that Chaul Chnam marks the Khmer New Year. As with Thai kids at Songkhran, Cambodian children run roughshod over the Chaul Chnam celebration, throwing buckets of water and pasting each others' faces with white chalk powder.

I suspect that Boon's young male friends have brought me to Chaul Chnam so they can use me to meet girls, but I am surrounded by little kids before we have a chance to do any tomcatting. Apparently, my reputation as Karate Man has spread, and now I can't walk anywhere without a gaggle of Cambodian kids trying to tackle me. Not up for a night of getting mobbed like a rock star (or, more accurately, a cast member of "Sesame Street Live"), I manage to neutralize the children by shaking hands with them in the manner of a charismatic politician. Since I can only shake hands with one kid at a time, this slows things down a bit.

Boon ultimately rescues me by taking me to a folding table, where he introduces me to a fierce-looking man called Mr. Song. Mr. Song has opted not to wear a shirt to the Chaul Chnam festivities; his chest is laced with indigo tattoos and his arms are roped with taut muscles. He looks to be in his forties, which inevitably means that he has seen some guerrilla combat over the years. Given our location, I wouldn't be at all surprised if he served his time in Khmer Rouge ranks. When I buy the first round of Tiger lager, Mr. Song is my buddy for the rest of the evening.

Although I am tempted to jump into the dance ring and take a shot at doing the graceful Khmer *aspara*, I end up holding court at the table for the next three hours. When Boon leaves to dance with his wife, Mr. Song becomes master of ceremonies, introducing me to each person who walks by the table. Everyone I meet tries to make a sincere personal impression, but it's impossible to know what anyone is trying to communicate. One man pulls out a faded color photograph of a middle-aged Cambodian couple decked out in 1980s American casual-wear. The back of the photo reads: "Apple Valley, California." Another man spends twenty minutes trying to teach me how to count to ten in Khmer. Each time I attempt to show off my new linguistic skills, I can't get past five before everyone is doubled-over laughing at my pronunciation.

It comes as a kind of relief when the generator suddenly breaks down, cutting off the music in mid-beat and leaving the *wat* dark.

On the way back to the neighborhood, Boon pantomimes that Mr. Song wants me to sleep with his family. Once we arrive at his house, Mr. Song lights some oil lamps, drags out an automobile battery and hooks it up to a Sony boom box. After a few minutes of tuning, we listen to a faint Muzak rendering of "El Condor Pasa" on a Thai radio station. This quickly bores Mr. Song, and he walks over to the corner and puts the radio away.

He returns carrying a pair of AK-47 assault rifles and four banana clips of ammunition. Motioning me over, he sits on the floor and begins to show me how the guns work. Three of the clips, he indicates, have a thirty-round capacity, and the fourth holds forty bullets. In what I assume is a gesture of hospitality, Mr. Song jams the forty-round clip into one of the rifles and hands it to me. I get a quick lesson on how to prime the first round, and how to switch the rifle to full automatic fire.

Mr. Song doesn't appear to realize that this is a doomed enterprise. Unless we are attacked tonight by Martians, or intruders who wear crisp white t-shirts that read SHOOT ME, I won't have the slightest idea how to distinguish a bandit from a neighbor. For good measure—and not wanting to sully his macho mood—I hand Mr. Song my camera, and indicate that I want him to take a picture of me with the AK-47. From the way he holds my camera, I can only conclude that this is the first photo he's ever taken.

When I finally fall asleep, I dream that I am renting videos from a convenience store in outer space.

Not wanting to overstay my welcome, and largely exhausted by my local-celebrity status, I tell Boon of my intention to leave Opasat the following morning. Boon indicates that he understands, and sends for a motorcycle taxi to take me to the overland-truck depot in the city of Sisophon.

To show my appreciation for all the hospitality, I give Boon's mother a $20 bill—figuring that she will know how to split it up among deserving parties. As soon as the money leaves my hand, I see Mr. Cham run off toward his house. When he returns, he is carrying a travel bag, and he's traded his Bon Jovi shirt for a purple polo top and a brown porkpie hat. Boon confers with him for a moment, then apologetically indicates that Mr. Cham wants me to take him from Sisophon to Angkor Wat. Not wanting to seem ungrateful, I shrug my consent.

When the motorcycle taxi arrives, I make my rounds and say my goodbyes. I save Boon for last. "Thanks, Boon," I say in English. "I wish I could tell you how much I appreciate all this." He can't understand me, of course, but he returns my pleasantry by bringing his hands together in a traditional Khmer bow. I give him a hug, knowing that I will probably never know why he invited me to come and see his family, or even what he does for a living.

I get onto the motorcycle between the driver and the eccentric Mr. Cham, and we take off in a flourish of dust. Opasat disappears behind me in a matter of minutes, and my thoughts move on to the sundry details of finding an overland truck and fulfilling my tourist agenda at Angkor Wat.

I am still not exactly sure what has just happened to me, but I know that I rather enjoyed it.

This will not stop me, however, from buying a new phrase-book the moment I see one for sale.

∾

ENDNOTES

1. **Page 267, paragraph 6:** *…I was invited to come here by Boon, a friendly young Cambodian*: This story came about as a happy accident, and it didn't occur to me to write about it until after it was over. I was penning biweekly travel dispatches for *Salon* at the time, and I'd gone into Cambodia with a number of story ideas for my column—most of which revolved around the nation recovering from years of civil war and genocide. While I was in Opasat, I kept wondering how life in the village might color a more serious story about Cambodia; later, I came to realize that my Opasat experiences were the story itself.

In this way, I believe travel reportage offers something standard journalism doesn't: unexpected glimpses into the human texture of a place, regardless of whether or not the place is "newsworthy."

2. **Page 269, paragraph 8:** *…kids doing their best to mimic my sober demeanor. Nobody blows up*: When I first arrived in the village, I was fascinated by the land-mine education posters that hung in most every house. Distributed by international aid organizations, these posters featured, say, a stern tiger in blue suspenders and plaid pants warning a naughty little rabbit not to play with land mines.

Other posters were not so whimsical. One had no words, and just three illustrations: the first frame showed a kid playfully kicking at a small metal object; the second frame showed the kid's leg getting vaporized in a blast of fire and blood; the third frame showed the kid sitting in a wheelchair, looking depressed. No doubt the kids I met in the village had lived their entire young lives in a keen state of wariness.

3. **Page 271, paragraph 3:** *…a dozen young men from the neighborhood have gathered at Boon's place*: I'd actually met these young men earlier in the day, but I didn't include the first encounter for two reasons: (1) not every interesting experience fits into the rhythm of a given story, and (2) this particular experience was so deeply humiliating it was pretty easy to leave out.

Not long after I met these young men, they'd taken me to a volleyball court just outside the village and asked me if I wanted to play a game. Or at least that's what I thought they said, so I gave them a thumbs-up. A game was already in progress, so they pulled a player off one team and put me in his place. Since I was a head taller than everyone else on the court, a big hoot went up from the spectators, and play resumed.

The game that ensued was certainly the most vicious thrashing the sporting world had seen since Christians took on lions in ancient Rome. Despite my height, it had been months since I'd played volleyball, and my first few bumps careened into the net. Under normal circumstances I would have written off these mistakes as part of the warming-up process, but the gleeful roar of ridicule that went up each time I shanked a volley threw off my confidence and concentration. Before long, the opposing team started serving the ball to me on purpose, and my own teammates began begging me to leave.

Out of courtesy alone I should have fled the court immediately, but I was determined to save face in front of the village. Increasingly desperate, I must have careened a dozen balls into peculiar directions before Boon's friends physically pulled me off the court. As I watched the rest of the game from the sidelines, I came to realize that this was no casual game of volleyball, but a very serious inter-village competition. Indeed, Boon's friends hadn't been asking if I'd wanted to play volleyball; they'd wanted to know if I was *good* at volleyball.

No doubt I'd turned out to be the worst "ringer" in village history.

4. **Page 271, paragraph 4: ...*a white-haired old man who Boon introduces as Mr. Cham*:** In the 1951 book *A Dragon Apparent* (which I'd been reading while I was in Cambodia), author Norman Lewis devotes a small section to Cambodia's ethnic Cham minority, noting how their religious beliefs combine elements of Islam, Hinduism, and animism. "They are inclined to give their children such names as Dog, Cat, Rat to distract from them the attentions of evil spirits," Lewis notes. "For this reason there were several Cham kings named Excrement."

I found this detail so delightfully strange that I actually wasted a couple of writing hours trying to concoct a story-tangent about how Mr. Cham might have been a Cham. Apart from his name, however, there was no evidence Mr. Cham was anything but Khmer, and in the end I had to drop the tangent and admit to myself that I suffer a serious weakness for quirky historical details.

5. **Page 274, paragraph 7:** ...*buying a new phrasebook the moment I see one for sale*: It's worth noting that, while this story is framed in the present tense, it could just as easily have been framed in the past tense. Why did I write it in the present? I can't really recall; I guess I was trying to capture the ongoing immediacy of my experience in such an unfamiliar place.

In general, I have no hard and fast method of choosing when to write a story in the present tense and when to use past tense. I usually just start writing in whichever tense feels most appropriate; sometimes I'll go back and switch tenses while I'm still writing the story. Editors rarely share a unified opinion about which tense works best: An *Islands* editor I worked with some years ago insisted on past tense; a *National Geographic Traveler* editor I wrote for around the same time invariably preferred present tense.

Of the twenty stories in this book, exactly half of them are past tense, half present tense. I didn't plan it that way; that's just how it turned out.

Some writers of a more traditional bent insist that present tense makes for an inferior travel narrative. In his introduction to *The Best American Travel Writing 2001*, Paul Theroux writes (or should it be "wrote"?), "I am puzzled by one tic in contemporary travel writing, a love of the present tense. What is it about this tense that turns travel writers' heads? I regard this as unfortunate—precious, self-regarding, a distraction—but there is nothing I can do except deplore it." Read the stories Theroux chose for *The Best American Travel Writing 2001*, however, and you'll find that one-third of them were written in the present tense, including selections by literary luminaries such as Salman Rushdie, David Quammen, and Gretel Ehrlich. Since two of my own past-tense stories were nominated for the anthology that year ("My Beirut Hostage Crisis" and "Islam's Bloody Celebration")—but passed over by Theroux for the main selection—I was left to wonder why he would so blatantly contradict himself. One can only conclude that many of the present-tense stories he read that year were in fact neither distracting nor self-regarding nor precious.

Moreover, one year after *The Best American Travel Writing 2001* came out, historian Timothy Garton Ash used Theroux as an example in examining just how complicated it can be to claim narrative purity in nonfiction. In an insightful *Guardian* essay entitled "Truth is Another Country," Ash notes:

> Paul Theroux's travel book *The Great Railway Bazaar*...concludes with an elaborate plea for its own strict, reportorial accuracy. He describes in detail the four thick notebooks in which he wrote things down as they happened, "remembering to put it all in the past tense." On this railway trip through Asia, he writes, he had learned "that the difference between travel writing and fiction is the difference between recording what the eye sees and discovering what the imagination knows. Fiction is pure joy— how sad that I could not reinvent the trip as fiction." At which I found myself thinking, "Well, you did, you did." Perhaps I am wrong, but even the production of four weather-stained notebooks containing words identical to those on the printed page would not dissuade me, for the invention can come at the moment of recording.

ᗏ 17 ᗏ

Islam's Bloody Celebration

SINCE I hadn't had time to change my clothes that morning, I arrived at the Jordanian customs station in Aqaba with bloodstains on my pants. No doubt I appeared a bit odd walking through the ferry station with scallop-edged black droplets on my boots and crusty brown blotches soaked into the cuffs of my khakis.

The blood was from the streets of Cairo, which at the time had been in the midst of celebrations marking the Islamic Feast of the Sacrifice, known locally as the Eid al-Adha.

As with everything in Cairo, the Eid al-Adha was an inadvertent exercise in chaos. For the entire week leading up to the holiday, the alleys and rooftops of the city began to fill up with noisy, nervous knots of livestock brought in for the feast. Cairenes paid little mind as cattle munched clover outside coffee shops, goats gnawed on empty Marlboro packs in alleyways and skittish sheep rained down poop from apartment building balconies. For Egyptians, this preponderance of urban livestock was part of the excitement of the feast—and it was certainly no stranger for them than putting a decorated tree inside one's house in anticipation of the winter holidays.

In Islamic societies, the Eid al-Adha is a four-day feast that commemorates Abraham's near murder of his son, Ishmael, to prove his obedience to God. Since tradition tells us that Allah intervened at the last minute and substituted a ram for Ishmael, Muslim families celebrate the Eid by slaughtering their own animal for the feast.

Consequently, on the first morning of the Eid, all of the thousands of sheep, cows and goats that have been accumulating in Cairo during the week are butchered within the span of a few bloody hours. In keeping with tradition, devout Islamic families are instructed to keep a third of the butchered meat for themselves, give a third to friends and family and distribute the final third to the poor. For Muslims, it is an honorable ritual.

For infidel visitors to Cairo, however, the Feast of the Sacrifice seems much more like a Monty Python vision of pagan mayhem. This has less to do with the intent of the holiday than with the fact that Cairo is a very crowded city where almost nothing goes as planned. Thus, on the first morning of this year's Eid, the lobby of my hotel resonated with vivid secondhand reports of gore: the lamb that panicked on the balcony at the last minute and avoided the knife by tumbling five stories to the alley below, the cow that broke free from its restraints with its throat half-slit and lumbered through the streets spraying blood for ten minutes before collapsing, the crowd of little girls who started puking as they watched the death spasms of their neighbor's sheep.

Regardless of how accurate these stories were, there was no disputing that free-flowing blood was as common as Christmas mistletoe on the first morning of the Eid. By the middle of that afternoon in Cairo, puddles of blood stood like rainwater around drainpipes, and doorjambs and minivans alike were smeared with clotted red-brown handprints.

I'll admit that there is much more to the Muslim Feast of the Sacrifice than public displays of carnage. Unfortunately, Cairo has a way of drawing one's attention away from nuance and subtlety. By the end of the day, I was so accustomed to seeing blood that I didn't even realize that my pants and boots had been stained until I boarded an overnight bus headed for the Gulf of Aqaba.

For most Westerners, Islam is a religion that doesn't quite make sense. No doubt this is largely the result of the Western press, which tends to portray Islam only in terms of its most extreme and violent factions.

When I first traveled to the Islamic world earlier this year, I'd hoped that the Arabs' legendary hospitality would break down such barriers to religious understanding in a direct and personal way.

After ten weeks of traveling through Egypt, I'd found that Islamic hospitality more than lived up to its reputation: Most of the Muslims I'd talked to were amiable, kindhearted people who practiced their faith with natural sincerity. By the same token, however, none of the Muslims I'd met seemed to know why they were Muslims; they just instinctively knew that their faith allowed them to live with a special sense of peace. Whenever I tried to qualify this faith in objective terms, people became defensive and impatient with me.

Reading the Koran didn't help. Perhaps when studied in its classical Arabic form, the Koran is a heart-pounding page-turner. Its English translation, however, has all the narrative appeal of a real estate contract. Nearly every page is crammed with bewildering sentences that seem to have been worded at random. An example: "But when they proudly persisted in that which was forbidden, we said to them, 'Become scouted apes'; and then thy Lord declared that until the day of the resurrection, he would send against them those who should evil entreat, and chastise them" (Sura 7:7).

After a while, my only reaction to such verses was to stare at the page while my mind wandered about aimlessly. In this way, I ultimately found that my reflections on Allah were being offset in equal portion by thoughts of breakfast, girls I should have kissed in high school but didn't, and the lyrics to "Rhymin' and Stealin'" by the Beastie Boys. I gave up on the Koran less than a tenth of the way through.

Thus, I considered my trip to Jordan on the second day of the Eid to be my most immediate and realistic chance of knowing the intimate ways of Islam. Just as a person can't know Christmas by interrogating shopping mall Santas, I figured my understanding of the Eid al-Adha lay outside the bloody distractions of Cairo. In Aqaba, I hoped, I stood a better chance of experiencing the Feast of the Sacrifice as an insider.

Aqaba, Jordan, owes much of its fate to the rather arbitrary international borders drawn up in Versailles, France, and London in the wake of World War I. Though the city had been used as a trading post since the days of the Edomites and Nabateans, its port and beaches never found much permanent distinction. This all changed in 1921, when Winston Churchill (who was the British colonial secretary at the time) oversaw the creation of a Transjordanian state that featured a mere eleven miles of coast on the Gulf of Aqaba. Nearly eighty years later, Jordan's only seaport has inevitably blossomed into a dusty, yet functional resort town. Jet skis and glass-bottomed boats ply its waters; weekend revelers from Amman, Jordan's capital, crowd its beaches; drab concrete buildings dominate its shore.

Upon arriving in Aqaba, I hiked into the city center in search of a hotel where I could change out of my bloodstained clothes. Because most hotels in Aqaba were full of Jordanians spending their Eid holiday on the beach, my only option was to rent a foam pad and sleep on the roof of a six-floor budget complex called the Petra Hotel.

I shared the roof with four other travelers, from Denmark and Canada. When I told them about my plans to celebrate the Feast of the Sacrifice in Aqaba, I got two completely different reactions. The Danes, Anna and Kat, were horrified by the thought that I would intentionally seek out Arab companionship. Both of them had just spent a week on the Egyptian beach resorts in Sharm el Sheikh and Dahab, where the aggressive local Casanovas had worn them both to a frazzle. The two spoke in wistful terms of getting back to the peace and predictability of their kibbutz in Israel.

Amber and Judith, on the other hand, stopped just short of calling me a wuss. The two Canadians had just returned from spending a couple of weeks with Bedouins in the desert near Wadi Rum. Not only did they celebrate the Eid as part of their farewell party, they personally helped butcher the goats. To experience the Feast of the Sacrifice any other way, they reasoned, would seem a tad artificial.

"And besides," Amber told me as I changed into clean clothes and prepared to hit the streets, "Aqaba is a tourist town. The only people you'll find here are college kids and paper pushers on vacation from Amman. You'd have better luck getting invited to the Eid in Toronto."

Amber had a point, but she was wrong: I was invited to celebrate the Eid before I reached the ground floor of the Petra Hotel.

My would-be host was Mohammed, a bespectacled sixteen-year-old who stopped me in the second-floor stairwell. "Where are you going?" he asked as I walked by.

"Well, I'm hoping to go out and celebrate the Eid al-Adha," I said.

"The Eid!" he exclaimed. "Please come and celebrate with us!"

It was that simple. Such is the gregariousness of the Arab world.

Unfortunately for my notions of authenticity, however, Mohammed's "Eid" consisted of him and two other goofy-looking sixteen-year-olds drinking canned beer in a tiny room on the second floor of the Petra. Mohammed introduced his two friends as Sayeed and Ali. Neither of them looked very natural as they grinned up at me, clutching their cans of beer.

I noticed there were only two beds. "Are you all sleeping in here?" I asked.

"Just Sayeed and Ali," he said. "I sleep at my uncle's house in Aqaba. My family always comes here for the Eid al-Adha."

Mohammed poured some of his beer into a glass for me and put an Arabic pop tape into his friends' boom box. The four of us sat in the room chatting, drinking and listening to the music. After about fifteen or so minutes of this, I began to wonder what any of this had to do with the Feast of the Sacrifice. "Aren't we going to celebrate the Eid?" I asked finally.

"Of course," Mohammed said. "This is the Eid."

"Yes, this is the Eid," I said, "but won't you be doing something special at your uncle's house?"

"It's not interesting at my uncle's house. That's why I came here."

I looked skeptically at my three companions. "But isn't there something traditional that you do when you celebrate the Eid?"

Mohammed thought for a moment. "We spend time with our family."

"But you just said that you didn't want to be with your family."

"Yes."

"So you aren't really celebrating the Eid, are you?"

"No. This is the Eid!"

"How?" I asked, gesturing around the tiny room. "How is this the Eid?"

"We're drinking beer. Many people drink during the Eid."

Ignorant as I was about Islam, I was positive that a true Muslim holiday would have very little to do with swilling beer. "I'm sorry guys," I announced, "but I think I'm gonna have to go now."

Mohammed looked hurt. "But you said you came here for the Eid!"

"Yes," I said, "but I could drink beer and listen to music back home in America. I want to do something different."

"Maybe you want to dance?"

"Maybe," I said. "Where can we dance?"

Mohammed reached over to the boom box and turned up the music. The three Jordanian teens leapt up and started to shake their hips to the music. There was no room to move, so they stood in place and waved their arms around. The Arabic music was as stereotypical as it could get: a snake-charming, harem-inspiring swirl of strings and drums and flutes. Mohammed took me by the arm; I stood and tried to mimic his dance moves.

"Is this an Eid dance?" I yelled over the din of the music.

"No!"

"Is this Eid music?"

Mohammed laughed. "Of course not!"

"Then why are we doing this?"

"Because it's the Eid! It's fun, yes?"

I told Mohammed that it was indeed fun, but that was a lie. As with freeze tag, heavy petting and bingo, many exercises in human joy are best appreciated at a very specific age. To truly understand the appeal of drinking beer and dancing with your buddies in a bland resort-town hotel room, I suspect you have to be sixteen years old. I danced halfheartedly to the music, politely waiting for it to stop.

When I sat down after the first song, Mohammed happily yanked me to my feet. Twenty minutes later, the young Jordanians had moved on to the Side B songs without any sign of fatigue. I weakly shuffled in place, desperate for an excuse to leave. It occurred to me that, technically, I could just sprint out of the room and never have to talk to these guys again.

Then the inspiration hit. Leaning across the bed, I shut off the boom box and unplugged it from the wall. Mohammed and his friends looked at me in confusion.

"Let's go," I said to them. Carrying the boom box with an air of authority, I led the Jordanian boys up the stairwell to the roof of the Petra Hotel. There, I introduced them to Anna, Kat, Amber and Judith.

Serendipity is a rare thing, so it must be appreciated even in its humbler forms. As Mohammed, Sayeed and Ali exchanged formal handshakes with the Danes and the Canadians, I saw that their faces were frozen into expressions of rapturous terror; they had probably never been that intimate with Western women in their lives. Perhaps charmed by the boys' awkwardness, the girls regarded the young Jordanians with sisterly affection.

I plugged in the boom box and announced that it was time to dance.

I'm not sure if that evening on the roof of the Petra Hotel meant much to any of the other parties involved, but I like to think that it was an all-around triumph: Anna and Kat were able to interact with Arabs in a charmed, unthreatening setting; Amber and Judith got to boss the boys around in colloquial Arabic and showcase their Bedouin dance steps; Mohammed, Sayeed and Ali—in their goofy, reverent, sixteen-year-old way— got to dance with angels on the heights of Aqaba.

For me, however, the night was a technical failure: I'd come to Jordan to experience the Islamic soul of the Eid al-Adha, and I'd ended up spearheading a secular sock hop on the roof of my hotel.

But, at a very basic level, even this was a bona fide extension of the Feast of the Sacrifice. After all, any holiday—when stripped of its identifying traditions and theologies—is simply an intentional break from the drab routines of life: a chance to eat or drink heartily with family and friends, an opportunity to give thanks to God or fate or randomly converging odds, a date to anticipate with optimism or recall with satisfaction.

With this in mind, I reckon that the ritual intricacies of feasts and festivals anywhere are mere decoration for a notion we're usually too busy to address: that, at the heart of things, being alive is a pretty good thing.

Six stories above Aqaba, the eight of us talked and joked and danced to the Arabic tunes, improvising our moves when we weren't sure what else to do.

ഠ

ENDNOTES

1. **Page 279, paragraph 3:** *...the Eid al-Adha was an inadvertent exercise in chaos*: Whenever I questioned the wisdom of bringing scores of hoofed animals into major cities to celebrate the holiday, Egyptians and Jordanians told me the festival simply wouldn't have felt right without live animals. In this way I suppose eating prepackaged meat during Eid al-Adha would have been the Muslim equivalent of displaying a fake tree during Christmas season.

Some Muslim cities come up with rather novel strategies to cut down on Eid al-Adha mayhem. In Istanbul, for instance, the city's veterinarians organize livestock-herding SWAT teams, which patrol the city with tranquilizer guns during festival season. Whenever runaway goats or panicked cattle threaten to jam traffic or trample schoolchildren during the Turkish Eid, residents just dial a special hotline and wait for help to arrive.

2. **Page 281, paragraph 4:** *Whenever I tried to qualify this faith in objective terms*: I found objective explanations of Islam difficult to come by in the Middle East. When I was in Egypt, I bought a number of English-language booklets created to proselytize Western visitors, but they all tended to sound like they'd been written by a committee of octogenarian theologians sometime around 1966. For example, a pamphlet called *Islam: The Only Way Out of Misery* described the faith as "a middle ground between bourgeois capitalism and Bolshevist communism," and insisted "polygamy is a social safety valve designed by the Supreme Law Maker to preserve society...from destruction, decay and moral disintegration."

In the end, my travel experiences in the Middle East taught me to understand and respect the Islamic faith not from its socio-theological apologetics, but from the humble sincerity and humanity of those who practiced it.

3. **Page 287, paragraph 1:** *...improvising our moves when we weren't sure what else to do*: My Eid al-Adha story is an example of how the briefest, most accidental situations can result in revealing travel tales. I probably spent no more than two hours with the Jordanian boys that day, but (coupled with a little context about the culture and holiday) my time with them allowed me to show a side of the Middle East that weeks of itinerary-driven travel and formal interviews might have missed.

∾ 18 ∾

Digging Mr. Benny's
Dead Uncle

From the outset, my reasons for moving to Ranong had nothing to do with the town itself. I hadn't moved there to shop in the fish markets, explore the tidal flats, or hike into the rainforest. I hadn't even moved there to meet the locals or learn about Thai culture. Rather, I'd moved to the sleepy south-Thailand border-town to rent a room for a few months and write my first book. Seeking the right blend of isolation and convenience, I'd located a cheap, quiet studio at the edge of town, where I set up my laptop on a wobbly kitchen table, spread my notes out on the worn wooden floorboards, and immersed myself in my work.

My plan had been to live like an obsessive and industrious hermit—and I regarded Ranong as little more than a static backdrop for my labors. Each morning I did a simple regimen of pushups and went for a run along a jungle-fringed road outside of town; the rest of the day was given to writing. Time spent away from my laptop, I reasoned, was time wasted—and apart from simple restaurant transactions, I didn't meet, talk to, or even think about anyone in the town. At night, when my work was finished, I would lie in my bed and stare at the ceiling until I fell asleep, content in my creative solitude.

Such blissful isolation might have lasted, too, had I not required a haircut ten days into my sojourn.

Although Ranong was home to several modern hair salons at the time, I opted for a dowdy old barbershop that fit my jungle-noir ideals: battered iron barber's chairs in a dim, humid store-front; slippery pomade bottles clustered around dented sink-basins; idle men in sweat-soured t-shirts puffing on cheroots in the corners. Lording over this scene was a thin, sexagenarian Burmese émigré who introduced himself as Mr. Benny. He wore thick spectacles and sported a wispy black mustache. Faded cru-cifix tattoos danced on his forearms as he pinned a frock around my neck.

"Where you from?" he asked in slow, slurry English. "Australia?"

"Nope," I replied. "America."

"America. I always want to go there and see cowboys." Mr. Benny paused in concentration as he took out a pair of shears and began to snip at the side of my head. "My great aunt was marry to a man from Boston once. His name is Benedict, same as me. He do a business for many years on the Burma side of the river."

"Did you know him well?"

"No, not well. He is much older than me. In 1993, I have to go find him and take him back to Thailand. Very difficult."

"Why was it difficult?"

"Well, nobody in my family can tell me where he is."

"Didn't he keep in contact with you?"

Mr. Benny let out a slurry giggle. "Of course not! My uncle Benedict been dead for forty years. But my England cousin write to me that year, and she ask to have his bones."

"So you went over and dug them up?"

"Yes, but it is a big problem. My cousin become angry with me."

"Why, what happened?"

The old Burmese barber paused and wrinkled his brow. "It's a difficult story. Maybe you not want to hear it."

"No, no, it sounds interesting," I said.

With a sigh, Mr. Benny started to snip at my hair again. "I hire a boat and go across to Burma. It is not hard to find my uncle Benedict. He's in a Christian cemetery at Victoria Point. But the cemetery mans want money to dig the bones. I not have any money, so I take a shovel and sneaked my uncle out when it get dark."

"You dug up the bones in the middle of the night?"

"Yes. It take me all night to dig, and then I leave Burma in the morning with my uncle in this sack. The border police stop and ask me what's in this sack, and I tell them it is Burma whiskey."

"Did they believe you?"

"No! They say 'open that sack!' I open that sack a little bit and give them one bottle of whiskey. Then they tell me, 'go home.'"

"But I thought your sack was full of bones."

The old Burmese barber raised an eyebrow and caught my eye in the mirror. "Mr. Benny is a clever man. He put one whiskey in with his dead uncle, because he knows how police mans think. You make present for them, and they not care what's in that sack."

"So you didn't get in trouble?"

"No problem with the police mans."

"So your story has a happy ending," I said. "You were a successful grave-robber."

Mr. Benny looked at the floor and blushed. "Happy ending," he repeated uncertainly.

The haircut ended up costing me forty baht (slightly less than a dollar), and left me with a close-cut whitewall coiffure that made me look like a Thai senior citizen. Bidding Mr. Benny farewell, I walked back out to my studio and went back to work.

Now that I'd heard Mr. Benny's story, however, my work wasn't quite so focused as it had been before. Sometimes, during my morning runs, or while organizing note cards in my studio, I'd get the urge to go back and ask Mr. Benny more about his uncle

Benedict. I wanted to know why the shadowy old Bostonian had come to Burma, and how he'd died. Moreover, I realized that I'd never coaxed Mr. Benny into telling me the entire story. What, I wondered, had happened to Benedict's remains once Mr. Benny brought them back to Thailand? Did the cousin just show up from England, plunk the old bones into a suitcase, and fly them home? Furthermore, why had Mr. Benny insinuated that his family was angry with him, when it was obvious he'd gone to so much trouble to help them out?

I did my best to ignore these issues as I toiled away on my book. The isolation of my little studio had allowed me to concentrate entirely on writing, and I was determined not to compromise this by walking back into town and delving into the apocryphal family-life of my Burmese barber.

After about three weeks of flawless discipline, however, I woke up one morning and decided that my hair looked a bit tousled at the edges. Seeing this as a fine excuse, I wandered into town to get a trim from Mr. Benny.

"I have a question about your story," I said as Mr. Benny pinned the frock around my neck.

"What story?"

"The story about going to Burma and digging up the bones of your uncle Benedict."

Mr. Benny gave me a quizzical look. "Do I tell you that story?"

"Yes, you told me the last time you cut my hair. It was very interesting. But I forgot to ask what happened when you got back to Thailand with your uncle's bones. Did your family come and get them?"

"No. They not get them."

"Why not? What happened to your English cousin?"

"It's difficult. Maybe you not want to hear about it." Mr. Benny took out his shears and silently started in on his work, as if hoping I'd change the subject.

"No, of course I want to hear about it," I insisted.

"It is a big problem," he said. "My family become angry with me."

"Yes, but *why* did they get angry?"

Mr. Benny sighed fatalistically. "Because I throw my uncle Benedict's bones into the sea."

This bit took me by surprise. "Why did you do that? Didn't your family want the bones?"

"Oh, my England cousin want those bones. She write me a letter and say she come to Ranong and get them from me. But when I come home from Burma with those bones I get scared. In Thailand, everyone is Buddhist—and Buddhist people burn up the body when it dies. Nobody ever see no bones except for in murders. So if the police mans come to my house and see my uncle's bones, I worry they think I kill him."

"So you decided to throw the bones in the sea?"

Mr. Benny blushed as he snipped at my hair. "Before I throw the bones in the sea, I drive them up to my cousin's cousins in Bangkok. Benedict is great *grandfather* to them, so I think maybe they can take those bones and wait them for my England cousin."

"So did they take the bones?"

"Well, I give them that sack and say, 'this is your great grandfather Benedict.' But my Bangkok cousins are Buddhists, so they think I'm giving them a goats."

"They thought you were giving them *goats*?"

"A goats."

"Oh, you mean a *ghost.*"

"Yes, a goats. They get scared and call a monk to chase the goats out from their house. They yell and tell me to take those bones and go home. So I took the bus back to Ranong."

"You took the bones back to Ranong on the *bus*?"

"Yes! Mr. Benny not have car! I hold that sack on my legs like a baby the whole way. Ten hours on that bus. And no sleep for Mr.

Benny, because he not want that sack to open and his uncle's bones fall out."

"But you made it home okay?"

"I make it home. But then I not know where to put those bones. There are many dogs in Ranong. They come and sniff that sack. They *know* about my uncle Benedict inside." Mr. Benny swapped his shears for a hard-razor and started shaping my sideburns. "When I fall asleep in my home that night, I dream of dogs eating those bones. So I wake up and get a rock for that sack and go find a boat."

"And you threw the bones into the sea?"

"Yes. I threw my uncle down into the sea."

"Wow. That's quite a story."

"Quite a story." Mr. Benny shot me a weak smile in the mirror. "Very difficult."

As Mr. Benny continued his work with the hard-razor, I quizzed him about his great uncle's life—but he didn't know much beyond the fact that Benedict was from Boston and had worked as a trader. Mr. Benny then proceeded to tell me about his own life in Burma: how the Irish priests at his grammar school had taught him English; how, at age fifteen, he'd been recruited to fight with Kuomintang nationalists against the Red Chinese in northern Burma; how he'd eventually raised a family in his troubled homeland but now spent most of his time working in Thailand.

I went home that morning with another garish senior citizen haircut, but I was happy I'd taken the trouble to chat up Mr. Benny. Now that my lingering questions about his dead American uncle had been addressed, I figured I could return my full energies to working on my book.

The problem, of course, was that I kept thinking up *new* questions for Mr. Benny. I found myself curious about the Irish priests who'd tutored him, and his days as a teen solider. I wanted to know why he'd spent so much of his adulthood working in

Thailand, and if he ever missed his homeland. What's more, I realized that I *still* hadn't let the recalcitrant old barber tie up the loose ends of his grave-robbing story. He'd dropped the bones into the sea, yes—but I suddenly remembered he'd left out certain details about his English cousin. What, I wondered, had she done when she arrived in Thailand to find the bones missing?

This time, I didn't have the discipline or patience to wait for another haircut. The following morning I walked into town and found Mr. Benny unlocking the iron grates in front of his barbershop. He cheerfully invited me in and served me a cup of coffee thickened with condensed milk. He asked me a bit about America, and when I told him I hailed from the prairie, he told me that his favorite English-language book was an old cowboy novel called *The Big Sky*.

Eventually, I steered the conversation over to his dead American kinsman. "I'm still curious about what happened with your uncle Benedict," I said to him.

Mr. Benny sipped his coffee and smiled cautiously. "I tell you: I throw his bones into the sea."

"Yes, but what about your English cousin? Wasn't she going to come to Ranong and get the bones? What happened to her?"

Mr. Benny gave me a bashful look. "It's difficult," he said. "A difficult story."

"You mean your cousin was angry to hear that you'd thrown the bones into the sea?"

"No."

"Oh. Then what's difficult about the story?"

Mr. Benny leaned in with just the trace of a smile. "I *never tell* my England cousin about throwing those bones in the sea."

"I don't understand. Didn't she come to Ranong?"

"Yes, she *did* come! But I feel too bad to tell her that grandfather Benedict is down under the water. So I say, 'see me tomorrow, and I give you the bones.'"

"But you didn't have the bones."

"Yes. I not have no bones. So I go to my Chinese friend and ask *him* for bones."

"Why would your Chinese friend have the bones? Was he a scuba diver?"

"He is a meat man."

"What, like a butcher?"

"Yes, butcher. He give me some *pig bones*. He say, 'tell your cousin that this pig bones is uncle Benedict.'"

"But surely your cousin could tell the difference between pig bones and human bones."

"Yes. So my Chinese friend and me, we smash up the pig bones and put them in a pretty jar. I give that pretty jar to my England cousin, and I say, 'these are the bones that I digged for you.' So she give me 1,000 baht and she go home with my uncle Benedict in that jar."

"But it wasn't really your uncle Benedict."

"Yes. And I didn't know about NDA."

"NDA?"

"I didn't know the scientist can check if those bones are her family."

"Oh, right. DNA testing."

"Yes. My cousin go to the NDA, and the scientist say to her, 'your grandfather is a pig.'"

"Wow. And she was angry with you?"

"Very, very. She send a letter and say I am a liar. She say I try and trick her for money. And I never heared from her again."

With a guilty giggle, Mr. Benny finished off his coffee and got up to prepare his barbershop for a day of business.

After that morning, my isolationist work ethic never quite recovered. In sharing the bizarre tale of his dead uncle, Mr. Benny had broken through my tunnel vision and allowed me to glimpse a piece of Ranong for the first time. In the weeks that followed, I found myself growing more gregarious and more distracted. One day in the central market, a passing conversation with a police-man led to a raucous evening at Ranong's kickboxing venue. Another time, a moto driver (whose English was as limited as my Thai) invited me to spend an afternoon with his family at a city park. I began to take my long-distance runs in the evenings, when I could join groups of Thai joggers along the road to the local hot springs. My landlady, sensing my new openness, had me over for dinners and offered to let me spend my weekends at her beach house on the Andaman Sea coast. Over time, I found myself lin-gering longer at restaurants and returning smiles on the street. Bit by bit, my loner pretensions dried up, and I began to feel more a part of Ranong.

Naturally, my writing output suffered as a result. What I'd hoped would be an intense four-month creative barnstorm ulti-mately ballooned into nine haphazard months. Rainy season stretched into dry season. Deadlines passed. Return-tickets were rescheduled and rent fees were renegotiated. Dry season began to stretch its way back into rainy season.

And, amidst all of this, I made a habit of visiting Mr. Benny's barbershop whenever I passed through central Ranong. There, we'd offhandedly talk about sports or politics, and I'd wheedle him into sharing more quirky tales from his life.

Sometimes, when the tales were particularly interesting, I'd even let him cut my hair.

∾

ENDNOTES

1. **Page 289, paragraph 1:** *From the outset, my reasons for moving to Ranong:* Note that this story involves the same Mr. Benny I describe in chapter 11. If some details of this Mr. Benny story seem different, keep in mind that these events happened almost two years prior to the events in "Death of an Adventure Traveler."

2. **Page 289, paragraph 1:** ...*I'd moved to the sleepy south-Thailand border-town to...write my first book*: The book in question was *Vagabonding: An Uncommon Guide to the Art of Long-Term World Travel*, which Random House published in 2003.

At that point in my travels I felt at home in many parts of Asia, and I could have written the book in any number of quiet, inexpensive provincial towns in Thailand (or Korea, or India, or even Egypt). Ranong made the most sense at the time because *Condé Nast Traveler* had recently commissioned me to write a story about the Moken sea-gypsies just over the border in Burma (a detail that seemed too tangential to mention in this story).

Because I spent several months there, I've since tried to track down what other travel writers have said about Ranong—but I haven't found much. Richard Halliburton (*The Royal Road to Romance*) briefly passed through after leaving Burma in the 1920s, and William T. Vollmann visited Ranong as part of his quest to buy a Burmese girl out of prostitution for *Spin* magazine in 1993. Past that, the only times I've seen the frumpy little Thai-Burmese border town mentioned in print is when some Japanese or Chinese conglomerate proposes to carve a Panama Canal-style shipping route through Thailand's Isthmus of Kra.

Should this ever happen, of course, Ranong will transform into a trade hub on a par with Singapore.

3. **Page 289, paragraph 1:** ...*I'd located a cheap, quiet studio at the edge of town*: This detail hints at a key contrivance of the story. In truth, my wooden-floored "studio" was located in a Thai hotel (the "Lotus Guesthouse" mentioned in chapter 11)—and living in a tourist guesthouse ensured that my life in Ranong wasn't always as solitary as I might have let on. When I wrote that I didn't "meet, talk to, or even think about anyone in the town," I was referring to the people who lived there. Townsfolk aside, I'd actually met plenty of travelers who were stopping off in Ranong on a visa-renewal run across the border to Burma.

Most of these travelers were backpackers, and whenever I needed company I could usually just trot down to the hotel's courtyard and strike up a conversation with whomever was hanging out by the mossy little swimming pool. As I came to know Ranong better, I would sometimes round up a group of travelers and take them to eat at my favorite restaurant, or watch Thai glam-metal bands perform at the Star Disco just up the road. Every so often a Norwegian or Singaporean backpacker lass would take a shine to me, and move into my room for a few days before continuing on to Bangkok or Phuket. The closest I had to an actual girlfriend during that time was a quiet, long-legged Swiss girl who stayed nearly a week before she realized that a travel writer's life in Thailand (which for me consisted of eight-hour days in front of my laptop) was not nearly so glamorous as it might have sounded.

Ultimately, I decided to gloss over this aspect of my social life in Ranong, since spelling out these details would only detract from the twists and turns of my barber's tale.

Either way, Mr. Benny helped me discover Ranong anew; the only difference was in the telling: In narrative reality, Mr. Benny inspired me to break out from utter social isolation; in lived reality, he helped me break out from the social bubble of my hotel.

~ 19 ~

The Living Museum of Everywhere and Nowhere

Having just journeyed to the remote corners of Asia as part of a life-altering two-year sojourn, I'll admit I wasn't expecting much when I returned to the United States and joined my sister on a weekend antique-shopping excursion to Minneapolis, Kansas.

Kristin, a city girl who'd recently moved with her husband and young sons to a farm in a neighboring county, sensed my lagging interest as we strolled the main drag of the small prairie town. "If you're not into shopping," she suggested, "there's a little museum here you might want to check out."

I considered her suggestion, my mind wandering back to Asia. One month before, in Burma, I'd bought a $40 bicycle with the goal of pedaling into the middle of nowhere. I'd hoped to find an experience as far from the tourist trail as that rickety one-speed bike could take me, and I felt I'd succeeded admirably. Rolling over dusty Burmese roads for three weeks, I'd feasted on two-cent mangoes, explored obscure caves, slept in out-of-the-way Buddhist monasteries, dodged secret police informants, and met plenty of warm and fascinating people.

Now that I was in Kansas visiting family, however—strolling around a town where I didn't look much different from the locals—I felt somehow more isolated than in any place I'd discovered in the hinterland of Burma. Admittedly, the town of Minneapolis (not to be confused with the major city in Minnesota) wasn't Timbuktu; it was a pleasant community of two thousand people—not far from a major interstate highway—home to a small newspaper, a grain elevator, a car dealership, a Pizza Hut, a couple banks, a bar, and (thanks to its aging population) a handful of antique stores.

Still, in terms of international travel, Minneapolis, Kansas was nowhere—a geographical nonentity, neither exotic nor familiar enough to tickle a wanderer's imagination. It was, I'd presumed, just another nondescript Great Plains community, one of many that had been slowly dwindling in size for half a century, each year losing a few more of its young people to places like Wichita and Denver and Kansas City. The few outsiders who strayed into this part of the United States came wearing smirks, looking for Middle American kitsch—record-setting balls of twine, Elvis impersonators, deranged religious zealots—but Minneapolis hosted no such oddities. Indeed, on paper, this part of Kansas was off-the-beaten-path in the least appealing sense of the phrase; I'd met plenty of fellow travelers who'd be happy to get lost on the nameless back roads of Burma, but none who viewed this flat, grassy stretch of America as anything more than flyover country.

Thus, faced with an afternoon of antiques and post-Asia ennui, I decided to try to prove my assumptions wrong about Minneapolis, Kansas. Even if it didn't promise the sublime wonders of backcountry Burma, I reasoned I could at least find something distinctive and telling about the place.

"I'm not in the mood for a museum," I told Kristin. "I think I'll just go get some coffee."

In truth, I was never much in the mood for museums, anywhere. Having lived in Asia and Europe, I'd come to regard museums as soulless cultural trophy cases, devoid of charm or surprise or epiphany. For me, an afternoon spent eyeing pretty girls in the

Jardin des Tuileries was far more rewarding than squinting at baroque maidens in the Louvre, and I'd found that people-watching in the food-stalls off Sukhumvit Road was more culturally revealing than anything in the palatial galleries of Thailand's National Museum. Even Cairo's Egyptian Museum, in all its cluttered, moldering frumpiness, wasn't half as charming as an evening of playing backgammon and smoking apple tobacco in a noisy Arab café a few blocks away.

Hence, I was confident that thirty minutes in a local coffee joint would show me more of small-town Kansas than an entire afternoon in the local museum.

When I arrived at the café, I noticed a thin, elderly man easing his way out of a white sedan parked out front. I knew I had to introduce myself the instant I saw the vanity tag on his front bumper. It read, WORLD WAR II VETERAN: CHINA * BURMA * INDIA.

"I couldn't help but notice your bumper tag," I said to him. "How long has it been since you were in Burma?"

The old fellow cocked an eyebrow. "Since never," he said. "I served in India. On an airfield near Calcutta."

"How was it?"

"If you're looking for war stories, you're outta luck," he said. "I was never in combat."

"That's O.K. I'm just curious to know what you thought of Asia."

The man thought for a moment, absently scratching under the brim of his ball cap ("D&M Body Shop," the cap read, "You Bend 'Em, We'll Mend 'Em"). "What I remember most about India was how poor it was," he said finally. "You had to be careful when you took your shower, because kids from the town would sneak up and steal your soap. Even the officers in the Indian army didn't have much money. One time I gave an Indian commander a pack of cigarettes, and he made his whole company bow down and worship me." He chuckled at the memory.

"Didn't that make you feel uncomfortable?"

"Oh, not really. I was too busy taking their photo. Wish I knew what happened to that one. Got some nice shots in Egypt, too, but they all got lost over the years."

"When did you go to Egypt?"

"About the same time. Egypt was full of military, and the Ayrabs knew we had money. Ask some fella on the street-corner where the Pyramids were, and pretty soon there were two dozen Egyptians fighting over who was gonna be your tour guide. I ended up hiring a couple fellas for next to nothing; they put me up on a camel, and took me all over Giza. When it was all done, they chopped off a chunk of the Great Pyramid of Cheops and gave it to me as a souvenir."

"Wow. I was in Egypt a couple years ago, and they kept a tight rein on that kind of thing."

The old war veteran sized me up. "You know, if you're interested in international stuff, you should see our museum. They've got a little bit of everything in there."

"I'm not too keen on museums," I said. "Your little chunk of Pyramid would be far more interesting to me than anything I'd find in a museum."

"Well then it looks like we've got a problem," he said. "Because that little chunk of Pyramid is sitting in the museum right now."

Trumped, I followed the man down a side street. He told me his name was Gus Ottland, and that he'd graduated from high school in Minneapolis back in 1931. "My family lived way out in the country," he said. "In the winter I lived in a boarding house so I wouldn't have to walk all that way in bad weather."

From the outside, the Ottawa County Museum looked like a glorified machine-shed—modern and functional, like something you might see in an industrial park. Inside, the museum was more like a carefully ordered attic, with narrow rows of period clothing, tools, army uniforms, sports trophies, souvenir plates, dolls, fossils, war medals, books, framed letters, and railroad equipment twisting maze-like from wall to wall under fluorescent lights. A vintage fire engine shared space with mammoth tusks and a collection of walking canes.

Gus took me to a glassed-in display case, where his white-tan chunk of the Great Pyramid sat alongside arrowheads, fossilized leaves, and small meteorites. "Kind of hard to look at that little rock and imagine the rest of the Pyramid," he said. "It's a little like showing you a mountain oyster and asking you to imagine the bull, I guess." He paused for a chuckle. "But that's where it came from."

Scanning the room, I noticed that the back corner of the museum was dedicated to George Washington Carver, the famed African-American botanist. "Did Carver live in Kansas?" I asked Gus.

"For a while," he replied, "when he was a teenager." Gus took me back to the Carver exhibit and showed me pictures and letters from the late nineteenth century, when the great science prodigy was a star student at Minneapolis High School. A wall display showed how, while at the Tuskegee Institute in Alabama, Carver had processed peanuts into instant coffee, margarine, mock oysters, rubbing oil, laxatives, shampoo, shaving cream, gasoline, plastics, glue, insecticide, and (perhaps most famously) peanut butter.

"Not many black families left in Minneapolis these days," Gus told me. "But I went to high school with some black kids."

"Was there much racism back then?"

"Oh, I'd reckon there was. We had a kid on the football team, by the name of Cooper. A good kid and a great athlete, but he always had to drink last from the water bottle. We didn't even think that was strange at the time; that's just the way it was."

Gus and I moved on to a display of fossils. A sign over a set of sturdy dinosaur bones read, "Silvisaurus Condrayi."

"Apart from the George Washington Carver stuff, I'd reckon those dinosaur bones are the most popular display here," he said. "I'll go get Jettie Condray, and he can tell you more about them."

"Who's Jettie Condray?" I asked.

"He's the curator. And it was his daddy who found those dinosaur bones."

Gus ambled off to the museum office and came back with a powerfully built, kind-faced man who sported a graying flattop haircut. Jettie Condray looked more like a farmer than a museum curator—and it turned out he'd been both. "I've been a teacher, too," Jettie said. "But I've been interested in museums ever since my dad found that dinosaur out on our land."

"How'd that happen?"

"Well, he was just riding his horse across the property, and he saw some white material sticking out of a ravine. Turned out to be the skeleton of a twelve-foot armored dinosaur that had never been identified by science."

"What did he do with it?"

"He called some officials from the University of Kansas, who came and dug it up and took it to the museum in Lawrence. Our display is just a plaster cast of the original bones, but they named the dinosaur after my dad. It shows up from time to time in dinosaur encyclopedias and kids books. It's not as well known as the more popular dinosaurs, like the T-Rex or the triceratops, but we're proud to have found it."

By this point, any resistance I had to the museum had vanished. I asked Jettie if he could show me around the exhibits; he took a laser pointer from his pocket and went to work, speaking with pride and enthusiasm about every display in the room. In addition to the Carver exhibit and the *Silvisaurus condrayi* bones, the marquee museum exhibits included a set of letters written to Abraham Lincoln by Ottawa County resident Grace Bedell Billings (who, at age eleven, reputedly convinced Lincoln to grow a beard), and a restored 1917 Fordson tractor that had once appeared in a 1984 issue of *National Geographic.*

Compared to the Louvre or the Smithsonian or the Hermitage, of course, the Ottawa County Museum was just a shed full of provincial miscellany. But, unlike in any of those world-famous galleries, it was easy to feel the human energy behind the displays in the little museum, and—on occasion—to meet the people whose lives were transformed by those objects. The regal, well-endowed international museums that had disappointed me in the past were the stuff of erudition and empire; this place was a haven of connection and continuity—a window through which a small town looked out at the world, and by which the world was brought home and held up for display by the people who lived there. Minneapolis, Kansas may have been "nowhere," in a certain sense, but this building, in its own, humble way, was a living museum of everywhere.

Later, when I met up with my sister, she was somewhat apologetic about keeping me waiting. "This place isn't exactly Burma, is it?" she said.

I thought back to Burma, and the pride I'd felt in straying off the beaten path there. Somehow, the thrill of that journey contained a hint of narcissism—an egoistic desire to see myself, vivid and unique, in the reflection of a land so unlike my own. Minneapolis, Kansas offered no such temptation; it had only offered itself, in all its understated and charming reality.

"You're right," I told her. "Burma it's not."

∽

ENDNOTES

1. **Page 301, paragraph 2: *...in terms of international travel, Minneapolis, Kansas was nowhere:*** As a native Kansan with keen affection for my home state, I should note that Minneapolis is not far from

Rock City, a Registered National Landmark consisting of two hundred or so sandstone boulders sitting in field a few miles south of town. Big rocks are a novelty in the Great Plains, and as a kid I enjoyed visiting Rock City to climb the boulders and check out the pioneer graffiti etched into their gritty contours. In this sense, Minneapolis does appear on the tourist radar (albeit in a quirky, not-exactly-Yosemite kind of way).

I used the word "nowhere" to describe the town because I originally wrote this story for a Lonely Planet anthology entitled *Tales From Nowhere*. Since I knew other contributors would share tales of physical isolation—Borneo, the Sahara, Antarctica—I decided to write about the touristic isolation of a county museum in small-town Kansas.

As it turned out, the "nowhere" theme was a great way to frame a story I'd been attempting to write since that first encounter with Gus and Jettie in the Ottawa County Museum. Whereas my early drafts of the story didn't effectively evoke the unexpected charms of the museum, the notion of "nowhere" created the perfect foil to illustrate how vivid travel experiences can be found where you least expect them.

2. **Page 302, paragraph 9: "*What I remember most about India was how poor it was," he said finally*:** By its very nature, narrative nonfiction requires that you condense rambling, open-ended conversations into concise beats of dialogue.

In truth, Gus didn't segue quite so smoothly into tidy observations about life in India and Egypt. Rather, he started out by sharing some of the more macabre details of his time in Calcutta: the G.I. from his unit who got drunk one night and drowned in a well; the hot-dogging fighter pilot who died in a fiery crash one week before he was scheduled to go home.

By leading off with these stories, I think Gus was just telling me what he thought I wanted to hear. As an ex-solider, he was probably accustomed to people curious about the tragedies of war. It wasn't until he saw my fascination with the details of India and Egypt that he began to share personal tales about his time overseas. At one point, when he was telling me how an Ay-rab had tricked his friend out of a ballpoint pen in Cairo, he stopped to marvel at how long it had been since he'd thought of that moment.

Months later, when I was trying to write about the experience, I realized how even the most casually told stories can carry a curious power of connection and synchronicity.

Indeed, in helping Gus to recall the stories he didn't usually tell, Gus had given me a story of my own—and were it not for events that had happened sixty years prior in India and Egypt, I might never have found reason to remember that day in Minneapolis, Kansas.

PART FIVE

Tutorial

Ͼ 20 Ͽ

The Art of Writing a Story about Walking across Andorra

I. MANY TRAVEL STORIES BEGIN AS AN ATTEMPT TO IMPRESS PRETTY WOMEN

A. Once you have walked across the small Pyrenean nation of Andorra, you should proceed to Barcelona. Here, you will look for a nightclub called L'Arquer. According to your guidebook, L'Arquer contains a fully functioning archery range, and you are intrigued by the idea that one can shoot bows and arrows inside a nightclub. As with Andorra, you are attracted by L'Arquer because you find it charming that such a place exists.

B. In actuality, of course, L'Arquer will not likely live up to your expectations. The archery range, for example, will probably be in a separate, cordoned-off area, and your fantasies of chugging beers while shooting arrows over crowds of drunken revelers will not come true. For this reason, you will not look very hard for L'Arquer, and you will end up settling for a pub called Shanghai. This way, L'Arquer will remain perfect in your imagination—unlike Andorra, the memory of which has now been tainted with jagged brown ridges, chintzy souvenirs and drunken Scotsmen.

C. In the Shanghai pub, you will meet a Canadian woman named Lisa, who has come to Spain for two weeks of vacation. Eventually, she will ask you what you're here for, and you will tell her that you just walked across Andorra. Lisa isn't exactly sure what Andorra is, so the implicit gag (that Andorra is in fact a very small country, quite easy to walk across) is lost on her. Instead, she asks a neutral question: "How was it?" You reply that it was quite interesting.

D. After this, there will be a pause, which implies that Lisa wants you to elaborate. This is when the real Andorra story begins. What immediately follows the pause will not be the final and definitive story, but it will set the tone for how you'll remember Andorra in the future. This is where you begin to pick and choose, to play games with reality, to separate the meaningful from the mundane and hold it up for display. Later, when you are writing the story down, you will add details of history and culture—but for now you just want to hold Lisa's attention, because she has clear blue eyes and a captivating smile.

E. Skipping over the actual details of the hike, you tell Lisa about the Festa Major celebration in Andorra la Vella. Here, a group of mentally handicapped Andorrans singled you out from the crowd and cheerfully bullied you into joining them in a Catalan dance called the *sardana*. You choose to reveal Andorra through this story because it's funny and self-deprecating, and you want to single yourself out to Lisa as a charmed person who is instinctively adored by retards.

F. The story goes fairly well upon first telling, save the fact that: (a) Lisa seems faintly offended when you use the word "retards"; and (b) You flub the phrasing near the end of the story, inadvertently implying (to Lisa's ears) that you were insensitive to the mentally handicapped Andorrans while you were dancing with them. You make a mental note to sharpen the clarity of your phrasing, since you were not, in fact, acting insensitive when it actually happened.

II. Historical Details Make It Look Like You Know What You're Talking About

A. After you have left Spain and returned to your home, you will decide you need to know more facts about Andorra before you properly begin to compose your story. Reference books and websites tell you that Andorra has 67,000 residents, only 33 percent of whom are Andorran citizens. Andorra has an area of 180 square miles. This is half the size of New York City, but two-and-a-half times larger than Washington, DC. Since you don't want to make your hike sound too easy, you will use the Washington comparison when composing your Andorra story.

B. You'll try to spruce up basic facts by clumping them together in a telling manner. Start by saying that Andorra has no airports, no trains, and no independent universities. Mention that Andorra's small army has not fought a war for seven hundred years, and that most of its ammunition consists of blank bullets used for public ceremonies. Point out that, while Andorra has a National Automobile Museum, it did not have substantial roads until the middle of the twentieth century. If possible, say: "More like a neighborhood than a country, Andorra's tourism boom has transformed it into a peaceful suburb of ski runs, luxury hotels and duty-free shopping."

C. Touch on the history of Andorra, but—since this is primarily a travel story—try to deal with it in a concise manner. Write: "Andorra is the lone remaining legacy of Charlemagne's 'March States,' which were created to keep Muslim Moors out of Christian France in the ninth century." Then jump forward a few centuries to describe how, in the 1200s, a local power struggle between a French count and a Spanish bishop led to a compromise that made Andorra nominally sovereign. "Called the 'Pariatges,'" you will write, "this treaty plays French and Spanish influences off one another, and has ensured Andorra's independence for centuries."

D. Mention that, to this day, power is officially shared by the president of France and the bishop of Urgell in Spain. Say: "Thus,

Andorra has the current distinction of being the only nation in the world to have two heads of state—neither of whom live in Andorra."

III. Editors Are Impressed by
Tidy Narrative Formulas

A. Now that you have prepared the historical facts, you must choose a manner of storytelling. Were you writing a book about Andorra, you might begin your story from a personal or emotional premise. You might say, for example, that your lover has just left you, and you resolved to walk across Andorra in an effort to heal your pain. Or, you might say that your home was lacking in good taste or authenticity, and you walked across Andorra to discover an older and more genuine way of life. Or, you might say that you've been fascinated with Andorra since childhood, and to walk its breadth would be to realize a lifelong dream.

B. You are not, however, writing a book. Nor did you go to Andorra to heal your pain, seek a more genuine way of life, or realize a lifelong dream. Rather, your Andorra sojourn was an extension of a trip to Paris, where you were teaching a seminar in (of all things) travel writing. As you walked across Andorra, in fact, your backpack contained a folder full of student papers. Every so often, you took these papers out and wrote things like: "Show how the villagers act, don't tell." Or: "Establish that you are inside the castle before you introduce the janitor." Or: "Describe what the geishas looked like." Or: "Don't give away the samba dancer's secret at the beginning." Or: "Tell me more about the one-legged man with the sausage."

C. Regardless of what happened to you in Andorra, you must choose a template.

You could, for example, present yourself as a connoisseur who traveled to Andorra to sample *Formatge de tupí* (a local specialty consisting of cheese fermented with garlic and brandy in an earthenware container).

You might present yourself as an avid hiker or skier, who came to compare the slopes of the Andorran Pyrenees with those of the French Alps. ("They are not as tall or dramatic," you might say, "but the lack of crowds lends a certain appeal.")

If you are good at humor, you could present yourself as a hapless wanderer in a tiny land full of baffling cultural differences and bizarre local folktales (be sure to mention the legend of L'Auvinyana, a feisty Andorran peasant who made her fortune as a prostitute in Barcelona and returned to her homeland, dressed in velvet and ostrich plumes, to seduce lumberjacks at gunpoint).

Another option is to follow in the footsteps of a famous historical, literary, or mythical traveler, making comparisons and contrasts as you go.

D. You are pleasantly surprised to find that a famous literary-historical traveler named Richard Halliburton walked across Andorra in 1921. "I wasn't sure whether the vaguely familiar word Andorra meant a fish or a fruit," Halliburton observed in his book *The Royal Road to Romance*, "until one day I ran across it by accident on the map, and found it was nothing edible, but an independent republic of six thousand people and one hundred seventy-five square miles, all lost for ten hundred years in the tops of the Pyrenees." Inspired, Halliburton traveled to the French border, rented a donkey named Josephine (which he promptly renamed Hannibal), and spent the next few days hiking the breadth of Andorra.

E. Thus, much as modern wanderers might seek to follow the trail of Marco Polo across Asia, you decide that your Andorra journey took place in the footsteps of Richard Halliburton.

IV. When Bogged Down in Description, Trot Out Some Colorful Characters

A. Think back to the beginning of your Andorra experience. Like Richard Halliburton, you started on the French side, in a village called L'Hospitalet. You hiked all day, slept your first night at Pedoures Lake, then crossed into Andorra at Ruf Peak, which is 8,500 feet high. From there, you hiked down the Vall d'Incles into the heart of Andorra. As usual, you have difficulty describing this hike, because you feel there is a sameness to describing mountains.

B. You want to just say: "There were a few pines and far-off forests of beech-trees on some of the mountainsides. I climbed up and up and crossed another high Col, and I saw a whole new range of mountains off to the south, all brown and baked-looking and furrowed in strange shapes." This seems such a simple and appropriate way to describe hiking in the Pyrenees. Unfortunately, it happens to be a direct quote from Ernest Hemingway's *The Sun Also Rises*, which you read on a series of bus rides from Paris to L'Hospitalet.

C. You don't want to resort to the usual clichés, however—the "jagged ridges," the "crystal clear lakes," the "quaint chateaux perched on hillsides"—so you check your notebook. Here, you have scribbled observations from the hike, such as "Yellow frogs, brown spiders, orange butterflies," and "French hikers carry what appear to be ski poles," and (to your own chagrin) "Crystal clear mountain lakes perched below jagged brown ridges."

D. In general, you are insecure about this first portion of your Andorran journey, because all you have is background and description, and (as you told your students) travel stories work better when they include characters and dialogue. Thus, you should hurry your narrative hike to the ski-resort town of Soldeu, where you met a retired Scottish ski instructor named Morrie. Morrie was very friendly, very colorful, and (by the end of the night) very drunk. Morrie clapped you on the back, bought you beers, and took you on tours of recently built hotels and bars.

Morrie pointed to the local elite and said: "Look at that bugger. A generation ago he and his family were dirt farmers. Now they own half the hotels in Soldeu."

E. In one pub, Morrie introduced you to a number of British, Spanish and Argentine ski instructors. In your notebook, you wrote: "Ski instructors arm-in-arm, singing along to 'Stuck in the Middle with You,' by Stealers Wheel." Beside this entry, in the margin of your notebook, you later added: "This could almost be the Andorran national anthem."

F. As it turned out, the ski instructors didn't know much about Andorra ("I think it became a country because France and Spain didn't want it," one Brit suggested). The best information you learned from these folks was that Andorra always wins lots of medals in the "Little Country Olympics."

G. Now that you've have a chance to confirm this, you are pleased to learn that there actually is a Little Country Olympics (officially called the "Games for the Small States of Europe"), which pits Andorra against Cyprus, Iceland, Liechtenstein, Luxembourg, Malta, Monaco and San Marino. The Vatican, you are somewhat disappointed to note, does not field a team.

V. BE SURE TO CONTRAST THE PURITY OF THE PAST WITH THE SUPERFICIALITIES OF TODAY

A. Since the Little Country Olympics is a tangent at best, you go back to your notes and scan for details about the hike from Soldeu to Canillo. "Trail to Canillo actually a thin path following a stream near the highway," your notebook reminds you. "Ski lifts and power wires. SUVs with French tags choking the highway." There is not much drama here, so you decide to mention smuggling.

B. Write: "Twisting down from the mountains, this trail is the legacy of Andorra's time-honored smuggling tradition. Due to her location between two larger neighbors, Andorra has always profited from monopolies and embargoes on both sides." Illustrate this with an example—say, the French match monopoly of the 1880s, when almost 2,000 pounds of matches were smuggled over from Spain each year.

C. Point out that the smuggling trade has given way to a somewhat bland trade in tourist souvenirs and duty-free goods. Say: "If a country expresses itself through its souvenirs, it's hard to tell what Andorra thinks it is." Describe how one can buy Scotch whiskey, Barcelona newspapers and even figurines of doobie-smoking Rastafarians (which, to your eye, look "disturbingly Sambo-like") in Canillo.

D. Imply that the superficialities of duty-free souvenirs in Canillo distressed you, and that you then had to find something authentic and redeeming. A church is always good for this. Our Lady of Meritxell would be ideal, since this is home to the patron saint of Andorra, who reputedly keeps her country safe from war and invasion. Unfortunately, you never visited this church.

E. Briefly consider pretending you went there, since you can easily patch together an account from tourist literature.

F. Choose instead, out of dull conscience, to describe St. Joan de Caselles, a twelfth-century Romanesque church that you actually did visit. Include the following phrases when describing the church: "rectangular nave with a wooden ceiling"; "semicircular apse with a Lombard-style bell-tower"; and "sixteenth century Italian-German renaissance-style altarpiece, which includes scenes from the life of St. John." Embellish the sense of history this evokes.

G. Since the hike from Canillo to Andorra la Vella is largely suburban, make a quick transition to the capital. Use this 1921 Richard Halliburton quote: "There, on the hillside, was Andorra City, climbing slightly above the verdant floor of this sunlit garden—the most pathetic, the most miserable capital city of any nation in the world."

H. Contrast above passage with the comparative modernity of contemporary Andorra la Vella. Mention luxury hotels, Spanish tourists driving Opel station wagons, and French middle-class shopaholics, who swarm the duty-free stores.

VI. Don't Forget to Talk to a Local

A. Since it is bad form to write a story about Andorra without producing an actual Andorran, it is now time to bring out Ms. Roser Jordana. Mention that she was a small, sharp, nononsense woman. Recall how her pearls and rhinestones glittered as she fielded phone calls and answered your questions in the office of tourism.

B. As it is somewhat lame for the Andorran in the story to be from the bureau of tourism, boldly bring this irony into the foreground. Say: "Andorra's tourist economy has turned the nation into a country of visitors. So much so, in fact, that the first true Andorran I meet heads up the office of tourism in Andorra la Vella."

C. Scan your notes from Ms. Jordana's personal tour of the Andorran parliament house. Condensing facts, write: "About the size of a large dining room, the Andorran parliament chamber seats representatives from each of the country's seven parishes. Before the days of roads, this small building doubled as a hostel, and representatives would often sit in the kitchen to eat their sack lunches and discuss politics."

D. Though your notes say as much, it's best not to mention that Marc Forne, the current General Syndic of the Andorran parliament, looks a lot like the father from the 1980s American sitcom *Family Ties*.

VII. Public Festivals are the Holy Grail of Any Travel Story

A. Festivals always lend color and climax to a travel story, so you should segue into the Catalan Festa Major, which you had the good fortune to experience on your second day in Andorra la

Vella. Establish the scene: orchestras and fireworks; a medieval market; Spanish wine for a dollar a bottle; rowdy parades with huge-headed Catalonian "giant" puppets.

B. Describe the traditonal *sardana* dances in a square near the park: the old Andorrans dancing in perfect step-step-step; the Spanish oom-pah band under the gazebo; the pretty young women in short skirts, singing. Mention that, because of geographical access, Catalan Spain has had a stronger influence over Andorra than France.

C. You have no choice now but to deal with the mentally handicapped Andorrans. Recall how they began their *sardana* with inspiring concentration, but soon shook free of their minders and flapped across the plaza with ecstatic abandon. Each of them wore a nametag, so you know that it was a hefty fellow named "Gordoneau" who fixed you in his small-eyed gaze and yanked you out into the plaza to join the dance—which by that point was rapidly disintegrating into a gleeful mosh-pit.

D. Jigging and swirling across the plaza, you slowly came to realize that the spectators regarded you and Gordoneau with the same bemused stare. When Gordoneau stopped at a plastic table and took a sloppy gulp of some stranger's beer, the old Andorran sitting there merely flinched and smiled up at you, as if you might do the same.

E. You think back to how you tried to explain this instant to Lisa two days later in Barcelona: how there was a wonderful freedom in the notion that—free of all expectations—anything you do in Andorra might be forgiven in advance. You intended no moral or quip-joke by saying this; you meant only to imply that one takes one's epiphanies where one can find them, and you were happy to be invited for a glimpse into Gordoneau's world.

F. You've since forgotten how long the dance went on before the harried minders corralled Gordoneau and his companions back into neat lines. No doubt it lasted mere minutes, but you realize that any accomplishment is relative, and that Andorra was somehow more knowable for the experience. What, after all, did Hillary know of Nepal? What did Armstrong know of the moon? More than most of us, perhaps—but neither of them had the chance to dance with Gordoneau along the way.

VIII. END WITH A TIDY GENERALIZATION, OR PERHAPS A KNOWING WINK

A. Since esoteric digressions make editors nervous, you must find a more conventional way to end your story. Uncertain how else to proceed, you search the Internet for one last detail that might sum up what you experienced in Andorra.

B. Stumbling upon a random webpage about traditional Catalan nativity scenes, you read about a peculiar figure called the *caganer*. The *caganer* is a harlequin of sorts, a grizzled old man who squats—trousers at his ankles, stogie in mouth—casually defecating in the background of the nativity. A sociologist, Xavier Fabregas, is quoted: "The *caganer* reminds us that even in the midst of the greatest mystery of humanity, the birth of the Redeemer, there are these ineluctable and physiological necessities."

C. It occurs to you that a travel writer is not unlike the *caganer* within his own narrative—an odd character, always squatting in the background, casually presuming the observer will ignore the fact that these brightly colored surroundings have been painted and positioned well after the events they represent.

D. Thus, from this metaphorical squat, you will write about how you packed your bags, bade farewell to Andorra la Vella, and made for the Spanish border.

E. You will write: "I know that I have only experienced the slightest taste of Andorra, but there is a certain joy in concise goals and knowable quantities—of entire nations that can be strolled across in the course of a long weekend."

ACKNOWLEDGMENTS

This book spans ten years of my life, so there's no room to acknowledge every single person who's inspired and assisted me. Still, I'd like to tip my hat to a few folks who helped these stories find an audience. On the editorial side, a huge thanks goes out to Don George, as well as Jim Benning, Bill Bryson, Tim Cahill, Sarah Jane Freymann, Klara Glowczewska, Lee Gutkind, Larry Habegger, Tim Leffel, Jen Leo, James O'Reilly, Stephanie Pearson, Christy Quinto, Christine Richard, June Thomas, Clint Willis, Jason Wilson, and Mike Yessis. In the online realm, I am grateful for the assistance of Mike Marlett, Justin Glow, Jeff Lebow, and all of my bloggers. I also appreciate the camaraderie and support of all my travel-writing colleagues—you know who you are (and I will name-check Ayun Halliday and Tony Perrottet for their many years of perfect attendance at my writers' brunches in New York).

Some of these stories previously appeared in different form in *Salon, Outside, Slate, Condé Nast Traveler, Islands, World Hum, The Smart Set,* and *Perceptive Travel*—as well as the following anthologies: *The Best American Travel Writing 2000; The Best Travel Writing 2005; The Best Travel Writing 2006; The Best American Travel Writing 2006; The Best Travel Writing 2008; The Best Creative Nonfiction Vol. 2; Adrenaline 2000; Encounters with the Middle East; Travelers' Tales Turkey; Wanderlust; By the Seat of My Pants; A House Somewhere; Tales From Nowhere;* and *The Kindness of Strangers.*

T

ABOUT THE AUTHOR

Rolf Potts has reported from more than sixty countries for the likes of *Salon, Slate, National Geographic Traveler, Outside*, the *New York Times Magazine, Condé Nast Traveler, The Believer*, and National Public Radio. His adventures have taken him across six continents, and include piloting a fishing boat 900 miles down the Laotian Mekong, hitchhiking across Eastern Europe, traversing Israel on foot, bicycling across Burma, and driving a Land Rover from Sunnyvale, California to Ushuaia, Argentina. He has won four Lowell Thomas Awards for travel writing, and his essays have appeared in over twenty literary anthologies, including *The Best Travel Writing, The Best American Travel Writing, The Best Creative Nonfiction*, and several collections of travel humor. His first book was *Vagabonding: An Uncommon Guide to the Art of Long-Term World Travel*.

Though he rarely stays in one place for very long, Potts feels somewhat at home in Bangkok, Cairo, Pusan, New Orleans, and north-central Kansas, where he keeps a small farmhouse on thirty acres near his family. Each July he can be found in France, where he is the summer writer-in-residence at the Paris American Academy.

For more information about the business and craft of travel writing (including interviews with over one hundred working travel writers), visit rolfpotts.com/writers.